DATE DUE

Unwin Critical Library
GENERAL EDITOR: CLAUDE RAWSON

HUCKLEBERRY FINN

Huckleberry Finn

HAROLD BEAVER

London
ALLEN & UNWIN
Boston   Sydney

Allen & Unwin (Publishers) Ltd,
40 Museum Street, London WC1A 1LU, UK

Allen & Unwin (Publishers) Ltd,
Park Lane, Hemel Hempstead, Herts HP2 4TE, UK

Allen & Unwin, Inc.,
8 Winchester Place, Winchester, Mass. 01890, USA

Allen & Unwin (Australia) Ltd,
8 Napier Street, North Sydney, NSW 2060, Australia

First published in 1987

British Library Cataloguing in Publication Data

Beaver, Harold
    Huckleberry Finn. – (Unwin critical library)
1. Twain, Mark. Huckleberry Finn
I. Title
813'.4   PS1305
ISBN 0-04-800077-9

Library of Congress Cataloging in Publication Data

Beaver, Harold Lowther.
    Huckleberry Finn.
(Unwin critical library)
Bibliography: p.
Includes index.
1. Twain, Mark, 1835-1910. Adventures of Huckleberry Finn.
I. Title. II. Series.
PS1305.B4 1986   813'.4   86-10946
ISBN 0-04-800077-9 (alk. : paper)

Set in 10 on 12 point by Columns of Reading
and printed in Great Britain by Billing & Son Ltd,
London and Worcester

GENERAL EDITOR'S PREFACE

Each volume in this series is devoted to a single major text. It is intended for serious students and teachers of literature, and for knowledgeable non-academic readers. It aims to provide a scholarly introduction and a stimulus to critical thought and discussion.

Individual volumes will naturally differ from one another in arrangement and emphasis, but each will normally begin with information on a work's literary and intellectual background, and other guidance designed to help the reader to an informed understanding. This is followed by an extended critical discussion of the work itself, and each contributor in the series has been encouraged to present in these sections his own reading of the work, whether or not this is controversial, rather than to attempt a mere consensus. Some volumes, including those on *Paradise Lost* and *Ulysses*, vary somewhat from the more usual pattern by entering into substantive critical discussion at the outset, and allowing the necessary background material to emerge at the points where it is felt to arise from the argument in the most useful and relevant way. Each volume also contains a historical survey of the work's critical reputation, including an account of the principal lines of approach and areas of controversy, and a selective (but detailed) bibliography.

The hope is that the volumes in this series will be among those which a university teacher would normally recommend for any serious study of a particular text, and that they will also be among the essential secondary texts to be consulted in some scholarly investigations. But the experienced and informed non-academic reader has also been in our minds, and one of our aims has been to provide him with reliable and stimulating works of reference and guidance, embodying the present state of knowledge and opinion in a conveniently accessible form.

C.J.R.
University of Warwick,
December 1979

CONTENTS

ACKNOWLEDGEMENTS

The chart and map in Chapter 10, first published in *Studies in the Novel*, vol. 12 (Fall 1980), pp. 196–7, are reprinted by kind permission of the author, Michael G. Miller, and the North Texas State University (Copyright 1980). 'Run, Nigger, Run' (Chapter 14), a much revised version of an article that first appeared in the *Journal of American Studies*, vol. 8 (December 1974), is here reprinted by permission of the Cambridge University Press.

PREFACE

The centenary of the publication of *Adventures of Huckleberry Finn* (1884–1885) was celebrated with a flurry of conferences and articles and collections of articles and bibliographies, capped by the appearance of a newly collated and annotated text from the Mark Twain Project of the Bancroft Library in Berkeley. That flurry, extending from 1984 to 1985, has still not subsided. For *Huckleberry Finn* enjoys a peculiar status. It is both a children's and an adults' and an academic classic. It is both widely loved and reviled. It remains the most consistently provocative bestseller, over a hundred years, that any American writer has ever produced.

Why? What is the secret of its popularity? Is it an adult novel or juvenile fiction? Does it mark a continuation of *The Adventures of Tom Sawyer* or a wholly new start? Is it a vernacular masterpiece or mere humorous burlesque? Does it offer a reconciliation between black and white or is it racist trash? Is Huck a new model hero from the West or just another amoral prankster and western rogue? Is his book part of the tall tales and journalistic buffooneries of the frontier or to be read in that grandest of all picaresque traditions linking *Don Quixote* to *Tom Jones*?

Mark Twain, disguised as General Grant, posted an imperious 'KEEP OFF' sign:

Persons attempting to find a motive in this narrative will be prosecuted; persons attempting to find a moral in it will be banished; persons attempting to find a plot in it will be shot.

That, however, has deterred no one. Books continue to proliferate. Yet no single book has ever confronted all these wide-ranging issues or attempted to review the whole debate. The time is ripe. As working text I used the Norton Critical Edition (second edition, 1977) with its skilfully selected source material and criticism. On the appearance of the Mark Twain Library edition (University of California, 1985), I double-keyed all quotations into that authoritative text. For despite the heat of political debates and the dust of scholarship, *Huckleberry Finn* remains as irresistibly fresh and joyous today as anything committed to words since Homer's *Odyssey*.

Amsterdam, May 1986   H.L.B.

For Jacob

Part One

CHAPTER 1

Missouri, Hannibal, Slavery

In my schoolboy days I had no aversion to slavery. I was not aware that there was anything wrong about it.

The Autobiography of Mark Twain, ch. 2

From the start it had rocked the Union. In 1821 the territory of Missouri was admitted as a slave state at the same time as Maine, by a tit-for-tat known as the Missouri Compromise (1820), entered as a free state. That was fifteen years before the birth of Samuel Langhorne Clemens in Florida, a hamlet on the banks of the Mississippi. But it was to affect the whole course of his life and that of his finest fiction. It is as well to begin here.

The territory had been set up in 1812, but settlement was slow. Missouri was primarily a fur-trading centre. Though slavery was early introduced by planters from the South, plantations were restricted to a small area. Tobacco and hemp were raised in the bottomlands of the Missouri river, but in the Ozarks and rich cornlands the slave system was uneconomic. The state faced west, Thomas Hart Benton declared, not south for its expansion. The great Mississippi, however, rolled south, and the hamlets on its banks quickly grew. Hannibal, with a population of thirty in 1830, had a population of just over a thousand by the time the Clemens family settled there in 1839 when Sam was 4. By 1847 the Hannibal *Gazette* reported the arrival of over a thousand steamboats annually. It was in this busy port, with a daily service (inaugurated in 1848) to Keokuk, that he grew up. The packets were named out of Sir Walter Scott.

This was to become the setting for *The Adventures of Tom Sawyer* and its sequel, *Adventures of Huckleberry Finn*. As he recorded among its preliminaries:

SCENE: THE MISSISSIPPI VALLEY

TIME: FORTY TO FIFTY YEARS AGO

Reckoned from the date of American publication, that means 1835 to 1845, or exactly the first decade of Sam Clemens's life. Those were the mythical years, the years of boyhood before his father's death, before the issue of slavery tore Missouri apart.

For there was civil war in Missouri long before the Civil War. The original constitution had prohibited freed slaves from entering the state; by the Compromise of 1820 this proviso was struck out. But legislation was passed and the number of free Blacks and mulattos remained small. In 1820 they made up only 347 out of a total population of 66,577. They were feared, nevertheless. They were a force, it was reckoned, capable of undermining the whole system. More and more stringent laws were passed. By 1847 free Blacks were prohibited from entering the state under any conditions. By 1850 a statement by a White under oath 'proved' ownership of a Black without freedom papers.

This explains something of the indignation of Huck's Pap:

Oh, yes, this is a wonderful govment, wonderful. Why, looky here. There was a free nigger there, from Ohio; a mulatter, most as white as a white man . . . And what do you think? they said he was a p'fessor in a college, and could talk all kinds of languages, and knowed everything. And that ain't the wust. They said he could *vote*, when he was at home.[1]

If this was execrable, then what about Missouri Blacks illegally crossing to Illinois or Ohio? Ten years after publishing *Huckleberry Finn*, Twain was to recall:

In those old slave-holding days the whole community was agreed as to one thing – the awful sacredness of slave property. To help steal a horse or a cow was a low crime, but to help a hunted slave, or feed him or shelter him, or hide him, or comfort him, in his troubles, his terrors, his despair, or hesitate to promptly betray him to the slave-catcher when opportunity offered was a much baser crime, & carried with it a stain, a moral smirch which nothing could wipe away. That this sentiment should exist among slave-holders is comprehensible – there were good commercial reasons for it – but that it should exist and did exist among the paupers, the loafers, the tag-rag & bobtail of the community, & in a passionate & uncompromising form, is not in our remote day realizable.[2]

There was no comparison between stealing a horse and stealing a slave; no comparison, either, between black and white. As Judith Loftus, a fine frontier type of a woman, makes clear after unmasking Huck:

> I ain't going to hurt you, and I ain't going to tell on you, nuther. You just tell me your secret, and trust me. I'll keep it; and what's more, I'll help you. So'll my old man, if you want him to. You see, you're a runaway 'prentice – that's all. It ain't anything. There ain't any harm in it. You've been treated bad, and you made up your mind to cut. Bless you, child, I wouldn't tell on you.[3]

Whites could expect such solidarity, it seems. Blacks confronted it. There was an absolute distinction between a 'runaway nigger' and a white runaway. Twain could recall 'the pater-rollers' of the 1850s patrolling the streets of Hannibal for abolitionists distributing leaflets or handbills or helping slaves escape. Every community had such a force of vigilantes. When he was 6, in 1841, his father served on a jury in a trial of three abolitionists from Quincy, Illinois. The charge was that they had 'tried to induce three negroes to leave and go with them to Illinois and thence to Canada and freedom'. The oddity of the trial was that the slaves themselves had helped capture the abolitionists. 'They testified to this in court, though legally at that time Negroes were not allowed to testify against whites. Crowds attended the trial, threatening to hang the prisoners. The verdict "guilty" was loudly applauded and the three men were sentenced to twelve years of hard labour. A subscription was taken up for the loyal slaves which netted $20.62½ cents.'[4]

Such was the state of tension when the Kansas–Nebraska Bill, in 1854, enflamed the slavery issue even further. Pro-slavery forces in Missouri became active in trying to win Kansas for their cause, contributing vigorously to the general violence. But anti-slavery elements were just as strong; and in the end they turned out to be triumphant. At the outbreak of the Civil War most Missourians remained loyal to the federal government, rallying behind strong

Unionists like Francis P. Blair (a founder of the Republican Party who presided over its first national convention in Pittsburgh). The state convention, which met in 1861, voted against secession. It shilly-shallied, though, by voting against coercion of the South; until in 1862 it assumed constituent powers and deposed the state government. For the pro-Southern administration of Governor C. F. Jackson, after refusing Lincoln's request for troops, had attempted to arm the state militia from the federal arsenal. This resolutely pro-Confederate force at first retreated, then won a victory at Wilson Creek (10 August 1861); but by March of the following year was routed, never to appear again except as guerrilla units making raids throughout the state. This lawlessness, bred by war, continued long after the war; and Missouri saw the rise of one of the most celebrated of all American outlaws, Jesse James.

How did Sam Clemens survive this era of belligerent confusion? With equal belligerence. His older brother turned Republican; but young Sam, true to his father, remained a staunchly old-fashioned Whig. He liked to mock Orion as a buffoon, the constant butt of his jokes. But it was Orion of whom he later said: 'born and reared among slaves and slaveholders, he was yet an abolitionist from boyhood to his death'.[5] In fact Orion was enough of a Southerner to despise Northern abolitionists and the Free Soil movement. But he regarded slavery as an evil, defended the civil rights of free Blacks and became a Lincoln Republican just before the outbreak of war.

So Orion, at least, had seen through Missouri's evasions. Brother Sam remained true to his state in *all* its multiplicity. He now seems like a one-man deposit of local sentiment – an archaeological site whose lowest layer bears an uncommon resemblance to Pap Finn. Perhaps he was only playing up to his mother, but letters from New York, written in 1853, when he was 18, voice the crudest prejudices of Huck's old man. He resented the liberties enjoyed in the North by Blacks. He resented having to push his way in Manhattan through crowds of mulattos, quadroons and other 'trash'. He wrote to his mother that 'to wade through this mass of human vermin, would raise the ire of the most patient person that ever lived . . . I reckon I had better black my face, for in these Eastern states niggers are considerably better than white people'. To Orion he exclaimed: 'I would like amazingly to see a good old-fashioned negro.'[6] Sam was outraged about the chains and soldiers needed to prevent the rescue of a fugitive slave from the Syracuse court-house 'by the infernal abolitionists'.

This distinctly unpleasant young man was put to the test by the outbreak of civil war. By that time he was a steamboat pilot on the Mississippi; and, as his 'Private History of a Campaign that Failed' (1865) confessed, he vacillated:

> During the first months of the great trouble . . . it was hard for us to get our bearings . . . My pilot mate was a New-Yorker. He was strong for the Union; so was I. But he would not listen to me with any patience; my loyalty was smirched, to his eye, because my father had owned slaves . . . A month later the secession atmosphere had considerably thickened on the Lower Mississippi, and I became a rebel, so did he . . . In the following summer he was piloting a Federal gunboat and shouting for the Union again, and I was in the Confederate army.

This need for a comic double – a twin for Twain – we shall see was a typical manoeuvre. But there is no need to doubt its essential truth. After three weeks' service as a Confederate volunteer, he deserted. Orion, newly appointed secretary to the Governor of the Nevada Territory by the Republicans, had urged him to come out West. The plan was 'to wean Sam away from his rebel cause'. It worked. He went.

But it was not exactly easy to live down. More than once, after the war, he was called 'a damned Secessionist'. His letters from Carson City are uncomfortably callous and mocking. He still thought it funny to indict a charity fund ball, held in Virginia City, for diverting funds 'to aid a Miscegenation Society somewhere in the East'. The humour remained callow. Revulsion came late. It was not until after the war that Twain held himself personally responsible. Then he charged himself with 'the wrong which the white race has done to the black race in slavery'. He paid a black Southerner through college as 'part of the reparation due from every white to every black man'. He paid to put another through Yale Law School. He proudly claimed Frederick Douglass as a 'personal friend'.[7] 'I was certainly glad to see *him*', he wrote to his wife in 1869, 'for I do so admire his spunk.' What he admired was the black leader's insistence on the need for extending political and economic civil rights far beyond the measure of Emancipation.

The conversion, when it came, then, was decisive. 'The idea of making negroes citizens of the United States was startling and disagreeable to me,' he wrote with mock-gravity on the Chinese question, 'but I have become reconciled to it, and the ice being broken and the principle established, I am ready now for all comers.'[8] The tone may be flippant, but the attitude behind it was deadly serious. Twain was always to remain the Southerner, the man in the white linen suit, but for all his complexities (the very complexities that made him such an unrivalled wit and raconteur) the volte-face cannot be doubted. The influence of his fellow-Southerner, George Washington Cable, has been urged; and he may well have added fuel to the flames.[9] But as early as 1869 Twain was already acting the renegade in public. 'What if the blunder of lynching the wrong man does happen once in four or five cases?' he caustically asked from distant Buffalo. 'Is that any fair argument against the cultivation and indulgence of those fine chivalric passions and that noble Southern spirit which will not brook the slow and cold formalities of regular law?'[10] The contempt expressed for 'the best regulated and most high-toned mobs' already heralds Colonel Sherburn's withering harangue of the Bricksville mob:

> Do I know you? I know you clear through. I was born and raised in the South, and I've lived in the North; so I know the average all around . . . Your newspapers call you a brave people so much that you think you *are* braver than any other people – whereas you're just *as* brave, and no braver. Why don't your juries hang murderers? . . . The pitifulest thing out is a mob; that's what an army is – a mob; they don't fight with courage that's born in them, but with courage that's borrowed from their mass, and from their officers. But a mob without any *man* at the head of it, is *beneath* pitifulness.[11]

A generation later, after a particularly grisly mass lynching in his own home state, he wrote his last despairing analysis, 'The United States of Lyncherdom'.[12]

By that time he was at work on his 'Autobiography'; and there he had to face the contradiction that he himself came from a slave-holding community and from slave-owning stock. But he softened the tints and mellowed the memories. He needed to protect himself. It was his way of guarding his childhood. His kith and kin, he averred, were simple, homely, affable – just plain folks:

In the small town of Hannibal, Missouri, when I was a boy everybody was poor but didn't know it; and everybody was comfortable and did know it. And there were grades of society – people of good family, people of unclassified family, people of no family. Everybody knew everybody and was affable to everybody and nobody put on any visible airs; yet the class lines were quite clearly drawn and the familiar social life of each class was restricted to that class. It was a little democracy which was full of liberty, equality and Fourth of July, and sincerely so, too; yet you perceived that the aristocratic taint was there It was there and nobody found fault with the fact or even stopped to reflect that its presence was an inconsistency.[13]

Slavery, too, was there, of course, but in a cheerful, innocent form: 'In Hannibal we seldom saw a slave misused; on the farm never.'

As I have said, we lived in a slaveholding community; indeed, when slavery perished, my mother had been in daily touch with it for sixty years. Yet, kind-hearted and compassionate as she was, I think that she was not conscious that slavery was a bald, grotesque and unwarrantable usurpation. She had never heard it assailed in any pulpit but had heard it defended and sanctified in a thousand; her ears were familiar with Bible texts that approved it but if there were any that disapproved it they had not been quoted by her pastors; as far as her experience went, the wise and the good and the holy were unanimous in the conviction that slavery was right, righteous, sacred, the peculiar pet of the Deity and a condition which the slave himself ought to be daily and nightly thankful for. Manifestly, training and association can accomplish strange miracles. As a rule our slaves were convinced and content.[14]

So the slaves were 'convinced'; yet earlier he had noted: 'if the slaves themselves had an aversion to slavery they were wise and said nothing'. Which was it? 'It was the mild domestic slavery,' he recorded, 'not the brutal plantation article'; yet within a paragraph he recalls how a White once 'killed a negro man for a trifling little offence'. Which was it? The text is rich in evasions and suppressions; and, when it does not quite repress, it only half-suggests. We must watch out for the bounds and rebounds, since Twain liked to

duplicate his texts in a series of double-takes. Quite deliberately he
plays Hide and Seek.

Four areas seem to be under discussion: the question of
drunkenness; the question of violence in general; the question of
violence towards slaves in particular; and surreptitious sex. All
overlap, of course; and I shall only partly disentangle them.

Mark Twain introduces four vagrants as town drunks: 'General'
Gaines, the elder Blankenship, Injun Joe and Jimmy Finn. But these
are essentially comic portraits. 'Whoop! bow your neck and spread!'
roars the General (a relic of the Indian wars). Drunkenness must have
been a good deal more terrifying. The Hannibal of Sam's youth
boasted a distillery and several saloons (locally known as 'dog-
geries').[15] A town ordinance, passed in 1845, made it a misdemeanour
to be 'found drunk or intoxicated in any streat, alley, avinue, market
place, or public square . . . or found a sleep in any such place not his
own'.[16] The opposition went further: it fielded a Temperance League
with junior Cadets of Temperance to which Sam briefly belonged. Here
is a portrait of the town as Dixon Wecter gives it:

> In addition to its two pork houses, Hannibal by 1844 took pride in
> four general stores, three sawmills, two planing mills, three
> blacksmith shops, two hotels, three saloons, two churches, two
> schools, a tobacco factory, a hemp factory, and a tanyard, as well as
> a flourishing distillery up at the still-house branch.[17]

This raw town, submerged in *Tom Sawyer*, half-emerges in *Huckleberry Finn*. Jimmy Finn endowed Huckleberry with his name; but it
was the Blankenships who fascinated Twain. The girls were 'charged
with prostitution', he later recalled; Tom Blankenship, he claimed,
was the model for Huck: 'the only really independent person – boy or
man – in the community'.[18]

Equally influential must have been Tom's older brother, Bence.
One day, in the summer of 1847, Bence came upon a runaway slave
hidden in the thickets of Sny Island, off the Illinois shore. Ignoring a
fifty-dollar reward which had been posted, Bence secretly carried food
across the river to the black man week after week. But woodchoppers
spotted him and chased him into a swamp where he disappeared. A
few days later Sam Clemens and a group of friends were poling about,
fishing near the island, when the corpse rose, head first, before their
eyes. In the words of the Hannibal *Journal* of 19 August:

While some of our citizens were fishing a few days since on the Sny Island, they discovered in what is called Bird Slough the body of a negro man. On examination of the body, they found it to answer the description of a negro recently advertised in handbills as a runaway from Neriam Todd, of Howard County. He had on a brown jeans frock coat, home-made linen pants, and a new pair of lined and bound shoes. The body when discovered was much mutilated.[19]

There seems no end to the shocks and horrors of Sam's boyhood. Three times he came close to drowning and before the age of 17 he had witnessed the abortive lynching of an abolitionist, a death by fire, a hanging, an attempted rape, two drownings, two attempted homicides and four murders.[20] No wonder Huck is haunted by death: he feigns his own brutal killing; he, too, discovers corpses on the river; he overhears a murder plotted; he witnesses the wholesale slaughter of the Grangerfords and the cold-blooded shooting of old Boggs. The casual violence is all-pervasive. Whether embodied in Pap, or Colonel Sherburn, or a criminal gang, or a lynch mob, it seems to typify this male world. Take a casual conversation: 'Mister, is that town Cairo?' Hucks asks a stranger setting a trotline from his skiff. 'Cairo? no. You must be a blame' fool.' Huck tries again: 'What town is it, mister?' Back slams a barrage of pent-up aggression: 'If you want to know, go and find out. If you stay here botherin' around me for about a half a minute longer, you'll get something you won't want.'[21]

Such was the South: bleak, arbitrary, destructive. Such is the scene of the Bricksville killing in chapter 21 of *Huckleberry Finn*. It was based on a real event, Hannibal's first deliberate murder, when Sam was 9. The killer was a prosperous merchant, William Owsley; the foolish farmer, one Samuel Smarr. The case is well documented since John Marshall Clemens, JP, Sam's father, took down twenty-eight depositions from eye-witnesses.[22] The murder was even more cold-blooded than Huck records. Smarr had shouted abuse, it is true, calling Owsley 'a damned pickpocket' and swearing to have him whipped. But it was days after this binge that Owsley came up behind him in the street. 'You, Sam Smarr!' he shouted. Smarr spun round and, seeing him draw at four paces, begged him not to shoot. Owsley fired. Smarr staggered. Without dropping his arm, Owsley fired a second shot, turned on his heel and walked off. He got away with it, too, acquitted on grounds of gross provocation.

Such gratuitous violence made for a mood of general apathy, of complete indifference. Twain admits as much in the case of a Black killed for some 'trifling little offence'. 'I think it stupefied everybody's humanity as regarded the slave,' he writes, 'but stopped there.' Did it? Only ten pages on he records a personal encounter with a 'slave man who was struck down with a chunk of slag for some small offence; I saw him die'. Such violence bore down ruthlessly on Blacks. It is as if, after all these years, Twain were still trying to answer Dickens's charge of the 'deformity and ugliness' of slave society. 'There were no hard-hearted people in our town' is his lame conclusion.[23]

For his mood remains determinedly bland. Cruelty may well have been rare; the 'nigger trader' loathed. Yet slave families *were* split and sold to different masters 'in the settling of estates', he admits, just as after the Wilks funeral:

> a couple of nigger traders come along, and the king sold them the niggers reasonable, for three-day drafts as they called it, and away they went, the two sons up the river to Memphis, and their mother down the river to Orleans. I thought them poor girls and them niggers would break their hearts for grief.[24]

Twain is coy about whether or not he recalls 'seeing a slave auction' in Hannibal; surely his beady eye would have taken that in; it certainly saw advertisements in his brother's own newspaper offering rewards for runaway slaves. His most vivid memory is that of 'a dozen black men and women chained to one another, once, and lying in a group on the pavement, awaiting shipment to the Southern slave market'. He adds: 'Those were the saddest faces I have ever seen. Chained slaves could not have been a common sight or this picture would not have made so strong and lasting an impression upon me.' Yet the sight of a manacled 'coffle' on the levee cannot have been that rare, either. William W. Brown, himself a fugitive slave, wrote in his memoir:

> Though slavery is thought, by some, to be mild in Missouri, when compared with the cotton, sugar and rice growing States, yet no part of our slave-holding country, is more noted for the barbarity of its inhabitants, than St Louis. It was here that Col. Harney, a United States officer, whipped a slave woman to death. It was here that Francis McIntosh, a free colored man from Pittsburgh, was taken from the steamboat *Flora* and burned at the stake.

He continues:

> A few weeks after, on our downward passage, the boat took on
> board, at Hannibal, a drove of slaves, bound for the New Orleans
> market. They numbered from fifty to sixty, consisting of men and
> women from eighteen to forty years of age. A drove of slaves on a
> southern steamboat, bound for the cotton or sugar regions, is an
> occurrence so common, that no one, not even the passengers,
> appear to notice it, though they clank their chains at every step.[25]

If Twain is evasive on the subject of slavery, he is most deliberately
and systematically evasive on that of his own family's slaves. It is
impossible now to glean the whole truth. The unpublished memoir of
his mother, Jane Lampton Clemens, provides a jumbled account;
there are some additional facts in the unpublished 'Villagers of
1840–3'; but self-censorship was wholesale. None of the bitter history
of the Clemens 'house servants' survived in the autobiography. It was
too discreditable to both his parents. His father's sale of a manservant
to the deep South is blandly reduced to: 'At first my father owned
slaves but by and by he sold them and hired others by the year from
the farmers.'[26] The sale of his own 'mammy' down-river is deleted
altogether. What he retained instead was a picturesque view of his
uncle John Quarles's estate (the prototype of the Phelps farm in
Huckleberry Finn) with its thirty slaves, including portraits of middle-
aged 'Uncle Dan'l' (the prototype of Jim) and superstitious old 'Aunt'
Hannah who tied up her hair in little tufts with white thread; and he
developed his sketch of young Sandy who would not stop singing. It
made 'Mars Sam' want to kill him. But his mother explained that
Sandy, too, had a mother in faraway Maryland:

> Poor thing, when he sings it shows that he is not remembering and
> that comforts me; but when he is still I am afraid he is thinking and
> I cannot bear it. He will never see his mother again; if he can sing I
> must not hinder it, but be thankful for it. If you were older you
> would understand me; then that friendless child's noise would make
> you glad.[27]

It's a sentimental little vignette which reflected well (Twain thought)
on his own mother.

Not so the case of Jenny. Jenny's presence in the Clemens

household long pre-dated Sam's. She had accompanied the Clemenses on their migration from Tennessee (where Orion was born) and later to Hannibal. She was nurse for all the Clemens children. But tension grew between the two women. The slave girl was uppity; she was insubordinate. On one occasion she snatched away the whip with which Jane Clemens was threatening her. The judge rushed home; her wrists were bound, and she was whipped with a bridle for her insolence. No wonder she 'took a notion that she would like to change masters'. Twain is at pains to emphasize that this was at *her* request: 'she wanted to be sold to Beebe, and was'. (Beebe had been luring her with all sorts of promises.) It was Beebe who 'sold her down the river'. Even in his most intimate notes Twain is anxious to exculpate his mother: his mother merely yielded and persuaded his father. The Clemenses had *not* sold their old 'mammy' down the river. No, in their high-minded and loving and unselfish way, they were not to blame. His mother merely accommodated a slave – even accommodated 'the whim of a slave, against her own personal interest and desire'. And with what result? 'Was seen, years later, ch[ambermaid] on steamboat. Cried and lamented.'[28] What a futile life! How she must have regretted leaving Mother! Yet the facts were awkward. Even the edited text as it appears in his mother's memoir is awkward. Jenny was no Dilsey for Twain, like Faulkner, to sentimentalize over. The memory hurt.[29]

The case of Charley was even more painful. A letter from his father (dated 5 January 1842) lay before him while he wrote:

> I still have Charley; the highest price I was offered for him in New Orleans was $50, and in Vicksburg $40. After performing the journey to Tennessee I expect to sell him for whatever he will bring when I take water again, viz., at Louisville or Nashville.

So his father, always a dab hand at a bad deal, was prepared to take the next slave-trader's offer. Unlike Miss Watson's $800, it wasn't even a bargain. Yet for a miserable forty dollars (a sum which accumulates a symbolic weight of Judas-like treachery in *Huckleberry Finn*) he was prepared to part with Charley on the river. None of this, I repeat, found a place in the autobiography. The emotional price was too great. But it found its surreptitious way into the fiction.

Such is the secret, or inside, history of a white conscience. Its sexual side Twain could not write at all. He was haunted in his dreams, as late as 1897, in London, by being accosted in a park by 'a negro wench' in a 'coarse tow-linen shirt that reached from her neck to her ankles without a break':

> She sold me a pie; a mushy apple pie – hot. She was eating one herself with a tin teaspoon. She made a disgusting proposition to me. Although it was disgusting it did not surprise me – for I was young (I was never old in a dream yet) and it seemed quite natural that it should come from her. It was disgusting, but I did not say so; I merely made a chaffing remark, brushing aside the matter – a little jeeringly – and this embarrassed her and she made an awkward pretence that I had misunderstood her. I made a sarcastic remark about this pretence, and asked her for a spoon to eat my pie with. She had but the one, and she took it out of her mouth, in a quite matter-of-course way, and offered it to me. My stomach rose – there everything vanished.[30]

Is all this fantasy? Or are there memories here, confused and tantalizing memories, sticky with Freudian insight? Perhaps Twain was recalling his apprentice days, flirting in the kitchen with the mulatto daughter of the slave cook, where it was 'well understood that by the customs of the slaveholding communities' it was his 'right to make love to that girl if he wanted to'.[31] The shenanigans of the young devils on the Hannibal *Courier* found their way into the *Autobiography*. Not a breath of scandal, hardly a whisper of smut, however, into *Huckleberry Finn*. That, too, was suppressed. But, then, as he liked to think, it was just 'another boys' book'.

NOTES:

1 *Huckleberry Finn*, ch. 6, pp. 26–7/33–4. All quotations are taken from the Norton Critical Edition of *Adventures of Huckleberry Finn*, ed. Sculley Bradley, Richmond Croom Beatty, E. Hudson Long and Thomas Cooley, 2nd edn (New York: W.W. Norton, 1977), but page numbers are given both to the Norton Critical Edition and to the Mark Twain Library edition, ed. Walter Blair and Victor Fischer (Berkeley, Calif.: University of California Press, 1985). The first page number refers to the Norton Critical Edition; the second to the Mark Twain Library edition. Page references for shorter quotations are given in the text; for longer quotations both chapter and page references are given in the notes.
2 Mark Twain Papers, Notebook 35, TS p. 35 (1895).
3 *Huckleberry Finn*, ch. 11, p. 52/73, cf. the two slave-catchers on the river: 'Well, there's five niggers run off to-night, up yonder above the head of the bend . . .' (ch. 16, p. 75/125).

4 Walter Blair, *Mark Twain & 'Huck Finn'* (Berkeley, Calif.: University of California Press, 1960), ch. 8, p. 110; cf. Murel and Crenshaw, in *Life on the Mississippi*, who enticed slaves to 'run away', promising to share with them the reward for their 'capture'. Blacks needed cash in order to buy their freedom; but were usually killed to prevent their confessing.

5 Philip S. Foner, *Mark Twain: Social Critic* (New York: International Publishers, 1958), ch. 6, pp. 253, 255, 257.

6 *Mark Twain's Letters*, ed. Albert Bigelow Paine, Vol. 1 (New York/London: Harper & Brothers, 1917), 28 November 1853, p. 29.

7 In a letter to James A. Garfield, then President-elect, urging him to retain Frederick Douglass as Marshall of the District of Columbia (12 January 1881).

8 'The Treaty with China', New York *Tribune* (4 August 1868).

9 'Cable has been here, creating worshipers on all hands. He is a marvellous talker on a deep subject . . .' (letter to W.D. Howells, November 1882). See Guy A. Cardwell, *Twins of Genius* (East Lansing, Mich.: Michigan State College Press, 1953), pp. 68–77. The January 1885 issue of the *Century* carried both an instalment of *Huckleberry Finn* and Cable's 'The Freedman's Case in Equity'.

10 'Only a Nigger', editorial in the Buffalo *Express* (August 1869), on the discovery that a black lynched in Tennessee for 'having ravished a young lady' was innocent.

11 *Huckleberry Finn*, ch. 22, pp. 118–19/190–91.

12 'The United States of Lyncherdom', planned for the *North American Review* (November 1901), was not published until after Twain's death by Albert Bigelow Paine in *Europe and Elsewhere* (1923).

13 *The Autobiography of Mark Twain*, ed. Charles Neider (New York: Harper & Row, 1959), ch. 7, p. 28.

14 ibid., ch. 7, p. 30. Originally written as part of Twain's memoir of his mother (1890), this passage was later incorporated into the autobiography.

15 See *Huckleberry Finn*, ch. 31, p. 166/266.

16 Dixon Wecter, *Sam Clemens of Hannibal* (Boston, Mass.: Houghton Mifflin, 1952), ch. 11, p. 151.

17 ibid., ch. 5, p. 60.

18 'Villagers of 1840–3' (notes on the inhabitants of Hannibal, written in 1897), in Walter Blair (ed.), *Mark Twain's Hannibal, Huck & Tom* (Berkeley, Calif.: University of California Press, 1969), p. 31; *Autobiography*, ch. 14, p. 68. Fred W. Lorch quotes reports in the Hannibal *Daily Messenger* (1861) that Tom Blankenship was sentenced to thirty days in the county gaol for stealing turkeys (21 April); and suspected of stealing onions (4 June); and two horses, a wash-tub of clothes, and a quantity of bacon, butter, molasses and sugar, in addition to robbing a chicken-house (12 June). See 'A note on Tom Blankenship (Huckleberry Finn)', *American Literature*, vol. 12 (November 1940), pp. 351–3.

19 Wecter, *Sam Clemens of Hannibal*, ch. 11.

20 Blair, *Mark Twain & 'Huck Finn'*, ch. 4, p. 55.

21 *Huckleberry Finn*, ch. 16, p. 77/129.

22 See 'Villagers of 1840–3', pp. 36 and 366; and Wecter, *Sam Clemens of Hannibal*, ch. 9, pp. 106–9.

23 *Autobiography*, ch. 7, p. 31; ch. 9, p. 41. See Charles Dickens, *American Notes for General Circulation* (1842), ch. 17.

24 *Huckleberry Finn*, ch. 27, p. 146/234.

25 *Narrative of William W. Brown, a Fugitive Slave* (1847), ch. 4, pp. 27–8 and 33–4.

26 *Autobiography*, ch. 1, p. 2.

27 ibid. ch. 2, pp. 6–7.

28 Blair (ed.), *Mark Twain's Hannibal, Huck & Tom*, pp. 39 and 50.

29 Aspects of Jenny were possibly transferred to Roxana (Roxy) of *Pudd'nhead Wilson* (1894), who also ends up on a Mississippi steamboat.
30 Mark Twain Papers, Notebook 30 (1897). See *Mark Twain's Notebook*, ed. Albert Bigelow Paine (New York/London: Harper & Brothers, 1935), ch. 31, pp. 351–2.
31 *Autobiography*, ch. 18, p. 88.

CHAPTER 2

The Making of
Huckleberry Finn

The huckleberries are in season, now. They are a new beverage to
me. This is my first acquaintance with them . . . (August 1868)

One of the treasures of the Buffalo and Erie County Public Library is
a 696-leaf manuscript which is clearly a first draft of *Huckleberry Finn*.
It is in Mark Twain's usual copperplate hand. But mysteriously it
contains only three-fifths of the completed text: from the middle of
chapter 12 to chapter 14 and from chapter 22 to the end. Why is a
mere three-fifths of the manuscript available? Much research has
centred on this problem.[1] The whole story of the composition of
Huckleberry Finn (even more than most other texts by Twain) remains
confused; for much has been lost, including the revised typescript for
the first edition. But at least a partial answer can now be sketched. It
runs something like this.

Huckleberry Finn was notoriously a long time in the writing. Years
of intermittent composition intervened between its inception in 1876
and that August day in 1883 when Twain reported from Elmira, New
York, to his old crony, William Dean Howells: 'I'm done work for
this season.' In the meantime he had written two travel books (*A
Tramp Abroad*, 1880, and *Life on the Mississippi*, 1883), a novel (*The
Prince and the Pauper*, 1882) as well as short stories, a couple of plays
and a run of magazine articles. But work on *Huckleberry Finn* had
continued by fits and starts. The 1876 fragment broke off near the end
of chapter 16 (though most of chapters 12 to 14 was as yet unwritten).
That is the point where a steamboat cuts into the raft. An insoluble
problem must have overwhelmed him, now that Huck was helping a
runaway slave plunge further and further into the deep South.

The very opening had been a headache. The first sentence of
Huckleberry Finn suggested that the new book was to be a sequel:

'You don't know about me, without you have read a book by the name of "The Adventures of Tom Sawyer", but that ain't no matter.' What mattered, though, was that the new book was not really a sequel at all. The problem had not been how to continue but how to detach it from the earlier 'Conclusion'. As was quickly apparent. On reading a manuscript copy of *Tom Sawyer*, Howells had written: 'I don't seem to think I like the last chapter.' Twain at once agreed, replying:

> As to that last chapter, I think of just leaving it off and adding nothing in its place. Something told me that the book was done when I got to that point – and so the strong temptation to put Huck's life at the Widow's into detail, instead of generalizing it in a paragraph, was resisted.[2]

Much of the material seems to have been transferred to the opening chapters of *Huckleberry Finn*. But there was a more pressing problem, that of voice.

It had long been his intention to write a story in a boy's own voice. Four months earlier he had written to Howells:

> I have finished the story & didn't take the chap beyond boyhood. I believe it would be fatal to do it in any shape but autobiographically – like Gil Blas. I perhaps made a mistake in not writing it in the first person. If I went on, now, & took him into manhood, he would be just like all the one-horse men in literature & the reader would conceive a hearty contempt for him. It is *not* a boy's book, at all. It will only be read by adults. It is only written for adults . . .
>
> By & by I shall take a boy of twelve & run him on through life (in the first person) but not Tom Sawyer – he would not be a good character for it.[3]

There are at least three issues here: the question of writing in the first person; the question of taking a boy into manhood; and whether he was writing children's fiction at all.

On the last question Howells was decisive:

> It's altogether the best boy's story I ever read. It will be an immense success. But I think you ought to treat it explicitly *as* a boy's story. Grown-ups will enjoy it just as much if you do; and if you should

put it forth as a study of boy character from the grown-up point of
view, you'd give the wrong key to it.

Again Twain promptly agreed: 'Mrs Clemens decides with you that
the book should issue as a book for boys, pure & simple – & so do I.
It is surely the correct idea.' For *Tom Sawyer*, of course. But for
Huckleberry Finn? He was to call it 'another boys' book' a year later,
yet he never quite made up his mind. On its title-page it was
advertised as '(Tom Sawyer's Comrade)', as if it were just a
companion volume to that bestseller; yet he allowed excerpts to be
printed, along with adult fiction by Henry James and Howells, in the
Century. Its status was to remain – and still remains – equivocal.[4]
The possibility of taking Tom on into manhood had already been
raised with Howells. It continued to haunt him; but it was not a
barrier he could ever cross. Anyhow not with Tom, as he said. Maybe
with Huck. As he had earlier written to Howells: 'Since there is no
plot to the thing, it is likely to follow its own drift, & so is as likely to
drift into manhood as anywhere – I won't interpose.'[5]
For by next year he was already at work on that 'autobiography'. I
'began another boys' book', he wrote to Howells:

– more to be at work than anything else. I have written 400 pages
on it – therefore it is very nearly half done. It is Huck Finn's
Autobiography. I like it only tolerably well, as far as I have got, &
may possibly pigeonhole or burn the MS when it is done.[6]

So at last he was writing in a boy's voice. An earlier first-person
manuscript had long lain abandoned; it was an embryonic sketch for
Tom Sawyer, whose boyish courtship rituals cutely parodied his own
recent courtship of Olivia Langdon.[7] But the temptation persisted.
The manuscript of *Tom Sawyer* shows that at least six pages of the
famous whitewashing scene were originally written in the first person.
For example:

And when the middle of the afternoon came, from being a poor,
poverty-stricken boy in the morning, I was literally rolling in
wealth. I had, besides the things I have mentioned, 12 marbles, part
of a Jew's harp, a piece of blue bottle glass to look through . . . I'd
had a nice good idle time.

Mark Twain simply crossed out 'I's and substituted 'he' all down the page. That arch, tautological phrase, 'from being a poor, poverty-stricken boy', suggests why Twain rightly concluded that Tom 'would not be a good character' for first-person narrative. He was too self-conscious, for one thing.

With Huck he had at last found his boy. Or had he? Why the despair? Perhaps he had already run into that impasse, the insoluble problem at chapter 16 that was to overwhelm him. But the violence of the response suggests his mingled dedication and frustration. Here he was in Hartford, Connecticut, and Elmira, New York, confronting the whole myth of his golden youth. Here he was re-creating the very accents of his Pike County past. Just as the book, begun in upstate New York, was to reach back to Mark Twain's roots in Missouri, so its working title, 'Huck Finn's Autobiography', from the start set up a double vibration. 'The huckleberries are in season, now,' he had written from Hartford in 1868. 'They are a new beverage to me. This is my first acquaintance with them . . .' Or again: 'I never saw any place where morality & huckleberries flourished as they do here.'[8] The very name of his hero, then, associated Hartford with Hannibal, huckleberries with Jimmy Finn, New England with the Midwest, the Atlantic seaboard with the Mississippi. No Missouri youngster of the 1840s ever saw a huckleberry in the Mississippi valley.[9]

At this testing juncture he drafted a vindictively unfair letter to his boyhood friend, Will Bowen (the original model for Tom Sawyer):

I can see by your manner of speech, that for more than twenty years you have stood dead still in the midst of the dreaminess, the melancholy, the romance, the heroics, of sweet but sappy sixteen. Man, do you know that this is simply mental and moral masturbation? It belongs eminently to the period usually devoted to *physical* masturbation, and should be left there and outgrown.[10]

The outburst was aimed solely at himself. He was facing the moral crisis of his career.

But he did not burn the manuscript. He simply stuffed it into his desk with all the other uncompleted manuscripts now in the Bancroft Library at Berkeley. Twain liked to call himself 'a faithful and interested amanuensis'. He would not push a work if it did not dictate itself. He just pigeonholed it. 'The reason was very simple – my tank had run dry', he would say; 'it was empty; the stock of materials in it was exhausted; the story could not go on without materials; it could not be wrought out of nothing'. The great discovery he made (while writing *Tom Sawyer*, he claims) was 'that when the tank runs dry you've only to leave it alone and it will fill up again, in time, while you are asleep – also while you are at work on other things'. In this, of course, he is rather like Huck. As Huck put it, confronting his own moral crisis at the Phelps farm: 'I went right along, not fixing up any particular plan, but just trusting to Providence to put the right words in my mouth when the time come; for I'd noticed that Providence always did put the right words in my mouth, if I left it alone.'[11]

By 1879–80 something apparently was stirring. Maybe the tank was filling up. At any rate Twain began making notes. He jotted down ideas. He tried to pick up the threads. Bernard DeVoto, who first published these notes, organized them into three groups (A, B and C), to which Walter Blair, after close scrutiny of the paper, the watermarks, the inks, etc., assigned rough dates. From which it appeared that chapters 17 and 18 (the Grangerford feud) were written between October 1879 and June 1880 in Hartford, Connecticut; chapters 19 and 20 (the arrival of the king and duke) possibly that same summer at Quarry Farm, Elmira; chapter 21 (the shooting of Boggs) in the spring of 1883. To general astonishment it was argued that Mark Twain had turned back to the manuscript even before his return trip to the Mississippi in 1882.[12]

Perhaps he just decided to ignore his impasse, just to let things drift. As Huck himself exclaims to the king and duke: 'Goodness sakes, would a runaway nigger run *south*?' (103/166) Shortly after passing Cairo, for example, there is talk of buying a canoe 'to go back in' (78/130). But that is the last we hear of their paddling back north. The idea is just dropped. When Huck eventually comes across a canoe, he simply paddles off 'to see if I couldn't get some berries' (98/158). As if dream-bound they float downstream.

But Twain never entirely let things drift. The working notes give a fascinating insight into his workshop as he turned from Jim's fate to a wider panorama of the old Southwest. I give here a selection from each group, as recorded by DeVoto and dated by Blair.

Group A (11 pages): mid-November 1879 to mid-June 1880

Negro campmeeting & sermon – 'See dat sinner how he run.'
Poor white family & cabin at woodyard in Walnut Bend.
     boys give bill of sale of Jim.

The Burning Shame at Napoleon, Ark.

Rich[ard] III – 15c – B[urning]. S[hame]. 50c.

Being in a close place, Huck boldly offers to sell Jim – the latter turns pale but dasn't speak – secretly is supported in the trial by firm belief that Huck is incapable of betraying him.

Huck gets decent suit of jeans.

Up a bayou where are alligators.

Tow-linen shirts or naked.

The scow with theatre aboard.

Dog fight – describe in detail.

The country cotillion.

The horse-trade.

Country quilting.

Candy-pulling.

Country funeral.

Describe aunt Patsy's house.

& Uncle Dan, aunt Hanner, & the 90-year blind negress.

(Jim has fever & is in concealment while Huck makes these observations.)

   (Keep 'em along.)

&c. The two printers deliver temp[erance]. lectures, teach dancing, elocution, feel heads, distribute tracts, preach, fiddle, doctor (quack)

The Circus – Huck's astonishment when the drunkard invades the ring, scuffles with clown & ring-master, then rides & strips.

Can't he escape from somewhere on the elephant?

An overflowed Arkansaw town. River booms up in the night.

George Jackson (Huck)		
Shepherdsons.		
Bob & Tom Grangerford	28 & 30.	~~abt. 30.~~
Old man (Saul) Col.	"	60
Betsy (negro)	"	
Old lady (Rachel)	"	
Buck	"	12–14
Emmeline (dead)	"	
Charlotte (proud & grand)	"	25
Sophia (sweet & gentle)	"	20
Harvney Shepherson		

Drunken man rides in the circus.

How *funny* the clown was – quote his jokes. & how the people received them – Huck envies him.

When did the raft pass St. Louis? Is there any mention of it? *Yes.[13]

Burning Shame *Do the mesmeric foolishness, with Huck ~~& the King~~ for ~~performers~~ Jim sawed in two.

po' $22-nigger will set in Heaven wid de $1500 niggers.

Back a little, CHANGE – raft only *crippled* by steamer.

* A lynching scene. * A wake.

L.A. punished her child several days for ~~disobedience~~ refusing to answer? & inattention (5 yr old) then while punishing discovered it was deaf ~~& dumb~~ & dumb! (from scarlet fever). It showed no reproachfulness for the whippings – kissed the punisher & showed non-comprehension of what it was all about.

After the raft was smashed, Twain may have considered continuing the adventure overland: thus the circus idea and the comic elephant (which reappears in the notes of 1883). In a miniature form, of course, the circus survived (chapter 22).

But the circus idea did not take fire. Or perhaps he had a kind of 'Kentucky Scenes' in mind, on the lines of Longstreet's *Georgia Scenes*, long a favourite.[14] Notes like 'Village school', 'Fire in village', 'The country cotillion', 'The horse-trade', 'Candy-pulling' suggest a cross-country miscellany of Southwestern humour in the making. Or perhaps Twain was even trying to combine such a miscellany with a burlesque detective plot that resolved his two initial murders: that of Pap Finn, which was real enough, and that of Huck. Such a plot might have centred on Jim (the runaway suspect), his capture, trial, the miraculous reappearance at the last minute by Huck, with Tom as *deus ex machina*: 'boys give bill of sale of Jim'.[15]

What in the end, however, seems to have fired Twain's imagination was the Grangerford family (in all its pride) and a jotting: 'The Burning Shame at Napoleon, Ark.' With that, whether he realized it or not, his book had found a new direction. His 'tank' slowly and steadily began to fill. Since 1865 he had been chuckling over Jim Gillis's romp, heard in his cabin at Jackass Gulch, California. In 1877 he had had ideas of working it into a novel. There, too, a 'printer tramp' was to be involved. Now two tramp printers emerge. Perhaps they should take over. Then the momentum is preserved: 'Keep 'em along.)' Then Huck and Jim can continue downstream. 'Back a little, CHANGE . . .' The raft needs to be resurrected and repaired. That's it. The printers *take over* the raft . . .

In some such fashion the text as we know it emerged. It emerged, that is, in 1879–80 before Twain's return to the Mississippi. At last his ideas were in ferment and he was able to compose the Grangerford chapters (17 and 18) by June 1880; perhaps that same summer to introduce the king and duke (chapters 19 and 20); and push the story ahead as far as Bricksville and the gunning down of Boggs (chapter 21) by the spring of 1883. A new panorama now spread before him, though the going was slow. He stopped, he started. After Huck's stay at the Grangerfords' the whole perspective shifted. Perhaps it was *both* to be an escapade *and* an anatomy of the Southwest. But how? On an elephant? With Jim in chains? Now that he was keeping that progress down the river, he could keep Huck as a *captive* observer and Jim could remain (somehow) at the centre of the whole drama, even if, for much of the time, necessarily invisible. So Twain adds: '(Jim has fever & is in concealment while Huck makes these observations.)'

Group B (2 pages): 1879–80
These notes suggest how confused and disconnected Twain now was from his 1876 manuscript:

~~Widow Douglas – then who is 'Miss Watson?'~~

Ah, she's W D's *sister.* – old spinster

– the dead man is Huck's father.

Let Jim say putty for 'pretty' & nuvver for 'never'.

In 1875 'Old Times on the Mississippi' (the account of his days as cub pilot on the river) had been published in the *Atlantic Monthly*. It was a great success. Now in 1882 he planned a return trip. He took a stenographer along. 'Stop at Cairo, Hickman or New Madrid (1 hour),' he dictated, 'and ask about old feuds.'[16] He spent a month that spring travelling on the river, first downstream from St Louis to New Orleans; then back upstream, stopping off three days at

Hannibal, as far as St Paul, Minnesota. Chat with a pilot elicited details of the Darnell–Watson feud. (Darnell was not a planter but a small farmer who employed a white 'hired man' and his wife. One family 'lived on the Kentucky side, the other on the Missouri side near New Madrid'; both carried their guns to church.) 'Once a boy 12 years old', he dictated, 'connected with the Kentucky family was riding thro the woods on the Mo. side. He was overtaken by a full grown man and he shot that boy dead.' All this was to be incorporated into *Life on the Mississippi* (1883); and if sections on the Darnell–Watson feud, the 'House Beautiful', on the tricksters and strolling players and assassins seem to anticipate *Huckleberry Finn* there is no knowing – even if chapters 17 to 20 were already written – whether Twain rewrote them on his return. The holograph is lost. What is certain is that he returned with a new zest to his seven-year-old manuscript. Now at last the decks were cleared for a final run at *Huckleberry Finn*.

Group C (some 13 pages): summer 1883, on the final resumption of work at chapter 22.

This is quite the longest group of jottings and queries. Again, details have grown rusty:

> Miss Watson, (goggles) sister to W^d Douglas.
> Becky Thatcher (or Bessie?)
> '*Bessie*' or Becky?

The interest in dialect spelling continues:

> Nuffn
> mouf.
> generly
> Huck says Nuther.   ef
> h'yer   reck'n
> ~~in defference~~ ⎱ to public opinion – don't know ~~which~~
> in defferunce ⎰
>   how to pronounce it. ~~He went through the motions of imprisoning~~
> ~~Tom in defferunce~~

As the muddle about Becky Thatcher's name suggests (she remains

Bessie in chapter 8), he is also tampering with the opening chapters, jotting down reflections for Huck which he never used:

> And bread cast *returns* – which it don't & can't, less'n you heave it up-stream – you let cast your bread downstream once, & see. It can't stem the current; so it can't come back no more. But the widow she didn't know no better than to believe it, and it warn't my business to correct my betters. There's a heap of ignorance like that, around.

The conclusion was still not settled:

> ~~& Jim can be smuggled north on~~ a ship? – no, steamboat.
> Jim cries, to think of his wife & 2 ch^n
> Talk among Ark family & visitors. – using snuff with a stick.

Some Arkansas scenes, sadly, were not to be used at all:

> Quilting. The world of gossip ~~of~~ 75 yrs ago, that lies silent, stitched into quilt by hands that long ago lost their taper & silkiness & eyes & face their beauty, & all gone down to dust & silence; & to indifference to all gossip.

Or less gloomily:

> He must hear some Arkansas women, over their pipes & knitting (spitting from between teeth), swap reminiscences of Sister this & Brother that, & 'what became of so & so? – what was his fust wife's name?' Very religious people. Ride 10 or 15 m to church & tie the horses to trees.
>   Let em drop in ignorant remarks about monarchs in Europe, & mix them up with Biblical monarchs.
>   Look through notebook & turn everything in.
>   ★ s'I, sh-she, s-ze,

But what these jottings show, above all, is the steady, inventive attention that Twain gave to details (those tiresome details so berated by critics) of the Evasion. Here is a final sample page:

> Tools too handy. ★(How'll we get this pen to him?) in a cake by Aunt Sally.

He ain't satisfied. Ought to be a watchman. Nonnymous note to recommend it. This when they are nearly ready.

*Get tin plates for Jim *Dig a moat.

Objects because tools & everything so handy.

*(Spend many nights in cabin with Jim.)

Saw there, too.

3 weeks getting him out. *make the pens – *Huck*.

Make rope ladder, now, hiding it as they work.

*Butter melts night of escape. *Ladder in *pie*

The dogs come in through the diggings – 11. *And themselves as ghosts. Nigger watchman faints.

Swallow the sawdust – *Huck* has to – & Jim. Gives them stomach ache. *Blow up* cabin? *aunt misses brass candlestick, shirt, sheet, flour &c (for *they* build the pie.) Uncle reads anonymous notes at table.

Much of this burlesque, it will be seen, found its way into Tom's grand finale.

From mid-June to August 1883, working in his octagonal study in Elmira, he scribbled on, in an inspired burst, to the famous conclusion: 'if I'd a knowed what a trouble it was to make a book I wouldn't a tackled it and ain't agoing to no more' (229/362). It was also now that he added most of chapters 12 to 14 (the *Walter Scott* and King Solomon episodes). In brief, it is the holograph of that final summer's work that has been preserved in Buffalo.

Twain was delighted by his flood of words. In July 1883 he boasted to Howells that he was averaging from 2,600 to 4,000 words a day. He must have been working on the so-called Evasion sequence (chapters 34 to 40), whose regular flow of lines shows few signs of afterthought or erasure. To his mother and brother Orion he wrote in high spirits:

> I haven't had such booming working-days for many years. I am piling up manuscript in a really astonishing way. I believe I shall complete, in two months, a book which I have been fooling over for 7 years. This summer it is no more trouble for me to write than it is to lie.[17]

Another eight months passed, however, before he finally informed his nephew, Charles L. Webster (in whose name he had set up his own publishing house): 'I sent the MS today.' He must have been tinkering with it since August. It was then that he not only regularized, but added further, phonetic dialect spellings: *seegars* for 'cigars', *considable* for 'considerable', *yaller* for 'yellow', *furrin* for 'foreign', *k'yer* for 'care', *mouf* for 'mouth', *g'yirls* for 'gals', *obleeged* for 'obliged', *bile* for 'boil', *afeard* for 'afraid', *awluz* for 'always', as well as occasionally adjusting the exact pitch and illiterate grammar for a colloquial speech with an *'uz* for 'was', *kin* for 'can', *de* for 'the', *s'pose* for 'suppose', *out'n* for 'out of', *nuther* for 'neither', *nuffin* for 'nothing'.[18] It was always his ear that dictated such changes, though deviant spelling follows deviant pronunciation far less frequently than it follows deviant diction. Perhaps a thousand substantive changes were made, not counting such economies as the elimination of italics for emphasis. Walter Blair, in *Mark Twain & 'Huck Finn'*, concluded that Twain worked over the manuscript three times before mailing it to his nephew.

It was at this stage, too, that the trend to revising for social propriety became marked. Years later Twain regretted having cleaned up the 'Burning Shame' (the king's lewd vaudeville turn for the men of Bricksville), though the manuscript shows only minor changes.[19] Howells was given 'carte blanche in making corrections'. His wife, Livie, as usual screened the galleys. But Twain, it is now agreed, was his own worst censor.[20] To his sexual discretions I shall return later. But there were other Victorian embargoes, especially those aimed at swearing and insobriety and impiety. The mildest oaths, he felt, had to be toned down: 'dam' is reduced to 'blame', 'dum'd' to 'derned', even 'derned' to 'ornery'. Though a fit of delirium tremens is graphically portrayed, 'drunker' and 'drunk' in a single passage are etiolated to 'tighter' and 'mellow'. It was now that the place of Jim's ultimate betrayal, a 'gin-mill', was euphemistically transformed to 'a little low doggery' (166/266). Religion, of course, had to be watched. Despite satirical set-scenes (such as the camp-meeting or the Wilks funeral), despite the whole import of the book, *detail* had to be respected. At the circus, the horse 'agoing like a house afire' was originally 'agoing like sin' (120/194). The king, all dressed up, originally looked as if 'he had walked right out of the Bible and maybe was old Leviticus himself'; this was ruined when 'ark' was substituted for 'Bible' (127/204). 'Judas Iscarott' was halved to 'Judus'; 'up towards the Throne' became 'up towards the sky'; even 'as mild as Sunday School' in Tom's mouth had to be changed to 'as mild as goose-milk' (184/292).

Such mealy-mouthed caution crept into some of his most vigorous passages. When on the third night of 'The Royal Nonesuch' a crowd gathers to break up the performance, the text originally read:

> I smelt rotten eggs by the barrel, and rotten cabbages and such things; and if I know the smell of a dead cat, and I bet I do, there was sixty-four of them went in. I shoved in there for a minute, but it was too rancid for me . . .

This was neutered to:

> I smelt sickly eggs by the barrel, and rotten cabbages, and such things; and if I know the signs of a dead cat being around, and I bet I do, there was sixty-four of them went in. I shoved in there for a minute, but it was too various for me . . .[21]

There was a wholesale deletion of words like 'putrid', 'rotten', 'rot', 'cuss', 'cussed'. Where Huck originally wrote that a conscience 'takes up more room than all the rest of a person's bowels', this density was casually evacuated to 'insides'. Even Tom was not allowed his recipe for prisoner's ink, 'iron-rust and spit', but palmed off with 'iron-rust and tears'. The duke's splendid parting shot at the king, 'you unsatisfiable, tunnel-bellied old sewer' (chapter 30), was sacrificed altogether.[22] At such moments Twain, the perpetually double man, lost confidence in his own soundest instincts. Little good did it do him!

The most significant changes, however, appear to have been due to structural worries. How could Tom Sawyer, last seen in St Petersburg, be reintroduced one thousand miles further down the river? Should there not be other children on the Phelps farm? Originally there had been a boy and a girl, called Phil and Mat. Huck had confided Tom's imminent arrival to Phil and Mat. But they had to go to prevent them from tagging along and undermining Tom's Evasion sequence. This left only a gaggle of youngsters, with the odd result that Silas and Sally became rather elderly parents for the Phelps brood. Should Colonel Sherburn's harangue to the lynch mob be quite so elaborately contemptuous? It was severely recast and reduced for political reasons, though all his most cutting sneers at the South were allowed to stand. The *Walter Scott* episode was added, in part, to provide the books for Huck to read from 'about kings and dukes'

(64/93), to pave the way for the real king and duke. He added Jim's story about the mistreatment of his daughter (at the end of chapter 23) and thoroughly revised Huck's crucial crisis of conscience (in chapter 31). Much of this revision was done on rereading the manuscript; much more – Huck's visit to the circus, for example – on correcting the typescript.[23]

By this time he was utterly fed up. He even inveigled Howells into doing the proof-reading. On 7 August 1884 he wrote to him:

> I have no doubt I am doing a most criminal & outrageous thing – for I am sending you these infernal Huck Finn proofs – but the very last vestige of my patience has gone to the devil, & I cannot bear the sight of another slip of them. My hair turns white with rage, at sight of the mere outside of the package.

Howells courteously, and no doubt sincerely, replied: 'If I had written half as good a book as Huck Finn, I shouldn't ask anything better than to read the proofs; even as it is I don't.' The detailed variety of phonic misspellings alone made this a complex and time-consuming task. In fact, Twain did rather more proof-reading than his letters to Howells suggest. But it is typical of him that he left so much to Howells's practised editorial eye, as he left so many other decisions to his nephew.

But that was still far from the end of the trail. For all his attention to detail, Twain could be sublimely vague. By the time unbound copies were ready in September 1884 still further changes had taken place. His nephew, an editorial greenhorn, played a remarkable role here. Twain delegated to him the whole matter of the running heads, the table of contents and possibly even chapter-breaks. But when, at his own suggestion, Webster signed up the 23-year-old E.W. Kemble as illustrator, for $1,200, Twain was immediately on his guard. He was testy about Huck's cover-portrait ('will answer; although the boy's mouth is a trifle more Irishy than necessary') and frontispiece ('an ugly, ill-drawn face'). Huck, he emphasized, 'is an exceedingly good-hearted boy, & should carry a good & good-looking face'. Though Kemble's work grew on him. Later he admitted that his pictures were 'mighty good, now', even 'rattling good'.

But there was nothing to suggest that he quarrelled with the captions: Pap's drunken tumble from the judge's porch, labelled 'FALLING FROM GRACE'; or the king and duke ridden out of town,

'TRAVELLING BY RAIL'. The running heads, too, with their pert play of language, are wholly out of keeping with Huck's world. Pap's demand for Huck's share of the loot, for example, is headed 'THE FOND PARENT'; Huck's pay-off by the slave-hunters 'FLOATING CURRENCY'; Huck's arrival at the Grangerfords', 'AN EVENING CALL'.[24] A recent examination of the correspondence and original drawings reveals that Kemble wrote the legends while Twain reworded them into their final form.[25] So that 'FALLING FROM GRACE' was *his* guffaw. The genteel jokiness – the smug Victorian omniscience – was *his*! And if these legends were his so, in all probability, were those cute running heads, too. It was just another case of his right hand not knowing what his left was up to.

A notorious incident occurred in November. An obscenity was discovered when copies had already been delivered to the subscription-canvassers and maybe as many as 30,000 sets of sheets printed by J. J. Little. An illustration for chapter 32, with the caption 'WHO DO YOU RECKON IT IS?', showed Uncle Silas proudly sporting an erection. All prospectuses and advance sheets (some bound) had to be withdrawn. The New York *World*, on 27 November, displayed the front-page headline:

MARK TWAIN IN A DILEMA – A Victim of a Joke He Thinks the Most Unkindest Cut of All.

A 'cut' (illustrating his new novel), it was explained, had been found to show 'a glaring indecency'. The New York *Tribune* (of 29 November) claimed that Webster had 'saved the first edition of 30,000'. In the New York *Herald*, that same day, Webster announced a $500 reward 'for the apprehension and conviction' of the mischievous engraver. 'The book was examined', he explained to a reporter,

by W. D. Howells, Mr Clemens, the proofreader and myself. Nothing improper was discovered . . . By the punch of an awl or graver, the illustration became an immoral one. Had the first edition been run off our loss would have been $250,000. Had the mistake not been discovered, Mr Clemens's credit for decency and morality would have been destroyed.

Luckily Twain was out of town, giving platform readings from

Huckleberry Finn. He was on tour, with George Washington Cable, throughout the United States and Canada, when *Huckleberry Finn* was published in England (4 December 1884), in Canada (10 December 1884), and finally in New York (18 February 1885). His favourite passages were the music-hall turns: the 'King Sollermun' dialogue from chapter 14 and Tom's rescue of Jim.

Twain's haphazard handling of what is now holy writ is best illustrated by the so-called 'Raftsmen's Passage'. It is a wonderful passage which Twain gratuitously lifted from *Huckleberry Finn* to enrich chapter 3 of *Life on the Mississippi*. On George Washington Cable's (excellent) advice, he restored it to chapter 16 of *Huckleberry Finn*, following the second paragraph. But when his nephew wanted it out again, since the book was 'so *much* longer than Tom Sawyer', out it went. Twain simply approved the cut by return mail:

Yes, I think the raft chapter can be left wholly out, by heaving in a paragraph to say Huck visited the raft to find out how far it might be to Cairo, but got no satisfaction. Even *this* is not necessary unless that raft-visit is referred to later in the book. I think it is, but am not certain.

That was his way. He was both the most professional and most cavalier of authors. He seemed to lose track of his own most considered views. Just as promptly he gave in to Richard Watson Gilder, then editing three pre-publication extracts for the *Century*.[26] It proved a memorable conjunction. Howells's *The Rise of Silas Lapham* was on its ninth and tenth chapters; George Washington Cable's 'The Freedman's Case in Equity' appeared in the January issue, 1885; in February, James's *The Bostonians* was beginning serialization. *Silas Lapham* Twain found 'dazzling – masterly – incomparable'. But James! 'I would rather be damned to John Bunyan's heaven than read that,' was his famous comment.

Encroaching chaos continued to haunt him. By early February 1885 he realized that they had neglected to send out review copies in time for the magazines: 'how in *hell* we overlooked that unspeakably important detail', he wrote to Webster, 'utterly beats my time'. His nephew coolly replied: 'In regard to press notices of the book; That was not overlooked, you remember you told me in the start that press notices *hurt* the last book before it was out & that this year we would send *none* until the book was out.'[27] The only comment he could surely have wished for on publication would have echoed his own welcome to Howells's *Indian Summer*: 'It is a beautiful story, & makes a body laugh all the time, & cry inside.'[28]

But sales figures, as supplied by Webster, must have helped cheer him up:

2 September 1884	Order from general agents: 9,000 copies
13 December 1884	The 'book is doing all that could be expected in these hard times'.
14 March 1885	39,000 sold, with orders bringing total up to 45,000.
18 March 1885	'We have sold *another* 1,000 "Hucks", making 42,000 sold to date and been out *just* a month today.'
24 March 1885	'We have sold about 1,500 "Hucks" since [21 March].'
6 May 1885	51,000 copies of *Huckleberry Finn* sold.[29]

America's most popular book of all time was launched. It was the advocacy of H. L. Mencken, a generation later, that established the claim for *Huckleberry Finn* to be 'the greatest novel ever written by an American'.[30]

NOTES

1 Begun by Bernard DeVoto in *Mark Twain at Work* (Cambridge, Mass.: Harvard University Press, 1942) and intensively developed by Walter Blair, 'When was *Huckleberry Finn* written?', *American Literature*, vol. 30 (March 1958), pp. 1–25. A two-volume facsimile of the Buffalo and Erie County Library manuscript, introduced by Louis J. Budd, was published by Gale Research (Detroit, Mich., 1983).

2 Howells to Mark Twain (21 November 1875), Mark Twain to Howells (23 November 1875), *The Mark Twain–Howells Letters*, ed. Henry Nash Smith, William M. Gibson and Frederick Anderson (Cambridge, Mass.: Harvard University Press, 1960), Vol. 1, pp. 110–13.

3 Mark Twain to Howells (5 July 1875), ibid., Vol. 1, p. 91. The 'story' is *The Adventures of Tom Sawyer*. *Gil Blas*, in fact, is not written autobiographically.

4 The New York *Sun* in its review, for example, called Huckleberry Finn 'the hero of what is neither a boys' book nor a grown-up novel' (15 February 1885).

5 Mark Twain to Howells (21 June 1875), *Twain–Howells Letters*, Vol. 1, pp. 87–8.

6 Mark Twain to Howells (9 August 1876), ibid., Vol. 1, p. 144.

7 Albert Bigelow Paine, filing it among the Mark Twain Papers, labelled it 'Boy's Manuscript'. It was probably written around 1870 or 1871. The first two pages are missing.

8   *Alta California* letter, August 1868.

9   See James L. Colwell, 'Huckleberries and humans: on the naming of Huckleberry Finn', *PMLA*, vol. 86 (January 1971), pp. 70–6. Note also how the final assonances on *k* and *n* link 'Huck Finn' to the pseudonym 'Mark Twain'.

10 *Mark Twain's Letters to Will Bowen*, ed. Theodore Hornberger (Austin, Tex.: University of Texas Press, 1941), pp. 23–4.

11 *The Autobiography of Mark Twain*, ed. Charles Neider (New York: Harper & Row, 1959), ch. 53, pp. 264–5; *Huckleberry Finn*, ch. 32, pp. 173/277.

12 DeVoto, *Mark Twain at Work*, pp. 61–81; Blair, 'When was *Huckleberry Finn* written?' extensively reworked in his *Mark Twain & 'Huck Finn'* (Berkeley, Calif.: University of California Press, 1960), passim. A schedule for the composition of *Huckleberry Finn* now looks as follows:
July to August 1876: chapter 1 to the middle of chapter 12 and chapters 15 and 16; i.e. from the opening to where the raft is struck by the steamboat, including the so-called 'Raftsmen's Passage' (later transferred to *Life on the Mississippi*, ch. 3).
October 1879 to June 1880: chapters 17 and 18 (the Grangerfords).
Summer 1880: chapters 19 and 20 (entry of the king and duke).
Spring 1882: Mark Twain returns to the Mississippi.
Spring 1883: chapter 21 (the shooting of Boggs).
Mid-June to August 1883: from the middle of chapter 12 to chapter 14 (the *Walter Scott* episode and King Solomon); chapters 22 to 43 (from Colonel Sherburn's speech to the end).

13 Asterisks indicate later interpolations.

14 Augustus Baldwin Longstreet's *Georgia Scenes* (1835) exhibited genre scenes like 'Georgia Theatrics', 'The Fight', 'The Horse-Swap'.

15 Such a plot might have been fleshed out from his unfinished novel, *Simon Wheeler, Amateur Detective* (1877–9). Franklin R. Rogers, in *Mark Twain's Burlesque Patterns as Seen in the Novels and Narratives 1855–1885* (Dallas, Tex.: Southern Methodist University Press, 1960), pp. 132–4, sets out the evidence. It includes Huck's own murder, which he so carefully contrives in Pap's cabin; the fact that local folk, as Huck learns from Mrs Loftus, suspect both Pap and Jim of the murder; and the fact that three days after Huck's disappearance Pap was seen with 'a couple of mighty hard looking strangers, and then went off with them' (49/69). The discovery of Pap's body in the floating house might also belong to this abandoned plot. See Blair, *Mark Twain & 'Huck Finn'*, ch. 17. See also *Tom Sawyer*, ch. 23, where Muff Potter is saved from hanging by Tom's testimony.

16 Mark Twain's Papers, Notebook 16, TS p. 13.

17 Mark Twain to Jane Lampton Clemens (21 July 1883), *Mark Twain's Letters*, ed. Albert Bigelow Paine, Vol. 2, (New York/London: Harper & Brothers, 1935), p. 434.

18 See Sydney J. Krause, 'Twain's method and theory of composition', *Modern Philology*, vol. 56 (February 1959), p. 176. I shall return to the question of dialects and dialect spellings in Chapter 12.

19 'I had to modify it considerably to make it proper for print and this was a great damage'; *Autobiography*, ch. 27, p. 139. The one considerable modification was that of the title to 'The King's Camelopard, or the Royal Nonesuch' (121/195).

20 See James M. Cox, 'The muse of Samuel Clemens', *Massachusetts Review*, vol. 5 (Autumn 1963), pp. 127–41, and Leland Krauth, 'Mark Twain: the Victorian of Southwestern humor', *American Literature*, vol. 54 (October 1982), pp. 368–84.

21 *Huckleberry Finn*, ch. 23, p. 123/198.

22 All examples are quoted from DeVoto, *Mark Twain at Work*, pp. 83–4.

23 Mark Twain, according to Victor Fischer, had the manuscript typed in two stages: the first two-fifth, put by since 1880, in late 1882 or early 1883; the remainder,

possibly in batches as he composed it, during the summer of 1883. The first two-fifth was later retyped under Howells's scrutiny. It was this typed copy, not the manuscript, which became printer's copy for the first edition. None of the typescripts are known to survive. A forthcoming volume of the Iowa/California edition of *The Works of Mark Twain*, collating variants line by line, will facilitate this comparison of the manuscript with the first printing.

24 See Allison Ensor, 'The contributions of Charles Webster and Albert Bigelow Paine to *Huckleberry Finn*', *American Literature*, vol. 40 (May 1968), pp. 222–7.

25 Beverly R. David, 'Mark Twain and the legends for *Huckleberry Finn*', *American Literary Realism*, vol. 15 (Autumn 1982), pp. 155–65.

26 'If you should ever carefully compare the chapters of *Huckleberry Finn*, as we printed them, with the same as they appear in the book, you will see the most decided difference. These extracts were carefully edited for a magazine audience with his full consent': *Letters of Richard Watson Gilder*, ed. Rosamund Gilder (Boston, Mass.: Houghton Mifflin, 1916), pp. 398–9. The three extracts for the *Century Magazine*, vol. 29, were: 'An Adventure of Huckleberry Finn: With an Account of the Famous Grangerford–Shepherdson Feud' (December 1884); 'Jim's Investments, and King Sollermun' (January 1885); 'Royalty on the Mississippi, As Chronicled by Huckleberry Finn' (February 1885).

27 See *Mark Twain, Business Man*, ed. Samuel Charles Webster (Boston, Mass.: Little, Brown, 1946), p. 300.

28 *Twain–Howells Letters*, Vol. 2, p. 533.

29 See Arthur Lawrence Vogelback, 'The publication and reception of *Huckleberry Finn* in America', *American Literature*, vol. 11 (November 1939), pp. 262–3. Vogelback's findings have recently been thoroughly revised by Victor Fischer: 'More than twenty contemporary reviews and well over a hundred contemporary comments on the book have now been found.' See 'Huck Finn reviewed: the reception of *Huckleberry Finn* in the United States, 1885–1897', *American Literary Realism*, vol. 16 (Spring 1983), pp. 1–57.

30 H. L. Mencken, 'The burden of humor', *The Smart Set*, vol. 38 (February 1913), pp. 151–4.

CHAPTER 3

A Civil War among Huck's Readers

Papa said the other day, 'I am a mugwump and a mugwump is pure from the marrow out'.

SUSY CLEMENS

The novel was written during the presidencies of Ulysses S. Grant, Rutherford B. Hayes and James A. Garfield. It was written, that is, not simply in the aftermath of the Civil War, during Federal Reconstruction, but in the aftermath of Reconstruction. Twain himself in 1873 gave the period its enduring name, the 'Gilded Age'.

Huckleberry Finn was begun the year after the passing of the Civil Rights Act which assured equality of treatment for Whites and Blacks. This sounded fine in principle, but was bitterly resented. Poor Whites teamed up against poor Blacks. Populist pressure assured a steady erosion of civil rights. The notorious Black Codes, introduced after the Civil War, were restored and new legislation passed that was to become a model for the 'Jim Crow' laws (segregating public transport, housing, etc.) of the 1890s. The Ku Klux Klan flourished.[1]

In November 1876, putting his manuscript aside, Twain actively participated in the Hayes campaign, rejoicing in the narrow (if electorally dubious) victory over the Democrat Tilden. Years later he was dismayed at the swindle. For 1877 was the year of betrayal, the year of Republican compromise with Southern democrats. In return for their electoral votes, the last federal troops were withdrawn from the South. The Supreme Court consistently defended states' rights to protect their public health, safety and morals – their police power, in other words – at the expense of the individual under the Fourteenth Amendment; and Blacks, increasingly denied their political rights, were forced into sharecropping.

Even in 1880, however (while working on the Grangerford feud and the entry of the king and duke), Twain was still an orthodox Republican. 'Garfield suits me thoroughly and exactly,' he wrote, despite mounting disgust with his henchmen. In 1883, the year *Huckleberry Finn* was finally finished, the Supreme Court declared the Civil Rights Act unconstitutional. The era of legal segregation was instituted. By now Twain had begun to detach himself from the Republican caucus. Through the autumn of 1884, while *Huckleberry Finn* was going to press, he worked with the rebel Mugwumps, chairing rallies and canvassing Nook Farm. Dismissing James G. Blaine, the Republican presidential candidate, as 'the filthy Blaine', Twain finally switched. He left the party of Lincoln for Grover Cleveland and the Democrats. It was a dramatic switch. It may even have been decisive. For Twain's political speeches were printed by both Republican and Democratic newspapers. Cleveland carried New York by only 1,149 votes, and it was the thirty-six electoral votes of New York State that won him the presidency.[2]

Yet *Huckleberry Finn* remained under the aegis of his hero, General Grant. It was published, as the peremptory 'NOTICE' indicates:

BY ORDER OF THE AUTHOR

Per G. G., CHIEF OF ORDNANCE.

By this time he was not only a personal friend but the General's publisher. Even while completing the final intricacies of publishing his own *Huckleberry Finn*, he was arranging the publication of the General's memoirs.[3] In a sense he had returned to the fold of his father. John Marshall Clemens had been a Southern Whig. Twain always remained a Whiggish Republican. Thus a Mugwump.[4] As his daughter Susy recorded – and Twain kept the record after her death – 'Papa said the other day, "I am a mugwump and a mugwump is pure from the marrow out". (Papa knows that I am writing this biography of him, and he said this for it.)'

Yet *Huckleberry Finn* must be viewed in an even wider context. The ante bellum South was founded on three great principles: (1) the rightness of hierarchical society; (2) which 'protected' Blacks by their subordinate status; (3) and which promoted Christian charity by its paternal guardianship of a race inherently childlike. *Huckleberry Finn* undermines at least two of these principles. That Blacks were somehow 'protected' by slavery is ruthlessly exposed by Miss

Watson's intended sale of Jim and destruction of his family. That Blacks are inherently childlike is more ambiguously treated. For, though linked to a 14-year-old boy as his social inferior, Jim transcends that childlike role by becoming, on occasion, Huck's guardian and ideal father. When it comes to a hierarchy headed by Judge Thatcher, the Grangerfords and Shepherdsons, the text is cutting.

Joel Williamson, in *The Crucible of Race*, divided the three broad strands of Southern White opinion into 'conservative', 'liberal' and 'radical'.[5] These terms denote what the French call *mentalités* rather than political platforms. The conservatives were the postwar paternalists, the white 'Redeemers' who toppled the Republican state governments in the 1870s. The liberal challenge was based on two great counter-principles: (1) that Blacks had no fixed place in a social and biological hierarchy; (2) and so should be granted the same public rights and opportunities as Whites. Under the slogans 'Equity' and 'Brotherhood' they strongly rebutted conservative orthodoxy. Mark Twain and George Washington Cable were leading liberals of the 1880s. The radical backlash developed later, only after *Huckleberry Finn* was published; but to a liberal propagandist like Twain it was early apparent. By mingling racist and sexual prejudices, it promoted the rapist stereotype: the Negro as Menace, the Negro as Beast. Before 1889 most lynchings occurred on the Western frontier and most victims, like the king and duke, were white. Then panic broke out. The number of lynchings soared. Between 1885 and 1907, Williamson writes, 'there were more persons lynched in the United States than were legally executed, and in the year 1892 twice as many'. In the 1890s an average of 138 people a year were lynched in the South, of whom 75 per cent were white. By 1900–10 lynchings declined to more like 70 a year, but 90 per cent of the victims were black.[6] The collapsing cotton economy of the late 1880s and early 1890s did not help. But by the late 1890s, when prosperity returned to the white South, racial violence continued. Mobs attacked defenceless Blacks in Wilmington, North Carolina, in 1898 and in Atlanta, Georgia, in 1906. This was now twenty years after the publication of *Huckleberry Finn*, but Twain was still alive; the book continued to sell alongside W. E. B. DuBois, *The Souls of Black Folk* (1903), and Thomas Dixon, Jr's *The Clansman* (1905). This was still the early period of its reception, in terms of which it was judged.

For despite its sales *Adventures of Huckleberry Finn* has never had an easy ride. It offended too many vested interests. In the late nineteenth century it offended the Northern bourgeoisie. By the early twentieth century it offended the white South. By the mid-twentieth century it offended Blacks everywhere, especially urban Blacks. By the late twentieth century it even offended urban Whites. There must, one cannot help thinking, be something right about a book that can offend quite so many diverse people, quite so many pressure groups, at various times. Concord, Massachusetts, launched the first attack. On 17 March 1885 the *Boston Transcript* published this notice:

> The Concord (Mass.) Public Library committee has decided to exclude Mark Twain's latest book from the library. One member of the committee says that, while he does not wish to call it immoral, he thinks it contains but little humor, and that of a very coarse type. He regards it as the veriest trash. The librarian and the other members of the committee entertain similar views, characterizing it as rough, coarse and inelegant, dealing with a series of experiences not elevating, the whole book being more suited to the slums than to intelligent, respectable people.

So the cat was out of the bag. Word was out from the transcendentalist Olympus. The home town of Emerson and Thoreau, Hawthorne and the Alcotts, had spoken. *Huckleberry Finn* was 'trash'. As Jim, in a memorable speech, had put it: 'Dat truck dah is *trash*; en trash is what people is dat puts dirt on de head er dey fren's en makes 'em ashamed' (72/105). Huck, he was saying, had stooped to a level of what even niggers called 'white trash'. The Concord library committee, without a jot of Jim's justification, felt the same. It felt ashamed of Huck; it felt as if Twain had poured dirt over their heads. So the book was banned.

Twain survived the anathema. He picked up his pen the very next day to write a gleeful letter to Webster:

> Dear Charley – The Committee of the Public Library of Concord, Mass, have given us a rattling tip-top puff which will go into every paper in the country. They have expelled Huck from their library as 'trash & suitable only for the slums'. That will sell 25,000 copies for us, sure. Yrs, S. L. C.

Much in the spirit of the duke sticking up posters for 'The Royal Nonesuch' with that huge bottom line:

LADIES AND CHILDREN NOT ADMITTED.

'"There," says he, "if that line don't fetch them, I don't know Arkansaw!"'(121/195).

In any case he was quickly revenged. Opinion in Concord was clearly split. A week later the Concord Free Trade Club offered him its membership. Twain pounced. A 'committee of the public library of your town', he wrote,

> have condemned and excommunicated my last book and doubled its sale. This generous action of theirs must necessarily benefit me in one or two additional ways. For instance, it will deter other libraries from buying the book; and you are doubtless aware that one book in a public library prevents the sale of a sure ten and a possible hundred of its mates. And, secondly, it will cause the purchasers of the book to read it, out of curiosity . . . and then they will discover, to my great advantage and their own indignant disappointment, that there is nothing objectionable in the book after all.

This letter was made public.[7] But Twain, as he well knew, was up against the entrenched snobbism of the Eastern seaboard, the elegant and respectable book-buying public. His book, it decreed, was subversive. It set a bad example to boys. Louisa May Alcott, too, was outraged. Unhesitatingly she backed the Concord decision: 'If Mr Clemens cannot think of something better to tell our pure-minded lads and lasses, he had best stop writing for them.' Between 1902 and 1907 the libraries of Denver, Omaha and Brooklyn, among others, banned *Huckleberry Finn* from their shelves. This must have had some effect. It certainly effected T. S. Eliot's parents in St Louis, Missouri. There, in Twain's own home state, they, too, considered 'that it was a book unsuitable for boys'. 'I suspect', T. S. Eliot was to write in 1950, 'that a fear on the part of my parents lest I should acquire a premature taste for tobacco, and perhaps other habits of the hero of the story, kept the book out of my way.'[8] Certainly he never read it as a boy.

By the mid-twentieth century the pendulum had swung the other way. It was Blacks who were up in arms. In 1945 the National Association for the Advancement of Colored People (the NAACP) linked *Huckleberry Finn* with *Little Black Sambo* for its 'racial slurs' and 'belittling racial designations'. By 1957 the New York City Board of Education had dropped *Huckleberry Finn* from its lists of approved textbooks for elementary and junior high schools, describing it as 'racially offensive'.[9] The use of the word 'niggcr' was the key trouble. In June 1976 it was also removed from required high-school reading lists in Illinois because of that same word.

The campaign has in no way abated. If anything, it has been stepped up. Throughout the 1980s public committees of both libraries and schools in states as diverse as Iowa, Pennsylvania and Texas have condemned *Huckleberry Finn* (in the words of one administrator from Virginia) as 'racist trash'. The most recent bid to ban the book from the high-school curriculum was made in Springfield, Illinois (1984). Universally condemned is the term 'nigger'; that common appellation for slaves at the time of slavery had long been a stumbling-block. Even before Twain was born, abolitionists were objecting to the term. Thomas Wentworth Higginson, in *Army Life in a Black Regiment* (1869), had deplored the common use of 'nigger' among freedmen.[10] Would Jews, for instance, approve a set text in which smear words like 'kike' and 'yid' were used between 160 and 200 times? (Dazed by this argument, its proponents seem to have trouble in establishing an exact word-count.) One thing, however, should be made clear: that the title 'Nigger Jim' (compounded, like 'Jud Süss', to form a proper name) is nowhere to be found in Mark Twain's writings. Devised by Albert Bigelow Paine for his biography (1912), it was picked up by Hemingway and transmitted by him to several generations of white Americans. We have learnt to be more sensitive. To us – as to millions of black Americans – the term 'nigger' connotes not only a role which is subservient, or a rank which is subordinate, but also a sub-species which is subhuman. Just property. That's all. As is clear from this exchange, about a riverboat accident, between Aunt Sally and Huck:

> 'Good gracious! anybody hurt?'
> 'No'm. Killed a nigger.'
> 'Well, it's lucky; because sometimes people do get hurt.'[11]

Huck had never before met Aunt Sally. He was spinning out a yarn. It was off the cuff – a reflex. But he is whip-smart. It was his instinctive idea of her idea of the conventions. He glibly exploited those conventions; and her reply promptly confirmed his assumptions. That – to spell it out – is the joke. He coolly evoked her bigotry. If that could be taught in American schools, then neither Jim (for all his limitations) nor Twain (for his) would be such a stumbling-block. For *Huckleberry Finn*, at heart, is a profoundly anti-racist book.

It belongs irrevocably, however, to its period, as the word 'nigger' belongs to that period. It cannot be wished away or ignored. But it can be read politically. The whole story, if clearly not an allegory, can be read through a wide range of political spectacles. There is a view from the North and there is a view from the South; and both are capable of different emphases and variations. There is the conscientious Huck of Reconstruction who brought back into fiction, as James M. Cox put it, 'not the Old South but an entirely new one which the Northern conscience could welcome back into the Union'.[12] But there is also the evasive Huck of the Evasion who eventually 'loses all but a spectator's interest in Jim'. Rather like a group of genteel Hucks, wrote George C. Carrington, Jr, 'the northern middle class, many of them former Radical Republicans who had fought to free the slaves, became irritated by the long bother of Reconstruction, became tired of Southern hostility, and were easily seduced by strong-willed politicians and businessmen into abandoning the freedmen for new excitements like railroad building.'[13] On this reading Jim's situation at the end of *Huckleberry Finn* reflects that of the Negro in the Reconstruction, then, 'free at last and thoroughly impotent, the object of devious schemes and a hapless victim of constant brutality'. He is the invisible man. 'Huck's liberation from the imperatives of racism', Neil Schmitz continues,

> is intensely realized, but his discovered love, it would seem, is not enough. The power of Tom's blindness, his simple inability to see Jim, intervenes. Huck is made a reluctant actor in a scenario that provides Jim with a spurious escape and an authentic mob of lynchers. The sordid history of the Reconstruction with its betrayal and humiliations of the black man pours into *Huckleberry Finn* at the end, inhibiting Twain as Huck is inhibited.[14]

Shift to the white South, though, and the view changes. There Tom looms larger as hero. In the words of Faulkner's lawyer, Gavin Stevens: 'That's what we are really defending, the privilege of setting [Sambo] free ourselves.'[15] Three times that phrase resounds at the conclusion of *Huckleberry Finn*. First Aunt Sally asks: 'Then what on earth did *you* want to set him free for, seeing he was already free?' (226/357) Next Huck asks himself why 'Tom Sawyer had gone and

took all that trouble and bother to set a free nigger free!' (227/358).
Finally he asks Tom 'what it was he'd planned to do if . . . he
managed to set a nigger free that was already free before?' (228/360).
Eric J. Sundquist, one of Faulkner's recent commentators, explains:

> The collapse into a melodrama of enslavement and liberation that
> Twain's novel enacts, some sixty years before *Intruder in the Dust*,
> reveals with all the irony Twain could bring to bear upon the
> emerging moral failure of his nation's own vision the utter
> necessity – *again, still, once more* – of setting free a people who had
> ostensibly been free for twenty years.[16]

That lurching parenthesis ('*again, still, once more*') might itself be a
comment on Tom's device for Jim's escutcheon: '*Maggiore fretta,
minore atto.*'[17] For the process of white liberation of the black man is
always inconclusive; its aim recede into the future. As Tom is coolly
aware:

> He said it was the best fun he ever had in his life, and the most
> intellectural; and said if he only could see his way to it we could
> keep it up all the rest of our lives and leave Jim to our children to
> get out; for he believed Jim would come to like it better and better
> the more he got used to it. He said that in that way it could be
> strung out to as much as eighty years, and would be the best time
> on record.[18]

Twain's revulsion is palpable. Who is this superior, white, romantic
saviour? Just the same old white delinquent with a new face. One who
by indulging in European fantasies and precedents effectively obscures
the basic issues of black slavery. And why is Jim 'pleased most to
death' (228/360)? Because he has learnt to truckle to such fantasies.
Because he must become a character in this production. Because he
has no choice but to shuffle and smile and accept Tom's farce.[19]
   'The negro has saved himself,' wrote Emerson years before the Civil
War, 'and the white man very patronizingly says I have saved you.'[20]
This Northern, liberal sentiment reached its most fervent expression
at the time of the Vietnam war:

> These chapters are a violent attack not only on slavery but on white
> people who think they are liberating black slaves; on what slavery

does to otherwise decent white people; and on what slavery does to otherwise decent black people . . .

The Negro is free by natural law – by virtue of being a man – and furthermore free by Emancipation (Miss Watson's will: she has freed him because of her guilty conscience). The white man, Tom Sawyer, knows he is free. But is the Negro ready for freedom? No, says Tom, he is illiterate and must be taught to write, under difficulties, to be sure – with a spoon on a grindstone, or *with his own blood*. The Negro (like the ordinary, simple, perceptive white man, Huck) does not 'understand' what must be done to be regular and right in attaining freedom. He must be taught by the superior white how to become free . . .

Slavery, in short, is an institution that makes callous jailers out of the sweet, gentle, ineffectual Phelpses; it makes a sadistic monster out of the normal, adventurous and romantic Tom Sawyer. While Huck, though he protests, goes along with white society's cruelty and folly.[21]

NOTES

1 Tennessee enacted laws prohibiting the intermarriage of races in 1870 and adopted the first 'Jim Crow' law in 1875. The Ku Klux Klan was organized in Pulaski, Tennessee, in December 1865. See C. Van Woodward, *Origins of the New South, 1877–1913* (Baton Rouge, La: Louisiana State University Press, 1951), pp. 205–34; and *The Strange Career of Jim Crow* (New York: Oxford University Press, 1955).

2 For Twain's shifting attitudes during the post-Reconstruction period, see Roger B. Salomon, *Twain and the Image of History* (New Haven, Conn.: Yale University Press, 1961), pp. 74–94.

3 See notebook entry for March 1885: 'Offer G.G's family $500 a month . . .' (Notebook 18).

4 See Kay R. Moser, 'Mark Twain – Mugwump', *Mark Twain Journal*, vol. 21 (Summer 1982), pp. 1–4. Mugwump Republicans wanted further reforms than Hayes had presented to clean up the party and government. The Hayes administration did nothing about wage cuts, the bitter strikes, nor the unemployment that rose to 4 million by the late 1870s.

5 Joel Williamson, *The Crucible of Race: Black–White Relations in the American South since Emancipation* (New York: Oxford University Press, 1984).

6 In 1882 public journals told of 114 lynchings, 68 of Whites, 46 of Blacks; by the end of 1883, the number had risen to 134 lynchings, 77 of Whites and 45 of Blacks, mainly for alleged murder. See James Elbert Cutler, *Lynch-Law* (New York, 1905), pp. 161–79, quoted by Walter Blair, *Mark Twain & 'Huck Finn'* (Berkeley, Calif.: University of California Press, 1960), p. 314.

7 Published in the Boston *Daily Advertiser*, 2 April 1885.

8 T. S. Eliot, introduction to *The Adventures of Huckleberry Finn* (London: Cresset Press, 1950), pp. vii.

9 Reported in the *New York Times*, 12 September 1957.

10 See David L. Smith, 'Huck, Jim and American racial discourse', *Mark Twain Journal*, vol. 22 (Fall 1984), p. 6.

11 *Huckleberry Finn*, ch. 32, p. 175/279; cf. Huck, a few pages earlier, hoodwinking the duke: '. . . and they've took my nigger, which is the only nigger I've got in the world, and now I'm in a strange country, and ain't got no property no more, nor nothing, and no way to make my living' (ch. 31, p. 171/272).

12 James M. Cox, *Mark Twain: The Fate of Humor* (Princeton, NJ: Princeton University Press, 1966), ch. 7, p. 179.

13 George C. Carrington, Jr, *The Dramatic Unity of 'Huckleberry Finn'* (Columbus, Ohio: Ohio State University Press, 1976), afterword, p. 190.

14 Neil Schmitz, 'Twain, *Huckleberry Finn*, and the Reconstruction', *American Studies*, vol. 12 (Spring 1971), pp. 60 and 65.

15 William Faulkner, *Intruder in the Dust* (New York: Random House, 1948; Vintage-Random, 1972), p. 154.

16 Eric J. Sundquist, *Faulkner: The House Divided* (Baltimore, Md: Johns Hopkins University Press, 1983), ch. 6, 'Half slave, half free: Go Down Moses', p. 148.

17 'Got it out of a book – means, the more haste, the less speed': *Huckleberry Finn*, ch. 38, p. 203/322.

18 ibid., ch. 36, p. 196/310. The figure is interesting. In the previous chapter Tom admired a prisoner who dug himself out of the Château d'If in '*Thirty-seven year*' (ch. 35, p. 192/304); and Tom's 'mournful inscription' for Jim repeats the sum: '*Here, homeless and friendless, after thirty-seven years of bitter captivity . . .*' (ch. 38, p. 204/322). Possibly Twain had a peculiar procrastination in mind. In 1863, only a month before the Emancipation Proclamation, Lincoln proposed to Congress the abolition of slavery by the year 1900 with financial losses reimbursed by federal bonds: i.e. a thirty-seven-year transitional period that would defer completion to the twentieth century. Here the period is even more protracted. It is extended to eighty years, perhaps to echo the eighty years between the peace treaty with England (in 1783) and the Emancipation Proclamation (in 1863). Since it took the United States eighty years to free men already declared free by the Declaration of Independence, Tom's 'fun' would of course not 'be the best time on record'.

19 cf. Neil Schmitz: 'The white man who defined his slavehood now dreams and defines the experience of his liberation, and in both roles the black man must act his part or perish' ('Twain, *Huckleberry Finn*, and the Reconstruction', p. 62).

20 *The Journals and Miscellaneous Notebooks of Ralph Waldo Emerson*, ed. Ralph H. Orth and Alfred R. Ferguson (Cambridge, Mass.: Harvard University Press, 1972), Vol. 9 (1843–1847).

21 Spencer Brown, '*Huckleberry Finn* for our time', *Michigan Quarterly Review*, vol. 6 (Winter 1967), pp. 42–4. See *Huckleberry Finn*: '"What do we want of a shirt, Tom?" "Want it for Jim to keep a journal on." "Journal your granny – *Jim* can't write"' (ch. 35, p. 190/301). 'Jim said . . . he didn't know how to make letters, besides; but Tom said he would block them out for him, and then he wouldn't have nothing to do but just follow the lines' (ch. 38, p. 204/323).

CHAPTER 4

What Kind of a Text?

'So now I got to go and trapse all the way down the river, eleven hundred mile . . .' (ch. 42)

All such interpretations converge on the final chapters of *Huckleberry Finn*, on the Evasion, on the dénouement by which Twain resolves his narrative problem. Yet a sense of an ending, as we saw in Chapter 2, was what had so long evaded him; it was what Twain had so long and desperately been seeking. It took him three years to continue his tale, seven years to complete it. He was always a tentative writer, working from unpredictable and short-term impulses. It was the impromptu performance that intrigued him, not the fuss and bother of the finished product. It cannot be right, therefore, to judge him by the canons of his contemporary, Henry James. The art of James lies precisely in a manoeuvring of his readers' expectations, of their precipitation into a vast and increasingly saturated quandary: how can all this end? Novels of his kind need to be probed both by foresight (of naïve calculation) and hindsight (of experienced judgement). They need to be both read and reread – read forward from the opening pages and backward from the closing pages – with a kind of simultaneous exposure. The art of dramatic irony was turned by James from the public tale in the public arena to all the confined and intense interstices of psychological fiction.

But Twain was a public performer. He loved to read aloud to his family from work in progress. He loved to give platform readings. As a storyteller he must be judged by his own 'How to Tell a Story' (1895), not James's 'The Art of Fiction' (1884). *Huckleberry Finn*, with its astonishingly sustained vernacular verve, is clearly a *tour de force*, but what kind of *tour de force*? It can be read, as his own reference to *Gil Blas* suggests, as picaresque fiction.[1] Both Lionel Trilling and T. S. Eliot, in celebrated introductions, called Huck a 'vagabond'.[2] In the very first chapter he puts out the light and

scrambles out of the window. His tale, that is, opens with flight; it is
overtaken by a couple of Rabelaisian roustabout tricksters; and the
whole ramshackle peregrination is docked, and ducked, in the end
with the 'evasion'. This episodic structure, however, is firmly linked
to a geographic structure. It opens in St Petersburg and Jackson's
Island, which is the world of Huck and Tom already familiar from
The Adventures of Tom Sawyer – a world seemingly without extended
families, dominated by the Widow Douglas, Miss Watson and Pap
(chapters 1 to 11). This is also the real world of Missouri and Illinois
and Glasscock's Island. It continues down the Mississippi from
Jackson's Island, past St Louis and Cairo, to the edge of the
Grangerford plantation, which is the world of Huck and Jim
(chapters 12 to 16); and from the Grangerford plantation, via
Pokeville and Bricksville, to Pikesville, which is the world of the king
and duke (chapters 17 to 31). It ends 'two mile below Pikesville'
(169/269) at the Phelps farm, returning Tom, 1,100 miles downstream, to the world of Huck (chapters 32 to 43). These three parts
are dominated by three full-scale portraits of extended families: the
Presbyterian Grangerfords;[3] the (possibly Anglican) Wilkses; and
(probably Baptist) Phelpses. Each part is again linked, but with
increasing vagueness, to a different section of the Mississippi: Huck
and Jim's solo voyage to the Illinois shore and Kentucky; the king and
duke's shenanigans to Arkansas; and the 'evasion' to Louisiana.[4]

Such a precise itinerary linked to such a casually haphazard scheme
seems the very mark of the picaresque as genre. But Twain, as we
saw, also had other models in mind. there was the boys' adventure
story as the subtitle (*Tom Sawyer's Comrade*) and opening paragraph
make clear. There was the attempt at juvenile monologue as a kind of
autobiography of a boy 'about as old as' Buck Grangerford, 'thirteen
or fourteen or along there'; later he seems to have settled on fourteen.
Then there was the epistolary model for a text which begins 'You
don't know about me' and ends with a flourish 'THE END. YOURS
TRULY, HUCK FINN.' Who *is* this 'you' to whom the book is
addressed? For the text firmly, if apologetically, is addressed to
someone. 'You see', it insists. 'You know what I mean – I don't know
the words to put it in' (32/42). There is a persistent pressure for
exposition and revelation behind this epistolary mode – for 'truth', in
a word, which is the key (three times repeated) of the opening
paragraph.

At least four models, then – the picaresque, the epistolary, the autobiographical and the adventure story – were fermenting in Twain's mind. Still others have been proposed. First and foremost the book has been read as a kind of *Bildungsroman* like *Tom Jones*, say, or *Candide*. It is this model ultimately that lies behind Leo Marx's influential essay, 'Mr Eliot, Mr Trilling, and *Huckleberry Finn*'.[5] As it lay behind Hemingway's familiar statement: 'All modern American literature comes from one book by Mark Twain called *Huckleberry Finn*. If you read it you must stop where the Nigger Jim is stolen from the boys [*sic*]. That is the real end. The rest is just cheating.'[6] But a great deal hangs on how much emphasis should be placed, as it was in the 1950s, on the river journey as a quest, a trial, an education, a ritual initiation, a pilgrimage even for revelation and grace. The moral claim is undoubted; but the extreme disappointment, the bitter sense of betrayal engendered, suggests that a too single-minded allegiance to such a model (whatever the moral consequences) is misguided.

Another model, used by Huck's earliest critics, was that of the historical novel. As Thomas Sergeant Perry, his first American reviewer, put it: 'the result is a vivid picture of Western life forty or fifty years ago . . . and the book is a most valuable record of an important part of our motley American civilization'.[7] *Huckleberry Finn* was written while Twain was between 40 and 50; its scene is set, as we saw, 'forty to fifty years ago'. Its era, therefore, by 1885 was already historic; for it pre-dated not only the Civil War, but also the Mexican war. It hardly comes past 1845, when Sam was 10.[8] Those were the golden years before the fall. Before the fatal date of 1849 (when Sam, like Huck, was 14): the year of the Gold Rush. 'To get rich', he was to daydream, 'was no one's ambition – it was not in any young person's thoughts . . . The Californian rush for wealth in '49 introduced the change and begot the lust for money which is the rule of life to-day, and the hardness and cynicism which is the spirit of to-day.'[9]

To some the book even seems a panegyric. The *roman fleuve* turns into a great prose hymn (as Twain himself called *Tom Sawyer*) to the Mississippi.[10]

> I do not know much about gods; but I think that the river
> Is a strong brown god . . .

T. S. Eliot began 'The Dry Salvages'. He called Twain 'a native' who 'accepts the River God'. Lionel Trilling entitled Huck himself 'the servant of the river-god'.[11] But *Huckleberry Finn* is not so much a lyric as an oral, an epic, an extempore performance. As Twain wrote in 1888 to the Finnish Baroness Alexandra Gripenberg:

> People are always losing sight of this pregnant fact: there is no merit in ninety-nine stories out of a hundred except the merit put into them by the teller's *art*; as a rule, nothing about a story is 'original', and entitled to be regarded as private property and valuable, except the art which the teller puts into the telling of it . . . Wherein lies a poet's claim to 'originality'? That he invents his incidents? No. That he was present when the episodes had their birth? No. That he was the first to report them? No. None of these things have any value; he confers upon them the only 'originality' that has any value, and that is his way of telling them.[12]

So Mark Twain fumbled forwards, seeking inspiration – epic breath – to continue. For it was momentum he was after, not destination. He was the last of the bards. If any text is oral, based wholly on the rhythm and tone of a speaking voice, that text is Huck's. A voice *has* no end: only pauses, slips, impersonations, quotations, digressions. Much as Chaucer and Boccaccio, Twain took over great hunks of his material. He shamelessly plagiarized Southwestern humour: Augustus B. Longstreet *and* Thomas Bangs Thorpe, Johnson J. Hooper's Simon Suggs *and* George Washington Harris's Sut Lovingood, as well as the whole baccy-chewing, loafing, hog-wallowing world of Bricksville.

In this sense *Huckleberry Finn* is a modern epic, an inexhaustible epic, as was early recognized. *Punch*, in 1896, called it 'a great book' and a 'Homeric book – for Homeric it is in the true sense, as no other English book is, that I know of'; the *Atlantic Monthly*, a year later, recognized 'that wild, youthful, impossible Odyssey . . . on a frail craft down the strong Mississippi' assuming 'in a manner epic proportions'.[13] Andrew Lang was both the first and most precise in drawing his Homeric parallel. For Huck is not only a Telemachus in search of a father, but the very heir of Odysseus as questing hero and disguised wanderer.[14]

But there is also an American term for such epic story-telling, with its own native American tradition: the 'tall tale'. As Twain himself wrote in 'How to Tell a Story':

To string incongruities and absurdities together in a wandering and sometimes purposeless way, and seem innocently unaware that they are absurdities, is the basis of the American art, if my position is correct. Another feature is the slurring of the point. A third is the dropping of a studied remark apparently without knowing it, as if one were thinking aloud. The fourth and last is the pause.

Twain's sense of a punch-line is always sure. Like that superb moment at the Wilks funeral when the undertaker

> glided, and glided, around three sides of the room, and then rose up, and shaded his mouth with his hands, and stretched his neck out towards the preacher, over the people's heads, and says, in a kind of coarse whisper, '*He had a rat!*' Then he drooped down and glided along the wall again to his place.[15]

But he had no sense of an ending, other than the anecdotal ending. All the key turning-points of Huck's *Adventures* – on Jackson's Island, on passing the Ohio at Cairo, the crisis of conscience near Pikesville – are without resolution. A voice, I repeat, has *no ending* – merely an adjustment of rhythm in its narrative expectations.

The whole adventure only makes boyish sense. Despite the river's current, Jim might have risked swimming the quarter mile channel from Jackson's Island to the Illinois shore.[16] By Illinois law, it is true, he would have been subject to arrest and (on conviction) indentured labour. Without freedom papers, that is, he would still have been on the run. Rewards were offered from way beyond the Ohio which made returning runaways profitable business. But the risks of going down-river seem far greater. Even if Huck and Jim had located the southern tip of Illinois and turned east up the Ohio river, what then? They could not go against the current. So they planned to take a *public steamboat* (67/99). A 14-year-old boy and 'his Negro' were to sail openly past slave territory on the Kentucky side! Of course they miss the Ohio, in fog as it happens (chapter 15), and only recognize the fact long past Cairo (77/129); so it seems as if Twain was never too concerned about that Ohio escape-route from the start. It was the Mississippi that he knew and there he meant to keep them, though only the devil knew (not Twain certainly) where such an 'escape' could take them.[17]

Where it takes them is on a circular tour leading from 'Pike County, in Missouri' (103/166) to Pikesville. It delivers them each to their separate fate on the Phelps farm. If we feel depressed at Tom's reappearance, Henry Nash Smith argues, so does Twain. For he invests a surplus of distraught feeling into Huck's arrival at the Phelps farm.

> When I got there it was all still and Sunday-like, and hot and sunshiny – the hands was gone to the fields; and there was them kind of faint dronings of bugs and flies in the air that makes it seem so lonesome and like everybody's dead and gone; and if a breeze fans along and quivers the leaves, it makes you feel mournful, because you feel like it's spirits whispering – spirits that's been dead ever so many years – and you always think they're talking about *you*. As a general thing it makes a body wish *he* was dead, too, and done with it all.[18]

The immediate cause of this depression is clear enough. Huck is alone once more; he is back in 'sivilization' once more; his run down the river 'all come to nothing, everything all busted up and ruined' (168/268). So it is more than formally appropriate that he returns to the state of nervous collapse of chapter 1. The wailing spinning-wheel seems the very sound of fate. In that circle of barking dogs 'I was a kind of a hub of a wheel' (173/277). Huck, in a word, is cornered. But so is Twain. Why?

Henry Nash Smith argues: 'As Huck approaches the Phelps plantation the writer has on his hands a hybrid – a comic story in which the protagonists have acquired something like tragic depth.'[19] True, but the conclusion hardly follows that Twain's own emotion was roused because the incipient tragedy of the failed mission had to be ditched or because a *comic* resolution was necessary and only Tom could supply this. As T. S. Eliot clearly perceived, for 'Huckleberry Finn, neither a tragic nor a happy ending would be suitable'.[20] Nor are the comic and the tragic exclusive as *Huckleberry Finn* had brilliantly displayed all along. For at their profoundest level – at the very roots of their perception – they are one. It is their resolution in art which Twain, in the end, failed to achieve. So again the question is: why?

Because with Tom's return Twain instinctively felt at home. With Tom he knew he could solve his problems. For Tom was always 'fun'. Tom could both thicken a plot and resolve it. Once Twain had Tom again in mind, his head simply teemed with ideas. There was no stopping him. His working notes (Group C) are by far the longest. The elaborate length of the 'evasion' sequence was one result. Far from gloom, he felt a tonic elation.

But the function of Tom as *deus ex machina* transcending *Huckleberry Finn* is wholly different from his function in his own *Adventures* – with disastrous consequences. As Robert Tracy has written, the organization of *Tom Sawyer*

> depends in large part on a kind of thematic resonance or echo: a myth, a superstition, or an incidence from romance is evoked, and this is followed by a sudden startling realization of that myth or romance. The boys pretend to be pirates and find themselves tracked by a murderer. They speculate about treasure according to Tom's half-baked romantic ideas, and behold, a treasure appears. The haunted house *is* haunted, by dangerous criminals. They dream of a 'Delectable Land' of freedom, and with the Jackson's Island episode they really do sojourn in that land. Tom imagines situations in which he will die for Becky, and then finds himself in a situation in which he must truly act heroically to save her life . . . Reality is continually interpenetrated by the mythic and the romantic worlds.[21]

Games in *Tom Sawyer*, that is, are a constant rehearsal for the affairs of the real world. Aesthetic play must be resolved in moral action.

But in *Huckleberry Finn* this sequence is radically reversed. Jim's flight for freedom merely proves a rehearsal for Tom's literary games. Instead of a myth being 'interpenetrated' by reality, Huck's reality is undermined by Tom's romantic dreams. If this frustrates Huck's so-called 'quest', or 'ritual initiation', it also makes a mockery of Tom's education. So again: why?

Because it was Tom Twain needed. This is what his euphoria implied. For Tom could interpret the dilemma as Huck never could. In his quandary over how to complete the text, Twain needed a *literate* hero. Huck can write, of course. He can write a letter, if need be; he can write his memoirs; he even on one occasion tries his hand at verse (86/141). But reading he finds 'tough' (83/137). He is not a habitual reader. What he does read instinctively are sensual signs, *natural* signs of the kind that figure in Mrs Judith Loftus's little quiz:

> 'Say – when a cow's laying down, which end of her gets up first?

Answer up prompt, now – don't stop to study over it.
Which end gets up first?'
  'The hind end, mum.'
  'Well, then, a horse?'
  'The for'rard end, mum.'
  'Which side of a tree does the most moss grow on?'
  'North side.'
  'If fifteen cows is browsing on a hillside, how many of them eats
with their heads pointed the same direction?'
  'The whole fifteen, mum.'[22]

What he cannot read instinctively are cultural signs, whether they be written texts ('I don't take no stock in dead people') or aesthetic artefacts (in the Grangerfords' parlour). A sense of symbolic interpretation is beyond his metonymic grasp, despite his vivid metaphoric imagination.

So Huck in *Tom Sawyer Abroad*, for example, is incapable of grasping that a map does not simply mirror the world; that Indiana is not necessarily pink or longitudes numbered on the ground.[23] All tokens, all arbitrary signifiers, are beyond him. That is precisely the beauty and mystery of Huck's literary style: that he writes without probing for wider (social, cultural, historical, political) designs. That is the unique value of his 'voice'. It can only push on from point to point, from day to day, in a potentially infinite series of circles. So, typically, his only 'plan' on the Phelps farm was to reproduce his earlier plan; and this, as he 'knowed very well', had no deliberate design at all:

> 'My plan is this,' I says. 'We can easy find out if it's Jim in there. Then get up my canoe to-morrow night, and fetch my raft over from the island. Then the first dark night that comes, steal the key out of the old man's britches, after he goes to bed, and shove off down the river on the raft, with Jim, hiding daytimes and running nights, the way me and Jim used to do before. Wouldn't that plan work?'[24]

Despite the plaintive tone, we can forestall Tom's reply. The answer is 'no'. We have been there before. The plan never did, or could have, worked. Not repetition was needed now, but *transformation*. That is why Twain turned to Tom. That is why Huck truckled to Tom. He truckled despite his foreboding that Tom's schemes, however stylish, were both cruel and daft and would probably get them 'all killed' into the bargain. But he could not counter them. He is his own worst victim.

Tom, on the other hand, can read every kind of sign (natural or symbolic), but he cannot write. He can only rewrite what he has read. Therefore he rewrites life in terms of books. His sense of 'style', so admired by Huck, is one of stylizing or codifying daily experience into a literary text. He is a master of codes. Twain alone can both write and read. He can read not texts only, but natural signs like 'the face of the water' as though it were a book – a book, he insists in *Life on the Mississippi*, 'that was a dead language to the uneducated passenger, but which told its mind to me without reserve'. *His* is the total authority, which is divided (twinned) in the text between Huck and Tom.[25]

To complete his book, then, Twain needed to resort to Tom, to this pseudo-literary performance, even if it put the whole momentum of *Huckleberry Finn* into reverse. Even if it stalled the book and effectively undercut it. For it offered a symbolic brake, however childish or vulgar. It produced, as a finale, the kind of symbolic and interpretative act for which Huck was always groping, but which was way beyond his powers. That, as he had always known, was the kind of thing Tom alone could handle.

The oral bard inevitably had to be overtaken by the literary hack who could impose any ending on any text anywhere. For an ending is itself a literary convention, dependent on various models of interpretation. Tom was soaked in such models. Literally soaked. Huck, deprived of all models, mastered a 'spoken' style, capable of recuperating his own experience, but as incapable as life itself of imposing a meaning, of registering a critical judgement, and so of reaching a conclusion. Huck's voice, left to itself, was incapable of concluding anything.

NOTES

1 See above Ch. 2, n.3.
2 Lionel Trilling, introduction to *The Adventures of Huckleberry Finn* (New York: Holt, Rinehart & Winston, 1948), pp. v–xiii. For T. S. Eliot, see above, Ch. 3, n.8.
3 They read the *Presbyterian Observer* (85/139) and hear a sermon on the two cardinal Presbyterian doctrines of predestination and foreordination (90/147).

4　If the Phelps farm, as Aunt Polly complains, is 'eleven hundred mile' south of St Petersburg (227/358), then it must be in either Mississippi or Louisiana. As is also implied by Huck's earlier remark: 'We begun to come to trees with Spanish moss on them, hanging down from the limbs like long gray beards' (ch. 31, p. 165/265). But Twain seems to persist in thinking of it as Arkansas. In *Tom Sawyer, Detective* (1896) the farm is in 'Arkansaw . . . not so very much short of a thousand miles at one pull' (ch. 2). In the *Autobiography*, too, he boasts of moving his uncle John Quarles's farm to Arkansas in *both* books: 'It was all of six hundred miles, but it was no trouble' (ch. 2).

5　Leo Marx, 'Mr Eliot, Mr Trilling, and *Huckleberry Finn*', *American Scholar*, vol. 22 (autumn 1953), pp. 423–40.

6　Ernest Hemingway, *Green Hills of Africa* (New York: Charles Scribner's, 1935), pt 1, ch. 1, pp. 22–3.

7　*Century Magazine*, vol. 30 (May 1885), pp. 171–2.

8　Though an occasional anachronism is made: for example, the two 'twenty dollar gold' pieces, floated by the slave-hunters down-river to Huck (ch. 16, pp. 76–127). The first regular coinage of the double-eagle was not minted until 1850.

9　'Villagers of 1840–3', in Walter Blair (ed.), *Mark Twain's Hannibal, Huck & Tom* (Berkeley, Calif.: University of California Press, 1969), p. 35.

10　In reply to a request for dramatization rights: 'This is a book, dear sir, which cannot be dramatized. One might as well try to dramatize any other sermon hymn. Tom Sawyer is simply a hymn put into prose form to give it a worldly air' (unmailed letter of 8 September 1887, in *Mark Twain's Letters*, ed. Albert Bigelow Paine, Vol. 2 (New York/London: Harper & Brothers, 1935), p. 477).

11　In their introductions, see n. 2.

12　Letter of 27 December 1888. See Ernest J. Moyne, 'Mark Twain and Baroness Alexandra Gripenberg', *American Literature*, vol. 45 (November 1973), pp. 370–8.

13　*Punch* (4 January 1896), pp. 4–5; Charles Miner Thompson, 'Mark Twain as an interpreter of American character', *Atlantic Monthly*, vol. 79 (1897), pp. 443–50.

14　Andrew Lang, *Illustrated London News*, vol. 98 (14 February 1891), p. 222. See also Ch. 7.

15　*Huckleberry Finn*, ch. 27, pp. 144–5/232-3.

16　Jim had already 'swum more'n half-way acrost de river' at night 'en kinder swum agin de current' (40/54). If the chute on the Illinois side was too strong, what remained? His best chance was to enter a free state at a *remote* point where he could neither be tracked nor traced. Now he could not even get off the island. His one idea had been to catch a ride on a passing raft and slip ashore twenty-five miles downstream. But, as Huck discovers, Jim is the prime suspect of his own murder. There was a $300 reward on his head. The situation was even worse than Jim realized.

17　cf. Roy Harvey Pearce: 'Letting Huck and Jim find Cairo and the Ohio River, Mark Twain would have realized his original intention and made Huck into the moderately "activist" type in terms of which he appears at first to have conceived him. Likely the story would have ended there. In any case, Mark Twain knew little or nothing about the Ohio River and almost everything about the Mississippi and would have been hard put to find materials with which further to develop the story' ('Huck Finn in his history', *Etudes anglaises*, vol. 24 (July–September 1971), p. 285).

18　*Huckleberry Finn*, ch. 32, pp. 172–3/276.

19　Henry Nash Smith, *Mark Twain: The Development of a Writer* (Cambridge, Mass.: Belknap Press of Harvard University Press, 1962), pt 6, 'A sound heart and a deformed conscience', ch. 6, p. 133.

20 T. S. Eliot, introduction to *The Adventures of Huckleberry Finn* (London: Cresset Press, 1950), p. xv.
21 Robert Tracy, 'Myth and reality in *The Adventures of Tom Sawyer*', *Southern Review*, new series vol. 4 (Spring 1968), p. 536.
22 *Huckleberry Finn*, ch. 11, pp. 52–3/73–4.
23 *Tom Sawyer Abroad* (1894), ch. 3 and ch. 6. I use these examples because they elaborate to the point of parody the tendency inherent in *Huckleberry Finn*.
24 *Huckleberry Finn*, ch. 34, pp. 183–4/292.
25 Their performances may overlap at times, but their essential 'grammatology' (to use Derrida's term) is very different. I shall return to the phenomenology of Huck's perceptions and the limitations of his literacy in Chapters 10 to 13.

Part Two

CHAPTER 5

Huck's World:
The River and Its People

'Soon as it was night, out we shoved . . .' (ch. 19)

The young Sam Clemens was enthralled by fraud, by the card sharks and vagrant hucksters along the Mississippi. His very pen-name was a fraud.[1] Impostors crowd his fiction from 'The Celebrated Jumping Frog of Calaveras County' to *King Leopold's Soliloquy*. The comic radiance of fraud, double-crossed with treachery, was to become the hallmark of his fiction.

For fiction itself was a fraud; and the ultimate con-man, for this renegade Southerner, was Sir Walter Scott. He damns him in *Life on the Mississippi* for 'his enchantments'.[2] He even named a foundering steamboat after him in *Huckleberry Finn* as if the great novelist were nothing but a sham-picturesque and sentimentally seductive dreamboat. Yet Twain, throughout his life, was easily taken in, just as young Huck was taken in by the king and duke, or young Sam (the cub pilot) by a nightwatchman who turns out to be 'a low, vulgar, ignorant, sentimental, half-witted humbug, an untraveled native of the wilds of Illinois'.

Sam's world, like Huck's, was all sham. Those imposing fluted columns with their Corinthian capitals adorning Southern mansions, for example, turn out to be 'made of white pine, and painted'. A dish of fruit in the parlour (as Huck, too, was to discover) proves to be 'all done in plaster, rudely, or in wax, and painted to resemble the originals – which they don't'.[3] But the greatest impostor of them all is the great Mississippi itself, that 'crookedest river in the world', continously doubling on itself and changing its course. Its very beauty is illusory, seen like a Claude at sunset, with 'the red hue brightened into gold, through which a solitary log came floating, black and conspicuous'. Such 'signs and symbols' conceal their dangers:

This sun means that we are going to have a wind tomorrow; that floating log means that the river is rising . . . that slanting mark on the water refers to a bluff reef which is going to kill somebody's steamboat one of these nights . . .[4]

The need for such sly semiology, such unceasing watchfulness, accounts for the uneasy threat in Mark Twain's landscapes. It is a lonely watch. The landscapes are as lonely as de Chirico's permanently sunny stage-sets. But in *Huckleberry Finn* there is little sunlight even; it is usually night:

Yonder was the banks and the islands, across the water; and maybe a spark – which was a candle in a cabin window – and sometimes on the water you could see a spark or two – on a raft or a scow, you know . . . Once or twice of a night we could see a steamboat slipping along in the dark, and now and then she would belch a whole world of sparks up out of her chimbleys . . .

We got away as soon as it was good and dark . . . We come in sight of the little bunch of lights by-and-by – that was the town, you know – and slid by, about a half a mile out, all right.[5]

'Where was Moses when the candle went out?' Huck's *alter ego*, Buck, quizzes him. Huck can't think. He can't think in riddles. 'Why he was in the *dark*! That's where he was!' (81/135) Huck Finn is always in the dark. *Huckleberry Finn* is a nocturnal adventure under black (often starless and moonless) skies: 'floating down the river by night and hiding in the willows by day'.[6] They are long nights *en route*, running 'between seven and eight hours' (55/78).

But not only the voyage, almost every major incident happens at night. Huck and Tom slip away from the Widow's at night (ch. 2). Pap suddenly reappears at night (ch. 5); gets drunk and has the d.t.'s at night (ch. 6). Jim escapes from St Petersburg on a night so dark that he can board and leave unseen a lighted raft: 'It clouded up en 'uz pooty dark for a little while' (40/54). The dead rattlesnake's mate bites Jim at night (ch. 10). Huck and Jim explore the *Walter Scott* (run aground in the night) to discover a gang of murderers at night (ch. 12). Cairo is shrouded in fog. Huck is lost in the fog and again separated from Jim at night when the raft collides with a steamboat: 'Well, the night got gray, and ruther thick, which is the next meanest thing to fog' (78/130). Sophia Grangerford elopes with Harney Shepherdson 'in de night' (93/151). The closing scene of the Wilks funeral is set in a thunderstorm at night: 'and it got awful dark, and the rain started . . .' (161/257). The king and duke are tarred and feathered by a torchlit rabble at night (ch. 33). The final 'evasion' chapters, making up one-fifth of the novel, are wholly set at night. Darkness is loneliness. Darkness is deception. Treachery and murder are hatched in the dark. It can spell friendship, even romance; but more likely violence: 'If any real lynching's going to be done, it will be done in the dark, Southern fashion' (119/191).

Yet the river is also the great highway of the book; it 'makes the book a great book', as T. S. Eliot said. Incidentally we learn a good deal about that 1,100-mile-long stretch of the Mississippi. It is a mile, 'sometimes a mile and a half', wide (96/156); after the spring floods often several miles wide from the Illinois to the Missouri shore:

> The river went on raising and raising for ten or twelve days, till at last it was over the banks. The water was three or four foot deep on the island in the low places and on the Illinois bottom. On that side it was a good many miles wide; but on the Missouri side it was the same old distance across – a half a mile – because the Missouri shore was just a wall of high bluffs.
> Daytimes we paddled all over the island in the canoe . . . We went winding in and out amongst the trees . . .[7]

It is the June rise which brings heaps of debris as well as those blanket fogs on the lower river. It is the June rise which floods down the canoe (in which Huck escapes from Pap) and the shack (in which Pap's corpse is found) as well as that section of a lumber raft (on which Huck and Jim make their way downstream); 'it is highwater and dead summer time', as Twain explains in introducing an excerpt from his unfinished novel into *Life on the Mississippi* (ch. 3). Huck and Jim float down the subsiding river after the June rise.[8]

We learn the technical terms which were the commonplaces of Twain's pilot days. We learn to distinguish 'chutes' (narrow, swift-flowing channels) from 'snags' (or sawyers) streaking the water; sometimes branches, or even whole trees torn from the banks, would lie half-covered with sand. We learn to tell tow-heads from islands. Islands might be as much as five or six miles long and more than half a mile wide; Jackson's Island was 'only three miles long and a quarter of

a mile wide' (43/58). Tow-heads were just sand-banks with cotton-
wood thickets and willows; some grew to sixty yards long and take
maybe ten minutes to pass on a current of 5 miles per hour. For we
also study the current. The river's speed for the second night is given
as 'over four mile an hour' (55/78); in the fog Huck reckons he is
floating at 'four or five mile an hour' (69/100). So the average speed of
the free floating raft works out at something like 4½ miles per hour.
We can also see the banks caving in and houses collapse:

> sometimes a strip of land as wide as a house caves in at a time.
> Sometimes a belt of land a quarter of a mile deep will start in and
> cave along and cave along till it all caves into the river in one
> summer. Such a town as that has to be always moving back, and
> back, and back, because the river's always gnawing at it.[9]

But, above all, we learn to take in the vast variety of the river's traffic:
the canoes and skiffs and trading scows; the wood-flats and lumber
rafts; the huge trading rafts or keelboats; and finally the ferry-boats
and wrought-iron paddle-steamers, potent industrial monsters such as
that which cut Huck's and Jim's raft in two.[10]

Huck is no river god, but his voyage is at one with the river, as is
his Celtic name. For 'in this connection it is worth noting', as
Chadwick Hansen observed, 'that Huck's last name is that of a pre-
Christian Celtic nature god who is "Fionn" in Irish, and who gave his
name to the cities of Vienna and Vienne'.[11] But it is neither such
supernatural nor such international resonances that matter here. The
Mississippi basin *was* America. The Midwest remains the backbone of
the nation to the present day. The great river had long been a national
totem to landscape painters. In the 1840s John Banvard had presented
a panorama of only its lower reaches, drawn to scale, on a three-mile
strip of canvas; Henry Lewis sketched the whole river on a circuit
1,325 yards long. Mark Twain's *Life on the Mississippi* and *Huckleberry
Finn* together more than matched such feats. But here it was not only
the river and its shifting banks that counted, but also the people on
the river and the Southern culture pushed 'back, and back, and back'
above those banks.

The world of *Huckleberry Finn* presents a curious mixture of
Calvinist principles and aristocratic ideals. The very name Twain gave
to his home town was paradoxical: both Christian and Russian. St
Petersburg was to evoke for him an uncomfortable twin resonance:

part heavenly city of God (the alpha and omega of his existence), part despotic capital of repression (of work, vanity and violence). We meet most of the fundamentalist Christian sects from their Sunday schools to their Methodist and Presbyterian churches; from Revivalist camp-meetings to lay preachers (like brother Phelps) and ministers (like the Wilks brothers). We meet representatives of all three classes from the upper and lower orders of the ruling Whites to Blacks. For that is the first division: Whites (who are 'people') and Blacks (just 'niggers'). 'People', in their turn, are further divided into two castes: 'the quality' and plain 'folks'. Let us look at each in turn.

The 'quality' are the ruling patricians and affluent Whites: the judges and colonels as well as the owner of a large 'store' (like Colonel Sherburn) or of the 'little drug store' (where Boggs dies). They include all the respectable, 'nice' townspeople: the Widow Douglas, Judge Thatcher, Miss Watson, even Mr Parker, the slave-hunter. They include Tom's family. Pre-eminently they include the two great clans of plantation-owners, the Grangerfords and the Shepherdsons. It is they who set the standard, who stamp their values on society with the visible presence of 'style'. As Colonel Grangerford has style; and Colonel Sherburn has style; and Tom Sawyer has style; and even Boggs attempts a pathetic dash of style.

It is this 'style' to which Huck again and again succumbs. He hero-worships Colonel Grangerford:

> Col. Grangerford was a gentleman, you see. He was a gentleman all over; and so was his family. He was well born, as the saying is, and that's worth as much in a man as it is in a horse, so the Widow Douglas said, and nobody ever denied that she was of the first aristocracy in our town; and Pap he always said it, too, though he warn't no more quality than a mudcat, himself.[12]

Pedigree counts. Huck is simply bowled over by the Grangerfords. He is goggle-eyed at their junketings: 'on the river, and dances and picnics in the woods, day-times, and balls at the house, nights . . . It was a handsome lot of quality, I tell you' (88/143–4). He is equally admiring of the Shepherdsons, 'another clan of aristocracy . . . as high-toned, and well born, and rich and grand, as the tribe of Grangerfords'. It is this that links Huck irrevocably to Tom. Even browsing through books, among the loot picked up from the *Walter Scott*, he 'read considerable to Jim about kings, and dukes, and earls, and such, and how gaudy they dressed, and how much style they put on . . .' (64/93) Style counts.

Though Huck rejects the Widow's 'mansion', he falls head over heels for the Grangerford place: 'It was a mighty nice family, and a mighty nice house, too. I hadn't seen no house out in the country before that was so nice and had so much style' (82/136).[13] Of course Huck is kindly taken in (the Grangerfords accept his absurd story of falling overboard off a steamboat at face value), but he is also thoroughly taken in. The picture, in all its complex irony, is a joke; but it is difficult to find an unbiased witness of the stagy charm of a well-bred Southerner to set against his. Take Poe, another Southerner, with his picture of Brevet Brigadier-General John A. B. C. Smith:

> He was, perhaps, six feet in height, and of a presence singularly commanding. There was an *air distingué* pervading the whole man, which spoke of high breeding, and hinted at high birth . . . His head of hair would have done honor to Brutus; – nothing could be more richly flowing, or possess a brighter gloss. It was of a jetty black; – which was also the color, or more properly the no color, of his unimaginable whiskers . . . Here was the most entirely even, and the most brilliantly white of all conceivable teeth. From between them, upon every proper occasion, issued a voice of surpassing clearness, melody, and strength.[14]

And here is Henry Adams's portrait of Roony Lee, son of Robert E. Lee, at Harvard from 1854 to 1858:

> Tall, largely built, handsome, genial, with liberal Virginian openness towards all he liked, he had also the Virginian habit of command . . .
>
> For a year, at least, Lee was the most popular and prominent young man in his class, but then seemed slowly to drop into the background. The habit of command was not enough, and the Virginian had little else. He was simple beyond analysis; so simple that even the simple New England student could not realize him. No one knew enough to know how ignorant he was; how childlike; how helpless before the relative complexity of a school. As an animal the Southerner seemed to have every advantage, but even as an animal he steadily lost ground . . .

Strictly the Southerner had no mind; he had temperament. He was not a scholar; he had no intellectual training; he could not analyse an idea, and could not even conceive of admitting two.[15]

Such was the 'aristocracy'. Such were the idols before whom Huck instinctively bowed.

From the 'quality' we descend to 'folks'; from '"baker's bread" – what the quality eat' to "your low-down corn-pone' (34/46). These are poor Whites like Pap Finn or the 70-year-old 'king' in his slouch hat and blue jeans. These are the tobacco-chewing, whittling loafers of Bricksville who turn as readily to whiskey as violence. These are the 'jeans-clad, chills-racked, yellow-faced' miserables of the spring rise:

Behind other islands we found wretched little farms, and wretcheder little log-cabins; there were crazy rail fences sticking a foot or two above the water, with one or two jeans-clad, chills-racked, yellow-faced male miserables roosting on the top-rail, elbows on knees, jaws in hand, grinding tobacco and discharging the result at floating chips through crevices left by lost teeth; while the rest of the family and the few farm animals were huddled together in an empty wood-flat riding at her moorings close at hand. In this flatboat the family would have to cook and eat and sleep for a lesser or greater number of days (or possibly weeks), until the river should fall two or three feet and let them get back to their log cabin and their chills again . . .[16]

Collectively they became the Southern mob: confronting Sherburn; massacring the Grangerford boys; riding the king and duke out of town.[17] Among the farmers, who have collared Jim, there is an explosive mixture of rage and financial savvy (222/352); among the poor Whites, just bloody-mindedness. They lynch the king and duke. They're out to lynch Pap Finn, 'but he was gone' (49/69). Twain pursues these bored and vicious desperadoes with a relentless vision. He is as minutely perceptive, and as passionate, as Breughel in detailing fatuous, gregarious, rural *indifference* to the possibilities of intellectual or spiritual transcendence in its midst.

Huck and Jim, who drift within – but apart from – this society, make the oddest couple. For poor Whites, like Pap Finn, did their damnedest to distance themselves from Blacks. But 'white trash' and 'nigger' here are linked. He is 'Miss Watson's Jim' (37/50). That's his name – his full 'nigger' name; and the term sticks. He is a bundle of stereotypes. How could he be otherwise since the term 'nigger' denotes not so much another class, or bottom rung, of Southern society as a mirror for Whites? As white man's property, even a 'nigger's' character was white man's property. Chadwick Hansen unravels it as follows:

> Jim is, in part, the comic stage Negro who can be made the butt of Tom's childish humor. But he is also a second Negro type, Mr Bones, whose cleverness enables him to turn the joke back on the Interlocutor. He is also a third Negro type, the kindly old colored Mammy, the protector of the white child. He is a fourth type, the sentimental family man who weeps for the suffering of his own child. And he is a fifth type, man in the abstract – natural man, if you wish – with the reasoning power, the dignity, and the nobility that belongs to that high abstraction.[18]

That sounds broadly right. Jim is easily cowed. Jim is readily victimized by children's pranks. Jim abjectly accepts his Arab role (from the duke) and transvestite clothes (from Tom). He remains something of a gullible golliwog who loves his children and stays loyal to Huck – even to Tom when Tom is wounded. But he is no 'Mammy' surely; his role is too paternal. Jim is handyman in cave and wigwam. Jim builds the shelter and protects Huck from the rain. He is experienced in skills of survival. As he remarks during the thunderstorm on Jackson's Island:

> 'Well, you wouldn't a ben here, 'f it hadn't a ben for Jim. You'd a ben down dah in de woods widout any dinner, en gittn' mos' drownded, too, dat you would, honey.'[19]

It is he who repairs the raft after the fatal collision. He can cook catfish and bake corn-bread.

I shall return to Jim at greater length in Chapter 14. But at least one side of his character is still missing. He is a seer. After Tom Sawyer's initial trick, 'Jim was most ruined, for a servant, because he got so stuck up on account of having seen the devil and been rode by witches' (11/8). After Huck's not dissimilar trick, Jim slips smoothly into his vatic role:

He said the first tow-head stood for a man that would try to do us some good, but the current was another man that would get us away from him. The whoops were warnings that would come to us every now and then, and if we didn't try hard to make out to understand them they'd just take us into bad luck, 'stead of keeping us out of it. The lot of tow-heads was troubles we was going to get into with quarrelsome people and all kinds of mean folks, but if we minded our business and didn't talk back and aggravate them, we would pull through and get out of the fog and into the big clear river, which was the free States, and wouldn't have no more trouble.[20]

A 'nigger', who cannot read books, reads nature's book. He inhabits a portentous, ominous spirit world, mainly malignant (if roused by the killing of a spider, for instance, or spilt salt), and swarming with ghosts.

This submerged world, lurking just below the threshold of visibility, needs both cautious scrutiny and astute interpretation. For it is an emblematic world, signalling hidden and mysterious messages. Huck, like Jim, is a wary native of this shadow world. If Jim is its shaman, Huck is his respectful acolyte. The decoding of dark meanings – not the local versions of Calvinism – is their true religion. It is that which binds them together and sends them together on a journey well beyond the official frontiers of St Petersburg.

NOTES

1 Stolen, he claimed, from one Captain Isaiah Sellers of New Orleans (*Life on the Mississippi*, ch. 50). But see Paul Fatout, 'Mark Twain's nom de plume', *American Literature*, vol. 34 (March 1962), pp. 1–7.

2 *Life on the Mississippi*, ch. 46.

3 cf. ibid., ch. 38, and *Huckleberry Finn*, ch. 17.

4 *Life on the Mississippi*, ch. 9.

5 *Huckleberry Finn*, ch. 19, pp. 97–8/158, and ch. 20, p. 104/167.

6 As Twain explains on introducing his interpolated chapter 3 into *Life on the Mississippi*. For stars, see *Huckleberry Finn*, ch. 12, p. 55/78, and ch. 15, p. 69/102; for a memorably starlit night, ch. 19, p. 97/158.

7 ibid., ch. 9, p. 44/60. Glasscock's Island, the original of Jackson's Island, is now completely eroded.

8 For the beginning of the 'June rise', see ch. 7, p. 29/37. As Bernard DeVoto makes clear: 'The time runs through two summers. One of them is the remainder of the summer in *Tom Sawyer* . . . and Huck floats down the river as the June rise is subsiding, the following year': *Mark Twain at Work* (Cambridge, Mass.: Harvard University Press, 1942), p. 89. I shall return for a more detailed look at the chronology in Ch. 10.

9 *Huckleberry Finn*, ch. 21, p. 114/183.

10 ibid., ch. 16, p. 78/130. It was an explosion on the *Pennsylvania*, as he writes in *Life on the Mississippi*, that cost Sam his younger brother's life.

11 Chadwick Hansen, 'The character of Jim and the ending of *Huckleberry Finn*', *Massachusetts Review*, vol. 5 (Autumn 1963), p. 65, fn. 9. Hansen continues: 'Joyce was, of course, aware of this, but it is unlikely that Twain was.' It was while working on *Finnegans Wake* that Joyce asked his brother's stepson to make notes on *Huckleberry Finn*: 'I need to know something about it. I never read it and have nobody to read it to me and it takes too much time with all I am doing' (8 August 1937). See *Selected Letters of James Joyce*, ed. Richard Ellmann (New York: Viking Press, 1975), p. 387. For the Fenian cycle of Finn, as poet and outsider, see Joseph Falaky Nagy, *The Wisdom of the Outlaw: The Boyhood Deeds of Finn in Gaelic Narrative Tradition* (Berkeley, Calif.: University of California Press, 1985).

12 *Huckleberry Finn*, ch. 18, pp. 86–7/142. Saul Grangerford is a Kentucky colonel who treasures 'Henry Clay's Speeches' (83/137). His plantation is set on the northern edge of the cotton and tobacco belts, far from the great plantations of the South. The double log-house, with its 'open space' between, was based on Twain's Uncle Quarles's Missouri homestead. Despite the household slaves 'and over a hundred niggers', despite those picnics and balls, it is clearly a small-scale affair. All its pseudo-effects are seen through Huck's dazzled eyes.

    Colonel Sherburn, who owns the largest Bricksville store, suggests a ruined planter with his patrician airs. See Louis J. Budd, *Mark Twain: Social Philosopher* (Bloomington, Ind.: Indiana University Press, 1962).

13 Her 'hill mansion the only palace in the town, and the most hospitable and much the most lavish in the matter of festivities that St Petersburg could boast . . .' (*Tom Sawyer*, ch. 5).

14 Poe, 'The Man That Was Used Up', in *Collected Works of Edgar Allan Poe*, ed. Thomas Ollive Mabbott, Vol. 2 (Cambridge, Mass.: Harvard University Press, 1978), pp. 378–9.

15 *The Education of Henry Adams* (1907), ch. 4. See also W. J. Cash, *The Mind of the South* (New York: Alfred A. Knopf, 1941), bk 1, ch. 2, sect. 9, and ch. 3, sect. 12.

16 *Life on the Mississippi*, ch. 11, 'The River Rises'. The passage is adapted from 'Old Times on the Mississippi'.

17 This was not just ignominous, but potentially lethal. The fence rail was wedge-shaped with a sharp and splintery edge. 'When a man was riding on a rail, with nothing between his body and the rail but a coat of tar and feathers, there would be very little left of his groin, and chances were that he would lose at least part of his genitals as well' (Hansen, 'The character of Jim and the ending of *Huckleberry Finn*', p. 63).

18 ibid., p. 55.

19 *Huckleberry Finn*, ch. 9, p. 44/60.

20 ibid., ch. 15, p. 71/104.

CHAPTER 6

Sam Clemens and Huck Finn

'A scow or a raft went by so close we could hear them talking and cussing and laughing . . .' (ch. 9)

Huck shares Jim's fears (whether of killed spiders or rattlesnakes) because they are the fears of the powerless; he is aligned to black superstition as a common folklore. For Twain's hero, and *alter ego*, is both empirical *and* logical *and* superstitious. He is both quick-witted and a failure as a con-man. 'I reckon a body that ups and tells the truth when he is in a tight place', he muses at one point, 'is taking considerable many resks, though I ain't had no experience' (148/239). But he takes just as many in telling lies: he forgets his assumed name when he masquerades as a girl at Mrs Loftus's; and again at the Grangerfords' he has to trick Buck into reminding him of it. Interrogation by Joanna Wilks or Aunt Sally easily rattles him and makes him falter.

Socially he is endowed with a low self-image: as one naturally depraved, naturally hell-bound.

> Well, I tried the best I could to kinder soften it up somehow for myself, by saying I was brung up wicked, and so I warn't so much to blame; but something inside of me kept saying, 'There was the Sunday school, you could a gone to it; and if you'd a done it they'd a learnt you, there, that people that acts as I'd been acting about that nigger goes to everlasting fire.[1]

He even compares himself to Judas in his humility when Mary Jane Wilks promises to pray for him: 'Pray for me! I reckoned if she knowed me she'd take a job that was more nearer her size . . . She had the grit to pray for Judus if she took the notion' (152/244). For

Huck is constantly under pressure: anxious, blue, depressed. Like Twain, he is haunted by death. Like Twain, he is permanently, suffocatingly *conscience*-stricken. Sam Clemens felt responsible for the death of his brother Henry blown up in the steamboat *Pennsylvania*; for the death of his 18-month-old son in June 1872; for a tramp burnt to death in the Hannibal gaol. In 'The Facts Concerning the Recent Carnival of Crime in Connecticut' he wrote: 'At last, and forever, my Conscience was dead! . . . Nothing in all the world could persuade me to have a conscience again.' One month later he began *Adventures of Huckleberry Finn*.

And Huck is *all* conscience, *all* sensitivity, *all* sentiment. Basically he is honest, kind-hearted, sympathetic to suffering. When he sees house lights burning late at night, for instance, he assumes 'there was sick folks, may be' (11/8). When he steals a chicken for his supper, he takes one 'that warn't roosting comfortable' (56/79). When he watches a circus performer fall off his horse, amid roars of laughter, he adds: 'It warn't funny to me, though; I was all of a tremble to see his danger' (120/93). He is worried even about the thieves on the *Walter Scott*: 'I says to myself, there ain't no telling but I might come to be a murderer myself, yet, and then how would *I* like it?' (61/87) He is sickened by the fate of the king and duke. He is haunted by the memory of the Wilks slaves, sold up and down the river: 'I can't ever get it out of my memory, the sight of them poor miserable girls and niggers hanging around each other's necks and crying' (146/234). Just as he is horribly haunted by Buck Grangerfords' death.

Leland Krauth has rightly called this refinement in Huck 'Victorian'. In him the more boisterous tradition of Southwestern humour is instinctively bowdlerized. 'Twain recreates the hero of that tradition in Huck,' Krauth argues, 'replacing the aggressive, violent male with a passive, loving one . . . Huck's delicacy and tenderness exceed, even today, the popular sense of what constitutes a man's feelings.'[2] Huck's gentleness – all appearances to the contrary – is that of a gentleman. And gentlemen, as Leslie Fiedler remarked long ago, are not genital men. Nor do they cuss and swear.

It is now widely argued that Twain was his own most demanding censor. In the original manuscript of *Tom Sawyer*, for instance, Injun Joe plans to rape the Widow Douglas. Twain altered this to 'slit her nostrils' and 'notch her ears like a sow' as apparently more acceptable. In chapter 20 he has a passage where Tom sees Becky Thatcher steal a glimpse of 'a human figure, stark naked' in the teacher's anatomy textbook. Reproached by Becky for sneaking up on her, Tom says: 'How could *I* know it wasn't a nice book? I didn't know girls even—' It is the single allusion to sex in *Tom Sawyer*. When Howells annotated the manuscript, 'I should be afraid of this picture incident,' out went Becky's sobbed reply as well as her thoughts and Tom's subsequent soliloquy. In all-male company Twain could be obscene. In 1876, the very year he started on *Huckleberry Finn*, he vastly amused himself with composing an Elizabethan pastiche on farting.[3] In February 1879 he delivered 'Some Thoughts on the Science of Onanism' to the Stomach Club in Paris. But in writing of boyhood he is resolutely pre-Freudian. Hannibal remains heaven itself, the city of St Peter. In his 'Villagers of 1840–3' – despite an adultery (John McDowell), a free union (Sam Bowen), a *crime passionel* (Jesse Armstrong) – he sums up as follows:

> *Chastity.* There was the utmost liberty among young people – but no young girl was ever insulted, or seduced, or even scandalously gossiped about. Such things were not even dreamed of in that society, much less spoken of and referred to as possibilities.
>
> Two or three times, in the lapse of years, married women were whispered about, but never an unmarried one.[4]

Even as late as 1897 – perhaps especially as late as 1897 – Twain did not want to dream of such possibilities. Adults were adults; and he dismisses their adult and adulterous humanity with rasping scorn. But his young people remained pure in tongue and body and mind. A 'nigger' might be hanged for raping and murdering a 13-year-old girl in the woods.[5] The Blankenship girls (Huck's real-life sisters, as it were) might be 'charged with prostitution'; but he adds: 'not proven'. Hannibal was to remain an idyll, an Eden before the Fall.

Profanity, too, as we saw in Chapter 2, had to be watched. Huck 'could swear wonderfully'. Then he 'stopped cussing, because the widow didn't like it'. Then he 'took to it again because pap hadn't no objections'.[6] Huck's passionate grievance against the Widow, in fact, originally culminated in the phrase: 'they comb me all to hell'. Inoffensive enough, one might think. Certainly Howells passed it without question. But Twain worried. He changed it to 'thunder'; then back to 'hell'; and then turned the worry over to Howells:

> There was one expression which perhaps you overlooked. When

Huck is complaining to Tom of the rigorous system in vogue at the widow's, he says the servants harass him with all manner of compulsory decencies, & he winds up by saying, 'and they comb me all to hell.' (No exclamation point.) Long ago, when I read that to Mrs Clemens, she made no comment; another time I created occasion to read that chapter to her aunt & her mother (both sensitive & loyal subjects of the kingdom of heaven, so to speak,) & *they* let it pass. I was glad, for it was the most natural remark in the world for that boy to make (& he had been allowed few privileges of speech in the book); when I saw that you, too, had let it go without protest, I was glad, & afraid, too – afraid you hadn't observed it. Did you? And did you question the propriety of it? Since the book is now professedly & confessedly a boy's & girl's book, that dern word bothers me some nights, but it never did until I had ceased to regard the volume as being for adults.[7]

Howells replied by return:

As to the point in your book: I'd have that swearing out in an instant. I suppose I didn't notice it because the locution was so familiar to my Western sense, and so exactly the thing that Huck would say. But it wont do for the children.[8]

So for children, at any rate, hell-fire had to be screened. Language that was familiar and appropriate (to Westerners) had to be purged. The new realism was for adults only – and hardly for them.

The raftsmen's 'cussing', overheard in the fog, is blanked out in Huck's mouth to a colourless 'dern the dern fog' (97/157). The word 'damn', in the Buffalo manuscript, is anxiously emended to 'dern'; 'damnation' jovially curtailed to 'nation'.[9] Twain first let his characters rip and swear, as came naturally to them. Then combed them all to thunder. In this, too, Twain was a double man. When he really meant to keep a phrase he had to remind himself insistently. 'Oh, de po' little thing!' Jim concludes the account of his deaf-and-dumb daughter, 'de Lord God Amighty fogive po' ole Jim, kaze he never gwyne to fogive hisself as long's he live!' (126/202) '*Lord God Amighty*' is underlined in the manuscript, with the marginal comment: 'This expression shall not be changed.'

Yet sexual antics were not altogether banned. A few erotic touches were slipped into *Huckleberry Finn*. Bernard DeVoto asked: 'Is it conceivable that a boy of Huck's upbringing, age, and curiosity would be totally unaware of sex?'[10] Of course, not; and on two, possibly three, occasions Huck does show a glimmer of awareness. For instance, when a corpse is found in the river, thought to be Pap's, Huck is stumped, knowing 'mighty well that a drownded man don't float on his back, but on his face' (15/14). Why is he so sure? Is it because he grasps the basis of the superstition: that male and female bodies float in their normal positions of coitus? It is impossible to say. Huck is always so delicate in his allusions. As when the house floats by which really is his Pap's last resting-place:

> There was heaps of old greasy cards scattered around over the floor, and old whiskey bottles, and a couple of masks made out of black cloth; and all over the walls was the ignorantest kind of words and pictures, made with charcoal. There was two old dirty calico dresses, and a sun-bonnet, and some women's under-clothes, hanging against the wall, and some men's clothing, too.[11]

The naked corpse, the whiskey, the women's underclothes: this certainly looks like a scene of debauchery. But Huck barely glances at the pornographic graffiti. He calls them 'ignorantest', which – however funny coming from him – proves how thoroughly he has internalized the Widow's ways to his own natural modesty.

Just once he gives himself away. He actually laughs; and Huck does not laugh easily. What was so funny?

> he rolled up the curtain, and the next minute the king come a-prancing out on all fours, naked; and he was painted all over, ring-streaked-and-striped, all sorts of colors, as splendid as a rainbow. And – but never mind the rest of his outfit, it was just wild, but it was awful funny. The people most killed themselves laughing; and when the king got done capering, and capered off behind the scenes, they roared and clapped and stormed, and haw-hawed till he come back and done it over again; and after that, they made him do it another time. Well, it would a made a cow laugh to see the shines that old idiot cut.[12]

This is the 'Thrilling Tragedy of THE KING'S CAMELOPARD OR THE ROYAL NONESUCH!!!', originally entitled 'The Tragedy of the Burning Shame', billed for men only. Clearly this was some kind of obscene, phallic romp. The duke called it 'ruther worse than low comedy'. The king originally declared, 'he judged he could caper to their base instincts; 'lowed he could size their style'.[13] But if the king was naked – especially 'stark naked' – how could he have been *outfitted*? How could there have been a 'rest' of an outfit? How can a naked man be outrageously fitted out? With some kind of phallic attachment, surely. In that case it was the codpiece which was the 'Burning Shame'. Possibly it was bright red. But would that be *so* funny? Would that alone make everyone clap and roar? Wallace Graves seems to have tumbled on the right solution: a lit candle was stuck upright in the king's arse.[14] If the king, that is, clutches a lighted candle in his rectum, he becomes a kind of bounding and buggered rebus, at once burning and shameful. Certainly Twain told and retold Jim Gillis's yarn; it struck him as permanently hilarious. And, for once, even Huck reveals an obscene sense of humour. He finds that swinging phallus and/or lit candle 'awful funny', enough to make 'a cow laugh'.

Otherwise the text is tame enough. Only two scenes introduce a hint of sex and they were thoroughly purged. The king's behaviour with the Wilks girls was once full of cuddly slapstick. But it is now quite anaemic. On three different occasions the king's kisses were deleted; nor is Mary Jane permitted to kiss him 'on the mouth'. The deletions themselves, too, are poor stuff.[15] A more potent deletion occurs in Colonel Sherburn's harangue. Originally it had contained a rare admission that prostitution existed on the banks of the Mississippi:

> Because you're brave enough to tar and feather poor friendless cast-out women that come along here, lowering themselves to your level to earn a bite of bitter bread to eat.[16]

That last revealing phrase was cut.

For Twain *was* very sqeamish. One of Kemble's drawings *would not do*. It was to illustrate the camp-meeting (chapter 20). The rest was admirable, he wrote to Webster:

> But you must knock out one of them – the lecherous old rascal kissing the girl at the campmeeting. It is powerful good, but it mustn't go in – don't forget it. Let's not make *any* pictures of the

campmeeting. The subject won't *bear* illustrating. It is a disgusting thing, & pictures are sure to tell the truth about it too plainly.[17]

He had himself already deleted the king bussing the Wilks girls and generally carrying on. He was still brooding on 'the Royal Nonesuch'; his comment 'scandalous' (crossed out) in the manuscript, by the description of the king's make-up, suggests that he had been wavering. But the effects, he must have thought, had been sufficiently camouflaged. Now here was young Kemble behind his back introducing such loose conduct all over again. Images were more embarrassing than mere talk. Words, for Twain, plainly implied fantasizing; pictures told 'the truth'.

So it was a kind of comeupance when Uncle Silas's mysterious erection appeared in that illustration to chapter 32. It was as if a printer's dirty joke was directly aimed at all Twain's self-imposed censorship, euphemisms and evasions. 'Delicacy – a sad, sad false delicacy', he once wrote to Howells, '– robs literature of the two best things among its belongings: Family-circle narratives & obscene stories.'[18] But he capitulated, without question, to his own inhibitions. It was such an instinctive self-censorship that years later, when writing his *Autobiography*, he imagined that he had actually written a more explicit version of the 'Burning Shame'. The Buffalo manuscript does not corroborate this.

Twain's mother had been a model for Aunt Polly in *Tom Sawyer*. In some sense she re-emerges as Aunt Sally of *Huckleberry Finn*; and it is immediately after the confrontation of Aunt Sally with Aunt Polly in chapter 42 that Huck makes his final, celebrated bid for evasion:

> But I reckon I got to light out for the Territory ahead of the rest, because Aunt Sally she's going to adopt me and sivilize me and I can't stand it. I been there before.[19]

For 'Aunt Sally she's', the Buffalo manuscript reads 'they're'. *They* are the women. The women are civilization; and civilization in *Huckleberry Finn*, as Leslie Fiedler wrote, 'is essentially a world of the mothers, that is to say, of what Christianity has become among the females who sustain it just behind the advancing frontier. It is a sufficiently simple-minded world in which one does not cuss or steal or smoke but keeps clean, wears shoes, and prays for spiritual gifts.'[20]

NOTES

1 *Huckleberry Finn*, ch. 31, p. 168/269.
2 Leland Krauth, 'Mark Twain: the Victorian of Southwestern humor', *American Literature*, vol. 54 (October 1982), pp. 377 and 384.
3 *1601, Conversation, As It Was by the Social Fireside, in the Time of the Tudors*, printed as a pamphlet (1880), but not published.
4 'Villagers of 1840–3', in Walter Blair (ed.), *Mark Twain's Hannibal, Huck & Tom* (Berkeley, Calif.: University of California Press, 1969), pp. 30, 32–3 and 35.
5 '*The Hanged Nigger*. He raped and murdered a girl of 13 in the woods. He confessed to forcing 3 young women in Va, and was brought away in a feather bed to save his life – which was a valuable property': ibid., p. 36.
6 *Tom Sawyer*, ch. 6; *Huckleberry Finn*, ch. 6, p. 24/30.
7 18 January 1876, *The Mark Twain – Howells Letters*, ed. Henry Nash Smith, William M. Gibson and Frederick Anderson, 2 vols (Cambridge Mass.: Harvard University Press, 1960), Vol. 1, p. 122. See also above, Ch. 2, n. 3.
8 The phrase was published as 'they comb me all to thunder', *Tom Sawyer*, ch. 35.
9 cf. Huck: 'Oh, that's all very fine to *say*, Tom Sawyer, but how in the nation . . .'; and the king: 'Looky here, Bilgewater, I'm nation sorry for you . . .' (*Huckleberry Finn*, ch. 2, p. 13/11, and ch. 19, p. 101/163).
10 Bernard DeVoto, *Mark Twain at Work* (Cambridge, Mass.: Harvard University Press, 1942), p. 96.
11 *Huckleberry Finn*, ch. 9, p. 45/61.
12 ibid., ch. 23, pp. 121–2/196.
13 This was deleted. But little else, despite Twain's later claims, was changed. The original text of the king's performance shows only three slight modifications, here indicated by square brackets:

   > the king come a-prancing out on all fours, [stark] naked; and he was painted all over . . . And – but [I won't describe] never mind the rest of his outfit, it was just [outrageous] wild, but it was awful funny.

14 Wallace Graves, 'Mark Twain's "Burning Shame"', *Nineteenth-Century Fiction*, vol. 23 (June 1968), pp. 93–8.
15 e.g. 'Soon as he could, the duke shook the hare-lip, and sampled Susan, which was better looking. After the king had kissed Mary Jane fourteen or fifteen times, he give the duke a show, and tapered off on the others.' Or here is Huck, conspiring to spirit away Mary Jane: 'Do you reckon you can face your uncles, and take your regular three or four good-morning smacks?'
16 *Huckleberry Finn*, ch. 22, p. 118/190, in the Buffalo manuscript version.
17 *Mark Twain, Business Man*, ed. Samuel Charles Webster (Boston, Mass.: Little, Brown, 1946), p. 260.
18 Twain to Howells: 19 September 1877.
19 Note how exactly the ending echoes the opening: 'The Widow Douglas, she took me for her son, and allowed she would sivilize me; but it was rough living in the house all the time . . . and so when I couldn't stand it no longer, I lit out' (7/1).
      The Territory is the Indian Territory, the future state of Oklahoma. In his abortive 'Huck Finn & Tom Sawyer among the Indians', begun soon after *Huckleberry Finn*, Twain sends them off on five pack-mules for those 'howling adventures amongst the Injuns'.
20 Leslie A. Fiedler, 'As free as any cretur . . .', *New Republic*, vol. 133, nos 7–8 (15 and 22 August 1955), pp. 17–18 and 16–18.

CHAPTER 7

Huck and Pap

'Pap always said, take a chicken when you get a chance . . .' (ch. 12)

Huck is a chip off the old block. To understand Huck one must begin with Pap. Pap is his one sure model. He often quotes the old man. After committing his own murder, he opts for the only life he knows, which is Pap's:

> All right; I can stop anywhere I want to. Jackson's Island is good enough for me; I know that island pretty well, and nobody ever comes there. And then I can paddle over to town, nights, and slink around and pick up things I want.[1]

What prevents this career of petty crime is Jim.

Old Man Finn, Pap Finn, is an Irish soak who has drifted to the frontier. A ragged, illiterate 50-year-old, with the gift of the gab, he boozes and snoozes in his hut on the Illinois shore. There was a wife once, but we do not know how she died.[2] When drunk, though, he feels persecuted by the dead. It seems that Huck is his only child. But he is paranoid about Huck, deliriously calling him the 'Angel of Death' and chasing him with a clasp-knife. He is paranoid about Blacks, too, ranting against mulattos and free 'niggers'. Just one recorded remark made by the real-life Jimmy Finn is among the depositions (made by Sam's father) in the Smarr–Owsley affair. On entering a store, where Sam Smarr (Boggs's prototype) had that moment let off a pistol, Finn remarked: 'That would have made a hole in a man's belly.'[3]

Pap's end is as mysterious as his beginning. Originally he was to have been Injun Joe's companion in grave-robbing. 'He became Muff Potter,' DeVoto thought, 'no doubt, to prevent Huck's oath from putting his father's life in jeopardy.'[4] His corpse is found drifting on the Mississippi: naked, shot in the back, among sleazy rubbish. The two black masks there suggest he was mixed up with gangsters.[5] But what kind of gangsters? Why was he naked? Why was he shot? Was it strip-poker they were playing? Had the flood-waters surprised them? Was he shot in a drunken brawl for not paying his debts? Or for rashly boasting that he was 'worth six thousand dollars and upards' (26/33)? There is no way of telling. Huck's father died out nigger-hunting, so he claimed, with a $200 reward (for murder) on his head.

That was Huck's pedigree. Such was his heritage, He, too, is slippery as an eel. He, too, is both a scoundrel and a con-man. White '*trash*', at a critical point, Jim calls him. He is fatally overreached in the end only by a couple of older, more experienced con-men, whom he instinctively admires. Though neither drunk, nor sexually active, nor a racist exactly, he carries both the paternal imprint (of that neurotic wreck) and social imprint (of a Southern White).

Pap's entry is scary; he had climbed through a window to catch Huck.[6] But Huck views the apparition (pasty face, black greasy hair) with chilly detachment: 'I stood a-looking at him; he set there a-looking at me' (21/23). Two long measured looks. Each is a kind of mirror image of the other. Each, throughout *Huckleberry Finn*, will seem a reverse image of the other. Whereas Old Finn will be officially alive (though actually dead), Young Finn will be officially dead (though actually alive). Whereas Old Finn had begun life as a grave-robber, Young Finn will become an active accomplice of grave-robbers. Whereas Old Finn (the confirmed bigot) rants at Blacks, Young Finn (the sentimental bigot) will accompany and shelter a Black on the run

But they have much in common. Pap may cuss and get roaring drunk; Huck just smokes. His very trademark in *Tom Sawyer* had been his corncob pipe. Here he smokes cheap chewing tobacco – even cigars when he can lay hands on them – but *never* touches liquor.[7] His superstitions, too, seem largely to derive from Pap. His belief in ghosts and the significance of 'signs' all sound like Pap. Huck entered the world of Tom Sawyer swinging a dead cat. Here he spots the sign of the cross, made with nails in Pap's left boot-heel, to ward off the devil.

But it is not only his superstitions, but also his saws and practices which he picked up from Pap. Take Pap's cautionary tale of the man who boasted that he had looked at the new moon over his left shoulder:

Old Hank Bunker done it once, and bragged about it; and in less
than two years he got drunk and fell off of the shot tower and
spread himself out so that he was just a kind of layer, as you may
say; and they slid him edgeways between two barn doors for a
coffin, and buried him so, so they say, but I didn't see it. Pap told
me.[8]

It was from Pap that Huck learnt this aggressive verbal energy as well
as his facility for spinning tall yarns. Huck is every inch Pap's son.

He was his apprentice, too, in the fine art of cussing. As Huck is a
champion in Tom's eyes, so Pap is in Huck's. Pap is a self-esteemed
master-craftsman of vituperation: 'his speech was all the hottest kind
of language' (27/34):

Then the old man got to cussing, and cussed everything and
everybody he could think of, and then cussed them all over again to
make sure he hadn't skipped any, and after that he polished off
with a kind of general cuss all round, including a considerable
parcel of people which he didn't know the names of, and so called
them what's-his-name, when he got to them, and went right along
with his cussing.

Huck glories in these epic demonstrations, as on the night Pap kicked
the pork-barrel:

and the cussing he done then laid over anything he had ever done
previous. He said so his own self, afterwards. He had heard old
Sowberry Hagan in his best days, and he said it laid over him, too;
but I reckon that was sort of piling it on, maybe.[9]

Huck lives in terms of this epic mythology, ruled by awesome
champions like Hank Bunker and Sowberry Hagan, lord of oaths.

Huck's use of the term 'borrowing', too, of course, is a family
tradition. Like the oaths and superstitions, Huck has assimilated
Pap's social prejudices; and, however abusive, Pap knows his place in
the hierarchy. He knows how to kowtow to the 'aristocracy' like Judge
Thatcher and the Widow. Even in *Tom Sawyer*, when Huck sneaks off
to eat meals with a 'nigger', he promptly adds: 'But you needn't tell
that. A body's got to do things when he's awful hungry he wouldn't
want to do as a steady thing' (ch. 28). That guilty reflex – that twinge

of Southern conscience – already evokes the whole wavering drama of
Huckleberry Finn.

Though not neurotic exactly, Huck is often 'lonesome'. More than
just 'lonesome', depressed. For a boy of 14 such severe depressions
seem cause for alarm. 'I felt so lonesome I most wished I was dead'
(9/14), he sighs. Or 'then I knowed for certain I wished I was dead'
(173/277). When a drunk on horseback weaves up to him to jeer,
'Whar'd you come f'm, boy? You prepared to die?' (115/184), we
already know the answer. Yes, Huck is prepared to die. He had begun
his *Adventures*, after all, with the staging of his own elaborate suicide.

Like father, like son. Pap has naturally had a poor press. But what
is the key difference between them? For one thing age, of course. Pap
Finn (*fl. c.*1790–1840) must have been of that same boisterous, hard-
drinking Jacksonian generation of Southern roustabouts and gamblers
who struck out West after the war of 1812. He might have heard Mike
Fink, that legendary keelboatman, roar:

> I can use up Injens by the cord, I can swallow niggers whole, raw or
> cooked . . . Whoop! holler, you varmints . . . or I'll jump right
> straight down yer throats, quicker nor a streak o' greased lightening
> can down a nigger's!

That was the language of his youth, not mealy-mouthed stuff about
'free niggers' and professors. It also suggests another difference, his
illiteracy. Pap, like Jim, cannot read; Huck, like Tom, can. 'Your
mother couldn't read,' he declaims,

> 'and she couldn't write, nuther, before she died. None of the family
> couldn't, before *they* died. *I* can't; and here you're a-swelling
> yourself up like this. I ain't the man to stand it – you hear?
> Say – lemme hear you read.'
>
> I took up a book and begun something about General
> Washington and the wars.[10]

Pap listens for half a minute; then swipes the revolutionary and
patriotic text out of Huck's hand. Pap is not drunk. This is not
knockabout farce. Twain knew exactly what he was about. Old Finn
bears a grudge, a deep grudge. He is a dispossessed White in an
embattled stance against the whole bookish establishment. For one
thing, the 'Widow Douglas, she took me for her son' (7/1): it is the

law which seeks to appropriate his child, backed by the courts. (The case has failed, but it is awaiting retrial.) Pap is up against the whole St Petersburg establishment, headed by Judge Thatcher. 'Here's the law', he roars, 'a-standing ready to take a man's son away from him – a man's own son' (26/33). Secondly, it is the law which seeks, by devious delay, to appropriate his right in Huck's $6,000 bonanza; that, too, is an affront. Thirdly, it is the law which has misappropriated his *vote*, as he sees it, by registering black voters.

But what makes him rage and roar is his complete helplessness, his total incapacity to defend his legal and financial and civil rights. Because he is illiterate. His performance is – necessarily and fluently and exasperatingly – *oral*:

'Yes, and I *told* 'em so; I told old Thatcher so to his face. Lots of 'em heard me, and can tell what I said. Says I . . .'

'Them's the very words. I says . . .'

'Look at it, says I . . .'

'. . . they said he was a p'fessor in a college . . .'

'I says I'll never vote agin. Them's the very words I said; they all heard me . . .'

'I says to the people . . .'

'And what do you reckon they said? Why, they said . . .'[11]

That, in a single burst, is how he addresses Huck. But he addresses Judge Thatcher and Mrs Thatcher, too, like a public meeting: 'Look at it gentlemen, and ladies all . . . You mark them words – don't forget I said them' (23/17). For in Pap's illiterate world, like Jim's, *speech matters*. Therefore the exact recollection and reportage of the spoken word is essential, since speech is testimony, the ultimate personal affidavit. Speech carries within it its own involuted marks of quotation, of ceaseless quotations within quotations. That is one function of speech: the quoting of a quotation. Human speech is transformed to a cento of quotations both for the historical record and for personal vindication. Such quotation is the ultimate proof – the only proof in an illiterate society – of a man's individual worth.

Huck can both read and write; but his role as a writer, too, is ultimately modelled on Pap. His, too, is an oral performance. His text, too, will offer an active collision, or collusion, of quotations. I shall return to this at length. Here it is enough to note that Huck, too, like Pap, is explicitly conscious of his own thought processes. Says Pap: 'And what do you think? . . . Thinks I, what is the country a-coming to?' (26–7/33–4). Says Huck to himself: 'Thinks I, this is what comes of my not thinking' (74/124). The very first sentences of *Huckleberry Finn* show something of this. Huck's gesture towards a text (*The Adventures of Tom Sawyer*) is remote and passive: 'That book was made by Mr Mark Twain'. What he instinctively and actively grasps is the text as spoken: 'and he told the truth, mainly. There was things which he stretched, but mainly he told the truth.'

Pap views this mirror-image, however, as a potential parricide. In a way, he is right. Huck *is* his 'Angel of Death'. Huck's suicide looks more like the symbolic murder of his own father. For it was Pap who slept 'with the hogs in the tanyard' (22/25). It was Pap who debased himself to the level of hogs. 'Look at it,' he declaimed, raising his hand. 'There's a hand that was the hand of a hog' (23/27). So that when Huck actually kills a wild hog, it seems like the most brutal Oedipal act: 'I shot this fellow . . . and hacked into his throat with the ax, and laid him down on the ground to bleed' (31/40). It is the first of his many rituals of death and resurrection; and even there, ironically, he remains very much the son of his father. Was not Pap the man who had 'started in on a new life'? Who had claimed to be 'clean' (23/27)? Had not Pap, too, masqueraded just such a moral and spiritual resurrection?

What for Pap, though, had been airy fiction, Huck turns into symbolic drama. He saws an escape-hatch at the back of the prison-cabin. He smashes the door and splashes blood over the floor. At the end of *Huckleberry Finn* the motif recurs in the ritual of Jim's 'escape' through a tunnel at the rear of *his* prison-cabin. The echo is quite deliberate: 'Jim's counterpin' (193/306) matches Pap's 'horse-blanket' (25/31) as screen. In *Tom Sawyer*, too, there had been scenes of rebirth and renewal. Tom, like Huck, too, rises from the dead. First he staged his own death, sneaking back from Jackson's Island to eavesdrop on his funeral, before revealing himself to the astonished congregation. Next he descended with Becky Thatcher deep into McDougal's Cave; lost, trapped, they spend a biblical three days and nights there, before finally crawling up a long tunnel towards the light to be literally 'reborn' (having been given up for dead).[12] This Return-from-the-Dead and the Cave-as-Tomb were permanent fixtures of Twain's imagination.[13]

The whole of *Huckleberry Finn* is a parody of Christian death and resurrection. In this sense it is a secular fable. Huck dies in his old self as Pap's son in Illinois to confront his new self as . . . But what self? That is where the real crisis begins. Who is he? His search for identity, through multiple rebirths and baptismal renewals in the Mississippi, is the story of *Huckleberry Finn*. The multiplication of selves itself becomes his resource against loneliness. He assumes nine incarnations: as Sarah Williams, Mary Williams, Sarah Mary Williams and George Peters (at Mrs Judith Loftus's); as Charles William Albright, alias Aleck James Hopkins (in the Raftsmen's Passage); as Mary Ann's brother (confronting the two slave-hunters on the river); as George Jackson (on parleying with the Grangerfords); as Adolphus (English valet to the king and duke); and finally as Tom Sawyer.[14] That is his last, absurd apotheosis: 'for it was like being born again, I was so glad to find out who I was' (177/282). Not a 'born again' Christian, but a 'born again' member of Southern society. The parody never slackens. When the real Tom Sawyer reappears, like his namesake Saint Thomas, he views the risen Huck with shocked awe:

'I hain't ever done you no harm. You know that. So then, what you want to come back and ha'nt *me* for?'
I says:
'I hain't come back – I hain't been *gone*.'
When he heard my voice, it righted him up some, but he warn't quite satisfied yet. He says:
'Don't you play nothing on me, because I wouldn't on you. Honest injun, now, you ain't a ghost?'
'Honest injun, I ain't,' I says.
'Well – I – I – well, that ought to settle it, of course; but I can't somehow seem to understand it, no way. Looky here, warn't you ever murdered *at all*?'
'No. I warn't ever murdered at all – I played it on them. You come in here and feel of me if you don't believe me.'
So he done it; and it satisfied him.[15]

This is Huck's last 'post-crucifixion' appearance. Up to this point, in a sense, he *had* been a ghost, ineffectively haunting the shores of the Mississippi. That is why 'The Raftsmen's Passage' is so crucial. As Kenneth S. Lynn first realized, it is a text within a text, a kind of parable for the whole of *Huckleberry Finn*. Like Charles William

Albright, whose identity Huck promptly adopts, Huck, too, has taken to the river in pursuit of a father:

> Drifting down the river toward a goal he can neither define nor scarcely imagine, Huck is in fact looking for another father to replace the one he has lost. And this quest is also a quest for himself, because once Huck has found his new father he will know at last who he himself really is.[16]

This quest is doomed to failure. Yet at the very point of his first Judas-like betrayal, he presents Jim instead (in the role of smallpox victim) as his father. 'I wish you would', he says to the slave-hunters, 'because it's pap that's there . . .' (75/126).

That had been Huck's problem all along. As Ben Rogers put it: 'Here's Huck Finn, he hain't got no family – what you going to do 'bout him?' (12/10) Huck's answer is to assume a series of alibis which he works into elaborate, thumbnail sketches. Twain brooded over these fictions. They are lavish with family names and details. They respond dramatically to the pressure of each occasion: Sarah Williams from Hookerville, seven miles south of St Petersburg, come to tell uncle Abner Moore that mother is 'down sick, and out of money' (48/68); George Peters, the 'runaway 'prentice', bound to a mean old farmer, looking for uncle Abner Moore in Goshen (52/73); Aleck James Hopkins, sent by Pap to contact 'a Mr Jonas Turner, in Cairo'; George Jackson, the Arkansas farmboy, fallen overboard off a steamboat, after a catalogue of disasters on the tenant-farm (82/135); and yet another orphan, from Pike County, Missouri, bound 'fourteen hundred mile' on $16 for Uncle Ben (103/166). Or there is his mercy mission at Booth's Landing where he thoroughly confuses the ferryman with his tale of Miss Hooker and her rich Uncle Hornback, contriving three fictitious deaths in the farrago for the robber trio aboard the *Walter Scott* (ch. 13).

For Huck – an only child, it seems – invariably invents tangled and complex family relationships, which are at once doomed to destruction. He is either an apprentice orphan; or a destitute orphan, deserted by his sister and brothers; or sole survivor of a collision. When a whole family, in one instance, does survive, it is down with smallpox aboard a raft. Huck consistently plays, that is, on others' sensibility as an outcast. For he *feels* his condition to be orphaned, even before learning of Pap's death. (Though, of course, some explanation was needed to account for a 14-year-old boy and a slave together on a raft.) These fictions, these hoaxes, these disguises are all masks. Huck is a creature of masks who sustains himself only in continual metamorphoses. It is when he returns to society at the end, 'appropriately trapped in the mask of Tom Sawyer (*the* mask of masks)', that he finally risks domination by the fixed concepts of civilization.[17]

Twain was a contemporary of Nietzsche, whom he went on to read, though well after the completion of *Huckleberry Finn*. In *Beyond Good and Evil* there is a passage that might almost be a commentary on Huck. The mask, Nietzsche argues, appropriates what is foreign; it arbitrarily falsifies certain traits to suit itself. But, just as arbitrarily, it shuts out and ignores other traits. It approves its own ignorance and even, on occasion, allows itself to be deceived with a joy 'in uncertainty and ambiguity'. For masks are capricious:

> Finally there also belongs here that not altogether innocent readiness of the spirit to deceive other spirits and to dissemble before them, that continual pressing and pushing of a creative, formative, changeable force: in this the spirit enjoys the multiplicity and cunning of its masks.[18]

'Larvatus prodeo': Descartes' motto might well be Huck's. But these 'feigned tales', hoaxes and disguises, as Andrew Lang recognized in 1891, are also essentially epic:

> In one point Mark Twain is Homeric, probably without knowing it. In the Odyssey, Odysseus frequently tells a false tale about himself, to account for his appearance and position when disguised on his own island. He shows extraordinary fertility and appropriateness of invention, wherein he is equalled by the feigned tales of Huckleberry Finn.[19]

Their performance is itself part of the oral tradition. What for Jim is just a 'dodge', or for the duke 'another little job', for Huck become 'yarns' or (on two occasions) 'stretchers'. For the yarn is literally *stretched*. The momentum of the narrative invades these fictions-within-the-fiction, inflating them, just as Homeric similes are dramatically indulged. There is no stopping such oral thrust. The narrative impulse extends every nuance, every play of circumstance – whether surrounding Hank Bunker or George Jackson.

Huck, in this sense, is the very heir of Odysseus as Cretan liar. With blithe self-confidence he proclaims: 'I'll go and fix up some kind of a yarn . . .' (61/87).

Even Jim is not immune to his hoaxes; or alibis even. But Huck goes unmasked for Jim. Jim accepts the white boy as a fellow-outlaw on the run; Huck learns to accept Jim as a black and loving father:

> Encountering the outcast colored man in hiding on the island, Huck is at first merely amazed and exasperated by the black man's stupidity, but part of the drama of their relationship is Huck's gathering awareness that Jim is 'most always right' about things that really matter, about how certain movements of the birds mean a storm is coming, about the dangers of messing with snakes, and the meaning of dreams. But while Jim's relationship to Huck is fatherly in the sense that he constantly is correcting and admonishing the boy, forever telling him some new truth about the world, he is identified even more unmistakably as Huck's father by the love that he gives him. As Huck is searching for a father, so Jim is attempting to rejoin his family, and he lavishes on the love-starved boy all of his parental affection.[20]

'Never you mind, honey,' he tells him. 'Don't you git too peart' (46/63). He stands his watch for him, and pets him, and picks the corn-shuck bedding while Huck sleeps on straw. But this, too, is a kind of 'evasion'. A white boy cannot ultimately have a black father. Once freed, Jim will have his own little Johnny. Freed from his own past, Huck will have to grow up. The compact is temporary and cannot resolve Huck's deepest needs: it is a compact of affectionate trust, on the open road, not a family tie.

Huck's awareness of Jim, moreover, was always limited. There were glimpses, throughout the *Adventures*, of a shrewd, wily, independent, even manipulative Jim. But had Huck noticed? Had he realized? Had he transcended his own desperate need for a lovable, hurt-but-chuckling Sambo (with a heart of gold)? Jim remains a stereotyped and sentimental figure. When Huck, sleeping naked outside the wigwam, is washed overboard, it 'most killed Jim a-laughing. He was the easiest nigger to laugh that ever was, anyway' (104/168). Instead of Tom, Huck now has his 'Uncle Tom' as a companion on the river, who will turn readily, when occasion offers, into a dignified (and humorous) Messiah.

That is the symbolic 'evasion' to which I shall return at length in Chapter 14. Its effect on Jim's role in the narrative, needless to say, is disastrous. For Huck, the outsider, who had betrayed his own community by siding with a slave, can only redeem his social role (as a pseudo-Tom Sawyer) by humiliating him. Jim must be reduced to a black scapegoat. Jim must suffer for white justice; for white renewal, that is, and reintegration. Jim must suffer for that ultimate Judas (Tom), who sells his conscience, like the two slave-hunters and huckster king, 'for forty dirty dollars'. It is Tom Sawyer who stages the second passion. Chained and stapled to his cabin, Jim Crow is transformed, for a bit of 'fun', to Jesus Christ. Not social fun, *aesthetic* fun to indulge Tom's boyish sense of the proprieties.[21]

Something of this already pre-dates Huck's arrival at the Phelps farm. The crux, as everyone acknowledges, occurs in chapter 31. After writing his letter to Miss Watson, Huck drifts into a daydream, a reverie, the only extended interior monologue in the book:

> and I see Jim before me, all the time, in the day, and in the night-time, sometimes moonlight, sometimes storms, and we a floating along, talking, and singing, and laughing. But somehow I couldn't seem to strike no places to harden me against him, but only the other kind. I'd see him standing my watch on top of his'n, stead of calling me, so I could go on sleeping; and see him how glad he was when I come back out of the fog; and when I come to him again in the swamp, up there where the feud was; and such-like times; and would always call me honey, and pet me, and do everything he could think of for me, and how good he always was; and at last I struck the time I saved him by telling the men we had small-pox aboard, and he was so grateful, and said I was the best friend old Jim ever had in the world, and the *only* one he's got now . . .[22]

It is an uncomfortable passage that Twain worked and reworked, piling on the effects: 'sometimes moonlight, sometimes storms, and we a floating . . .' Stylistically it *sounds* false. Because psychologically it *is* false. For once Huck meditates on the past, and the meaning of the past, with free poetic leaps of association. He calls it 'thinking'. But we know from earlier where such thinking leads. This is fantasy. This is dreaming. This is the decisive dream itself, feeding on itself, gathering momentum in its ecstasy, until desire inverts the facts in the triumphant recollection.

Jim had called Huck 'de bes' fren' Jim's ever had' and 'de *only* fren' ole Jim's got now' and (here suppressed) 'de on'y white genlman dat ever kep' his promise to ole Jim' (74/125) *before* his potential betrayal, not *after* the successful evasion. Huck transposes what had, in part, pre-empted his Judas-like decision. His memory is self-congratulatory and self-protective. As he had just observed: 'everybody naturally despises an ungrateful nigger' (168/268). On the jubilation of that inverted recollection – so flattering to him and his sense of their mutual dependence and intimacy – Huck makes his celebrated decision. It is both lyrical and (like all extended lyricism as a basis for action) a trifle farcical. For it stretches the truth in the way Huck most complacently and adroitly and painfully and longingly desires. Once Huck has made his decision to '*go* to hell', he never looks back.

NOTES

1 *Huckleberry Finn*, ch. 7, p. 32/41.
2 See *Tom Sawyer*, ch. 25: 'Look at pap and my mother. Fight! Why, they used to fight all the time. I remember mighty well.' For a vague mention of a wider family circle (all dead), see *Huckleberry Finn*, ch. 5.
3 Dixon Wecter, *Sam Clemens of Hannibal* (Boston, Mass.: Houghton Mifflin, 1952), p. 106.
4 Bernard DeVoto, *Mark Twain at Work* (Cambridge, Mass.: Harvard University Press, 1942), p. 17.
5 cf. ch. 11: '. . . that evening he got drunk and was around till after midnight with a couple of mighty hard looking strangers, and then went off with them' (49/69).
6 Just as Huck had predicted in *Tom Sawyer*. He thought then there was no point in his finding treasure: 'Pap would come back to thish yer town some day and get his claws on it if I didn't hurry up, and I tell you he'd clean it out pretty quick' (ch. 25). DeVoto called this the germ of *Huckleberry Finn*.
7 Huck makes off with 'Pap's whiskey jug', though, which comes in useful for Jim. Note his scorn for the baccy-chewing Bills and Bucks of Bricksville (ch. 21).
8 *Huckleberry Finn*, ch. 10, p. 47/65.
9 ibid. ch. 6, pp. 25/31 and 27/34.
10 ibid., ch. 5, p. 21/24.
11 ibid., ch. 6, pp. 26–27/33–4; cf. Old Mrs Hotchkiss in ch. 41: 'I says so to Sister Damrell – didn't I, Sister Damrell? – s'y, he's crazy, s'y – them's the very words I said. You all hearn me: he's crazy, s'y . . .' (218/345).
12 The half-caste, Injun Joe, alone is entombed in McDougal's Cave without hope of resurrection: 'When the cave door was unlocked, a sorrowful sight presented itself in the dim twilight of the place. Injun Joe lay stretched upon the ground, dead, with his face close to the crack of the door, as if his longing eyes had been fixed, to the last moment, upon the light and the cheer of the free world outside' (*Tom Sawyer*, ch. 33).
13 cf. Twain's famous *bon mot*: 'The report of my death was greatly exaggerated'; or, as originally framed: 'The report of my death was an exaggeration' (June 1897). Already in the *Early Tales & Sketches* (1863) there is a joke about someone reported

dead: 'I asked him about it at church this morning. He said there was no truth in the rumor.'

14 Peter G. Beidler has put the definitive case for the restoration of 'The Raftsmen's Passage' from *Life in the Mississippi* to *Huckleberry Finn* in 'The raft episode in *Huckleberry Finn*', *Modern Fiction Studies*, vol. 14 (Spring 1968), pp. 11–20.

15 *Huckleberry Finn*, ch. 33, pp. 177–8/283.

16 Kenneth S. Lynn, *Mark Twain and Southwestern Humor* (Boston, Mass.: Little, Brown, 1959), ch. 9, p. 213.

17 John Carlos Rowe, *Through the Custom-House: Nineteenth-Century American Fiction and Modern Theory* (Baltimore, Md: Johns Hopkins University Press, 1982), ch. 6, pp. 164–5.

18 Nietzsche, *Beyond Good and Evil*, trans. R.J. Hollingdale (Harmondsworth: Penguin Books, 1972), pp. 141–2; cf. also Claude Lévi-Strauss in this quasi-paraphrase of Nietzsche: 'Un masque n'existe pas en soi; il suppose, toujours présents à ses côtés, d'autres masques réels ou possibles qu'on aurait pu choisir pour les lui substituer . . . Un masque n'est pas d'abord ce qu'il présente mais ce qu'il transforme, c'est-à-dire choisit de *ne pas* représenter. Comme un mythe, un masque nie autant qu'il affirme; il n'est pas fait seulement de ce qu'il dit ou croit dire, mais de ce qu'il exclut' (*La Voie des masques*, 1975).

19 See above, Ch. 4, n. 14.

20 Lynn, *Mark Twain and Southwestern Humor*, pp. 214–15.

21 See Harold Beaver, 'Time on the cross: white fiction and black messiahs', *Yearbook of English Studies*, vol. 8 (1978), p. 50.

22 *Huckleberry Finn*, ch. 31, p. 169/270.

CHAPTER 8

Huck Adrift

'But I go a good deal on instinct . . .' (ch. 32)

T. S. Eliot was right. 'Huck we do not look at', he declared, ' – we see the world through his eyes.' Now we must try to turn the tables round. Instead of looking *through* Huck, we must try to look *at* Huck. We must look into those wary, curious, roving, matter-of-fact, anxious eyes.

By his own estimation, Huck is 'ignorant', 'so kind of low-down and ornery' (15/14). But he is not stupid. He takes pride in his practical intelligence. When Jim tells him 'bees wouldn't sting idiots', for example, he is sceptical. Because he has personal experience of bees. Because, he says, 'I had tried them lots of times myself, and they wouldn't sting me' (41/55). Nor is the chuckle in that sentence Huck's; the touchstone of his personal experience is absolute.

Yet even to a boy of his own age he can seem dumb. When Buck asks him the Moses riddle, Huck is stuck:

'I said I didn't know; I hadn't heard about it before, no way.'
'Well, guess,' he says.
'How'm I going to guess,' says I, 'when I never heard tell about it before?'[1]

Huck has severe limitations, even as an observer. If he has no previous experience of something, he is at a loss. He cannot make a guess. He just gives up. Even the nature of a riddle – the very concept of intellectual play – is beyond him.

'Well, if you knowed where he was, what did you ask me for?'
'Why, blame it, it's a riddle, don't you see?'

But Huck doesn't.

He is wholly empirical. His role, in the initial chapters, is to play Sancho Panza to Tom's quixotic imagination. Where Tom sees 'julery' and 'rich A-rabs', Huck sees only turnips and Sunday-school picnickers. Playboy Tom calls him a 'numskull' for his pains, a 'perfect sap-head'; devout Miss Watson a 'fool'. But, if a fool, he is a holy simpleton, a wise fool.

Take the opening paragraph of chapter 16, which originally introduced 'The Raftsmen's Passage' (lifted into *Life on the Mississippi*):

We slept most all day, and started out at night, a little ways behind a monstrous long raft that was as long going by as a procession. She had four long sweeps at each end, so we judged she carried as many as thirty men, likely. She had five big wigwams aboard, wide apart, and an open camp fire in the middle, and a tall flag-pole at each end. There was a power of style about her. It *amounted* to something being a raftsman on such a craft as that.

Huck is always on the alert. He is always closely observant of detail. He has a quick, practical grasp. There is enough detail here to construct a model from his report. Of their own raft, which he knows from bow to stern, he can give the exact measurements: 'It was twelve foot wide and about fifteen or sixteen foot long, and the top stood above water six or seven inches' (44/60). One trusts such figures, such easy precision. Huck seems utterly reliable as witness. But he is more than a mere witness. His mind is charged with activity. He is always thinking and judging. Observation is backed by practical inference and rapid calculation. So 'we judged she carried as many as thirty men, likely': around four men to each oar, that is, and six to a wigwam.

His is a detective skill, moving from inference to observation as well as from observation (or reported observation) to inference. 'I knowed mighty well that a drownded man don't float on his back,' he comments on a corpse claimed to be his father's. Or on the origin of stars, with Jim arguing for creation and Huck for evolution:

I judged it would have took too long to *make* so many. Jim said the moon could a *laid* them; well, that looked kind of reasonable, so I didn't say nothing against it, because I've seen a frog lay most as many, so of course it could be done.[2]

Huck is always logical, always reasonable on his own empirical terms.

What most impresses him, however, is 'style'. In this he is a true Southerner. He loves to cut a dash. He adores a swagger, a hint of bravura, a touch of class. (Twain allows a rare italic emphasis to the verb '*amounted*'.) Huck is infallibly awed by style. But he, too, can put on panache. His own 'style' is stylish. Though mainly metonymic, in its temporal and local sequences, it is capable of metaphoric flights: 'as long going by as a procession'. The fact that the raft is 'monstrous long' and so almost literally passing by – from flag-pole to oars to wigwams to camp-fire to wigwams to oars to flag-pole – like a procession makes the simile peculiarly Huck-like. For it evokes not only the details but also the exact *impression* produced. We see, that is, as always through Huck's eyes.

For Huck is all eyes and hands and nostrils and ears. He *sees* things with precision. He *handles* things experimentally. He *hears* things exactly: '*plunkety-plunk*' (horses coming); '*k'chunk!*' (sound of an axe across water); '*h'wack!*' (crack of thunder). He even *smells* the essence of night: 'Everything was dead quiet, and it looked late, and *smelt* late. You know what I mean – . . .' (32/42).

Or take his description of the parlour in the Grangerford house:

> Well, there was a big outlandish parrot on each side of the clock, made out of something like chalk, and painted up gaudy. By one of the parrots was a cat made of crockery, and a crockery dog by the other; and when you pressed down on them they squeaked, but didn't open their mouths nor look different nor interested. They squeaked through underneath. There was a couple of big wild-turkey-wing fans spread out behind those things. On a table in the middle of the room was a kind of a lovely crockery basket that had apples and oranges and peaches and grapes piled up in it which was much redder and yellower and prettier than real ones is, but they warn't real because you could see where pieces had got chipped off and showed the white chalk or whatever it was, underneath.[3]

Huck not only studies all the ornaments on the mantlepiece, he touches them and presses on them; and obviously picks them up to examine their manufacture from underneath. He probes the world around him. He scrutinizes it. He tests it with his hands. Huck is the practical American boy, matching hand and eye. He exposes himself to experience. He plunges into water and into the woods. Much like

Thoreau, his contemporary, another tramp in the woods. Like Emerson even, shorn of transcendentalism. For Emerson supplied the symbols. The very stuff of language, he argued, was revealed in hieroglyphs and puns. Hand and eye, research and rhetoric, life and letters are one. Meaning itself becomes transparent. The seeing 'eye' is transformed to 'I', the experimental 'hand' to 'and'. In the sequential handling of our world the 'I' is for ever linked to 'and'.[4]

Not that Huck would have cared. His problems are almost never semiotic; they are profoundly moral. As a contemporary American critic put it:

> What Huck really is . . . is simply the usual vagabond boy, with his expected shrewdness and cunning, his rags, his sharp humor, his practical philosophy. The only difference between him and his type would be found in his essential honesty, his strong and struggling moral nature . . .[5]

His characteristic trait is loyalty. He remains loyal, at heart, to Pap. He remains loyal to Tom. In all his confusion, he remains loyal to Jim. He is loyal to Sophia Grangerford. He even remains loyal, in the end, to the king and duke. His heart aches for reconciliation and love. It aches for the two tricksters, tarred and feathered, straddling a rail. He breaks down in tears at Buck's death and at the loss of Jim. This spontaneous overflow of feelings affects his relationship to almost all the characters. His sympathy extends to the Widow, who 'looked so sorry that I thought I would behave a while if I could'. To the gang aboard the *Walter Scott*: 'I begun to think how dreadful it was, even for murderers, to be in such a fix.' To the Grangerfords: 'I liked all that family, dead ones and all, and warn't going to let anything come between us.' To the circus 'drunk'. To victims of the king and duke. To Mary Jane Wilks: 'It made my eyes water a little, to remember her crying there all by herself in the night.' To Aunt Sally: 'I wished I could do something for her, but I couldn't, only to swear that I wouldn't never do nothing to grieve her any more.' Finally even to that 'poor old woman' (Miss Watson) and 'the poor old king'. Huck scorns self-conscious preaching ('all about brotherly love and such-like tiresomeness'), but he is no slouch himself at universal brotherhood, bidding this adieu to the king and duke:

> Well, it made me sick to see it; and I was sorry for them poor pitiful

rascals, it seemed like I couldn't ever feel any hardness against them any more in the world. It was a dreadful thing to see. Human beings *can* be awful cruel to one another.[6]

But his response is *all* feeling. It is solely by feeling. It is nothing but feeling. There seems to be no cohesion between Huck's sympathies and his actions. No intellectual awareness. No consistency between what he *feels* and what he *does* at all. That is why he has no sense of history, no active memory, no sense of time even. His very tenses wobble indeterminately between the past and historic present. Spatially Huck is always in control. Geographically each episode is explored with absolute precision. But the intervals between episodes are left vaguely adrift: 'Two or three nights went by'; 'Two or three days and nights went by; I reckon I might say they swum by'; 'Soon as it was night'; 'pretty soon'; 'One morning'; 'by-and-by'. In this context Tom's final revelation, that 'Old Miss Watson died two months ago', seems extraordindary. For all Huck ever registers is sequence.[7]

As the raft drifts, Huck drifts. He is hopelessly fatalistic. Now he is 'lazying around', now on the jump. One by one, things just happen. There are good signs; there are bad signs. There is good luck and bad luck. Huck lives in a predetermined world where 'the good and the bad are the things that happen to you, not the ways you choose to behave'.[8] In fact, there is a total lack of connection between Huck's actions and any *ideas*. All he realizes is that there is: (1) something wrong with Miss Watson's version of Christianity in general and the Grangerford version of Presbyterianism in particular; (2) something wrong with the conventions of morality as a system; (3) something wrong with slavery as an institution.[9] All he has is a negative conscience (THOU SHALT NOT) which is haphazard and wholly unpredictable in its spontaneous irruptions. As he concludes:

> it don't make no difference whether you do right or wrong, a person's conscience ain't got no sense, and just goes for him *anyway*. If I had a yaller dog that didn't know no more than a person's conscience does, I would pison him. It takes up more room than all the rest of a person's insides, and yet ain't no good, nohow.[10]

This undogmatic, drifting, spontaneous approach to life is what makes Huck so endearing, of course. His problems may be moral, but he does not confront them as moral problems. Not as complex and demanding issues. A 'thing that had some good in it' (like smoking) simply means something that makes him feel good. His is a wholly sensual register of 'right' and 'wrong'. It is all a matter of expedience. The questions are never remotely speculative but can be reduced, on their lowest terms, to: what makes Huck feel comfortable? What makes him feel uncomfortable? Conscience is such a 'yaller dog' because it invariably makes him feel uncomfortable. It is really this discomfort, rather than what is discreditable, that troubles him. This is why he tells himself (it is his major imperative) always to 'do whichever come handiest at the time'. What he asks himself on the key issue of betraying Jim is:

would you felt better than what you do now? No, says I, I'd feel bad – I'd feel just the same way I do now. Well, then, says I, what's the use of you learning to do right, when it's troublesome to do right and ain't no trouble to do wrong, and the wages is just the same?[11]

Huck is a philosopher of a kind in that he likes to relax a good deal and smoke and meditate: 'I laid there in the grass and the cool shade, thinking about things and feeling rested and ruther comfortable and satisfied' (34/45). But he can only really think about what is in front of his nose. In the long run, he is pragmatic. He is a fatalist. In a word, a hedonist.[12] James M. Cox put it well:

Freedom for Huck is not realized in terms of political liberty but in terms of pleasure. Thus his famous pronouncement about life on the raft: 'Other places do seem so cramped up and smothery, but a raft don't. You feel mighty free and easy and comfortable on a raft.'[13]

Or, again, he avoids tangling with the king and duke by observing: 'what you want, above all things, on a raft, is for everybody to be satisfied, and feel right and kind towards the others' (102/165).

Huck's ultimate principle, then, is the pleasure principle: lounging, 'talking, and singing, and laughing'. It is a wholly passive principle. It even affects his language. Huck has a trick of transforming adjectives, describing a passive state like 'lazy' or 'sad', into active verbs: 'And afterwards we would watch the lonesomeness of the river, and kind of lazy along, and by-and-by lazy off to sleep' (97/157). It is as if passivity, experienced deeply enough, can itself become an active principle. As if even to 'drift' might become an active verb. As if rafting were responsibility. Yet the raft inevitably drifts and cannot initiate action. For that reason Huck, despite his quick-change defence mechanisms, is such easy prey for active predators like Tom, or the king and duke.

Twain first published his thoughts on rafting in his book of German travels:

> The motion of the raft . . . is gentle, and gliding, and smooth, and noiseless; it calms down all feverish activities, it soothes to sleep all nervous hurry and impatience; under its restful influence all the troubles and vexations and sorrows that harrass the mind vanish away, and existence becomes a dream, a charm, a deep and tranquil ecstasy.[14]

There has been general jubilation all round among critics at the beauty of raft society and of raft relationships, especially of the relationship between Huck and Jim. But Jim, as it were, has been hijacked on to the raft. For him this raft-as-idyll is merely a means to an end: to safety and self-possession. Freedom for him can only mean political freedom. (Both Huck and the majority of his critics are peculiarly thick-skinned about this.) For Huck, of course, there is a charm, a dream, an ecstasy. This soothing of feverish activity, this calming 'all nervous hurry and impatience', is a kind of harmonious self-indulgence. It means, for a start, an emptying out of 'conscience'. That is his temporary bliss. He can now *both* help another *and* look out for him all the time, yet think continually about himself (which the Widow had expressly warned him against).

Such are the positive blessings for Huck in the drift; for Jim there are none. To that extent T. S. Eliot was right: 'Huck is the passive observer of men and events, Jim the submissive sufferer from them; and they are equal in dignity.' Or as Jonathan Raban more robustly phrased it: Huck 'tries to transfer this passive acceptance into situations which demand moral and intellectual discrimination'.[15] It leaves him singularly unprepared to meet crises. His reaction is to duck. He avoids confrontations wherever possible. When the king and duke, for example, board the raft, his main concern is to 'keep peace in the family':

But I never said nothing, never let on; kept it to myself; it's the best way; then you don't have no quarrels, and don't get into no trouble . . . If I never learnt nothing else out of Pap, I learnt that the best way to get along with his kind of people is to let them have their own way.[16]

To troubles which he cannot duck, he abjectly surrenders. When the king and duke unexpectedly reappear after the Wilks funeral, he just wilts. He never fights back. It is all he can do 'to keep from crying' (163/260).

In other tricky situations he blindly forges ahead. He simply trusts in 'Providence'. This confused and fatalistic residue of conflicting versions of predestination, as presented in the Watson–Douglas household, is his only resource. He has no other moral or intellectual map to guide him. At the critical moment, on approaching the Phelps farmhouse, he is without a plan, without an initiative, without a safeguard. He just goes right along, 'trusting to Providence to put the right words' in his mouth. It is a parlous predicament.

His empirical quick wits and acute observations are not much help, either. Huck is interested in *what* things are (how they work, how they are made), not in *why* they are there in the first place. As Huck lies in the cool shade of Jackson's Island 'thinking about things', the play of light catches his eye; the cause of those shifting, dappled sunspecks is the kind of 'thing' he thinks about:

I could see the sun out at one or two holes, but mostly it was big trees all about, and gloomy in there amongst them. There was freckled places on the ground where the light sifted down through the leaves, and the freckled places swapped about a little, showing there was a little breeze up there.[17]

He is always observant, always inquiring. But his pragmatic mind stops short at practical questions. It can make certain deductions. It reasons from visible shifts below to an invisible breeze above. But that is all. It never probes this causal chain. It never pushes beyond immediate cause and effect. That is why Huck can so shrewdly observe society and still be taken in. As he is taken in by the Grangerfords. As he is taken in by the circus 'drunk'; and the ringmaster as well:

> Then the ring-master he see how he had been fooled, and he *was*
> the sickest ring-master you ever see, I reckon. Why, it was one of
> his own men! He had got up that joke all out of his own head, and
> never let on to nobody. Well, I felt sheepish enough, to be took in
> so . . .[18]

That is why Huck is so often a victim of events, or incompetent or
ineffectual in his undertakings. However observant, his naïvely
objective mind is naturally credulous. He notes that the fruit in the
Grangerford parlour is fraudulent, artificial, made of plaster; but
leaves us, his readers, to ponder the social and moral implications. He
inspects and explores and tests his world, but he does not interpret it.
He does not translate it. He does not read it. He is literate, but too
literal-minded. So, unlike Tom, he is a halting rather than a habitual
reader. Leafing through *Pilgrim's Progress* is a puzzling experience: 'I
read considerable in it now and then. The statements was interesting,
but tough' (83/137). Tough, that is, for someone without an
instinctive symbolic imagination. Huck seems not even to recognize
that this book 'about a man that left his family it didn't say why'
might have symbolic implications for his own mysterious departure
from Pap and St Petersburg.[19] But by his same literal standards he is
impressed by Emmeline Grangerford's doggerel 'Ode to Stephen
Dowling Bots, Dec'd'. 'It was very good poetry,' he asserts. It is his
one unqualified critical judgement.

As Locke might have put it, Huck possesses sensibility, imagination
and memory, but little power of reflection since he cannot compare
ideas or reason abstractly.[20] So naturally he cannot grasp the abstract
idea of fiction, only of the practical disguises (or fictions) by which he
sustains his life. Introducing himself, oddly, as a reader (of a book)
and a character (in that book), he is at once its most formidable critic:

> You don't know about me, without you have read a book by the
> name of 'The Adventures of Tom Sawyer', but that ain't no matter.
> That book was made by Mr Mark Twain, and he told the truth,
> mainly. There was things which he stretched, but mainly he told
> the truth.

The sole test of fiction for Huck is truth. He is no Pirandello-like
character in search of an author. Decisively he *verifies* Mark Twain:
'he told the truth, mainly'. *The Adventures of Tom Sawyer*, he insists,

'is mostly a true book'; then again modifies the claim: 'with some stretchers, as I said before'. Untruths nag. When qualified to judge a text, he qualifies his critical judgement not aesthetically, not morally, but with the evidence of his senses, of his memory, with first-hand proof. Twain may be a literary author, that is, but Huck remains the living authority. Though often and easily fooled, especially by close friends, Huck never fools himself. He just fools others with his fictions.

A 'huckleberry', in contemporary parlance, was a person of no consequence. Huck, who is of 'mudcat' status like Pap, is basically a survivor. At a pinch he can mount a dramatic action. Just as Jim decisively left Miss Watson, so Huck planned his own very stylish and incontravertible murder. But his active interventions tend to misfire. For they tend to be based on the Sawyer model (his only model for dramatic action); and Huck is no Tom. Unlike Tom, for one thing, he never comes on 'ca'm and important, like the ram' (179/285). Unlike Sherburn, too, with a double-barrel gun on his porch roof: 'ca'm and deliberate, not saying a word' (118/189). He bungles the visit to Mrs Loftus. He bungles the boarding of the *Walter Scott*. He bungles disastrously with the dead rattlesnake; and even more disastrously in the attempt to locate the Ohio at Cairo.

Only at the Wilks funeral does he successfully initiate an action and energetically intervene. His participation there, though, is an exception that proves the rule; and even then it misfires. He is torn by puppy love. The rival claimants put in their appearance. He feels threatened, whichever way he turns, by the extraordinary rigmarole woven round him by the king. For once he has no idea what to say. He is hedged in by truth. He is hedged in by lies:

here's a case where I'm blest if it don't look to me like the truth is better, and actuly *safer*, than a lie. I must lay it by in my mind, and think it over some time or other, it's so kind of strange and unregular. I never see nothing like it.[21]

Exposed to questioning, therefore, he is hopelessly out of his depth:

Then the doctor whirls on me and says:
    'Are *you* English too?'
    I says yes; and him and some others laughed, and said, 'Stuff!' . . . And by-and-by they had me up to tell what I knowed.

The king he give me a left-handed look out of the corner of his eye,
and so I knowed enough to talk on the right side. I begun to tell
about Sheffield, and how we lived there, and all about the English
Wilkses, and so on; but I didn't get pretty fur till the doctor begun
to laugh; and Levi Bell, the lawyer, says:

'Set down, my boy, I wouldn't strain myself, if I was you. I
reckon you ain't used to lying, it don't seem to come handy; what
you want is practice. You do it pretty awkward.'[22]

Which is much what Mrs Loftus told Huck in drag: 'You do a girl
tolerable poor, but you might fool men, maybe' (53/74). Still, he does
outsmart the king and duke by hiding the gold in Peter Wilks's coffin.
They reckon the '*niggers*' stole it; and even when it turns up in the
exhumed coffin they mutually suspect each other sooner than suspect
Huck of outwitting them both.

It is ignorance, incompetence, powerlessness that bedevils Huck.
That is why he is so overawed by the Grangerfords and the king; why
he kowtows to Tom. For they are all endowed with a 'demonic
force'.[23] Poor Huck is far from demonic. Leslie Fiedler called him
'the most non-violent of American fictional children'. Unlike Tom, he
observes, he never fights with his fists: 'He runs, hides, equivocates,
dodges, and, when he can do nothing else, suffers.'[24]

NOTES

1 *Huckleberry Finn*, ch. 17, p. 81/135.
2 ibid., ch. 19, p. 97/158.
3 ibid., ch. 17, p. 83/136-7.
4 To this wondering 'I' with wandering hands I shall return, for a full discussion of
   Huck's style, in Chapter 13.
5 Charles Miner Thompson, 'Mark Twain as an interpreter of American character',
   Atlantic Monthly, vol. 79 (1897), pp.443–50. But I omit the racist conclusion: 'his
   strong and struggling moral nature, so notably Anglo-Saxon'. This adds a new
   twist to the debate surrounding the genteel reception of the book. See above, Ch.
   3.
6 *Huckleberry Finn*, ch. 33, p. 182/290.
7 See Alan Trachtenberg, 'The form of freedom in *Adventures of Huckleberry Finn*',
   Southern Review, new series vol. 6 (October 1970), pp. 965–6.
8 Jonathan Raban, *Mark Twain: Huckleberry Finn* (London: Edward Arnold, 1968),
   ch. 1, p. 18.
9 Even this is arguable. His main worry at the end is why Tom can act like a 'low-
   down abolitionist': 'I couldn't even understand, before . . . how he *could* help a
   body set a nigger free, with his bringing-up' (227/358).
10 *Huckleberry Finn*, ch. 33, p. 183/290.

11 ibid., ch. 16, p. 76/127–8.
12 A 'lazy hedonism' was Lionel Trilling's phrase (1948).
13 James M. Cox, *Mark Twain: The Fate of Humor* (Princeton, NJ: Princeton University Press, 1966), ch. 7, p. 178.
14 Mark Twain, *A Tramp Abroad* (1880), ch. 15.
15 T. S. Eliot, introduction to *The Adventures of Huckleberry Finn* (London: Cresset Press, 1950), p. xi; Raban, *Mark Twain: Huckleberry Finn*, ch. 1, p 17. 'Dignity' hardly seems an appropriate word for Huck; but even 'passive' seems to offend some critics. 'The very last word one should use to describe Huck is "passive",' wrote Gilbert M. Rubenstein. 'He is no drifter but a plucky, lovable boy who, after painful self-examination, achieves an iron determination to help his friend Jim reach free territory.' See 'The moral structure of *Huckleberry Finn*', *College English*, vol. 18 (November 1956), pp. 72–6, which is a reply to Lauriat Lane, Jr, 'Why *Huckleberry Finn* is a great world novel', *College English*, vol. 17 (October 1955), pp. 1–5. Iron determination? To reach free territory? 'Passive' seems to alarm some readers as much as if one had called Huck 'queer'. See Leslie Fiedler's notorious essay, 'Come back to the raft ag'in, Huck honey!', *Partisan Review*, vol. 15 (June 1948), pp. 664–71.
16 *Huckleberry Finn*, ch. 19, p. 102/165.
17 ibid., ch. 8, p. 34/45.
18 ibid., ch. 22, p. 120/194.
19 This may also be something of a private joke. Twain's own first book was entitled *The Innocents Abroad, or The New Pilgrim's Progress* (1869). Huck is yet another 'New Pilgrim', or Innocent Abroad.
20 John Locke, *An Essay Concerning Human Understanding*, ed. Peter Nidditch (Oxford University Press, 1975), p. 160.
21 *Huckleberry Finn*, ch. 28, p. 148/239.
22 ibid., ch. 29, pp. 157–8/252–3.
23 George C. Carrington, Jr., *The Dramatic Unity of 'Huckleberry Finn'* (Columbus, Ohio: Ohio State University Press, 1976), ch. 2, p. 55.
24 Leslie Fiedler, *Love and Death in the American Novel* (New York: Criterion Books, 1960; London: Paladin, 1970), ch. 13, pp. 426–7.

CHAPTER 9

Huck and Tom

'Gentlemen, I will reveal it to you, for I feel I may have confidence in you.' (ch. 19)

In most other respects, though, Huck is a normal 14-year-old boy: self-indulgent, unreliable, forgetful. Another joker, like Tom. His joking is compulsive. He is committed to Jim, but at least twice cannot resist fooling him for 'fun'. His initial schoolboy oath is an oath of honour, a true bond:

> I'll stick to it. Honest *injun* I will. People would call me a low down Ablitionist and despise me for keeping mum – but that don't make no difference. I ain't agoing to tell, and I ain't agoing back there anyways.[1]

But he has no idea what he has committed himself to.

For Huck is conditioned by the whole white Southern culture – by everyone from Pap to the Widow Douglas and Judge Thatcher – to regard 'niggers' as *sacred property* and anyone who tampers with such property as 'a low down Ablitionist'. I quoted earlier a passage from Twain's notebooks where he compares stealing a horse or cow to the unspeakable crime of stealing, or helping to steal, a slave. It continues:

> That this sentiment should exist among slave-holders is comprehensible – there were good commercial reasons for it – but that it should exist and did exist among the paupers . . . and in a passionate and uncompromising form, is not in our remote day realizable. It seemed natural enough to me then; natural enough that Huck and his father the worthless loafer should feel and approve it, though it seems now absurd. It shows that that strange thing, the conscience – that unerring monitor – can be trained to

approve any wild thing you *want* it to approve if you begin its
education early & stick to it.[2]

The 'conscience', for Twain, is 'the creature of *training*', as he calls it
elsewhere: that is, of social indoctrination. Only the 'heart' is
something God-given and incorruptible. So Huck's self-image as a
white Southern boy is deeply incriminated by his association with Jim.
His self-respect in Jim's company is bound to be wobbly, rocking
from personal affection – even devotion – to a wild kind of aggressive
indifference, expressed in pranks. That is the covert psychology
behind his pranks. That is why he curls the dead rattlesnake on Jim's
bed. That is why he compels Jim on to the *Walter Scott*. That is why
he releases his own pent-up anxieties by mercilessly teasing Jim after
the fog. That is why he is oblivious of Jim at the Grangerfords' and
again ignores him at the Wilkses'. That is why he can condone the
duke's cruel treatment of Jim as he condones Tom Sawyer's
complacent and ruthlessly sustained sadism.

In his working notes Twain had pondered a possibly more liberal
approach for Silas Phelps towards his 'nigger' prisoner:

> Uncle S wishes he would escape – if it warn't wrong, he'd set him
> free – but it's a too gushy generosity with another man's property.[3]

Though not written in Huck's vocabulary, this certainly spells out his
problem. Wasn't he also, perhaps, being too gushily generous with
Miss Watson's property? Had she ever taken his property? Had she
ever harmed him? Huck and Silas have much in common: both share
the same white Protestant conscience; both are steeped in the same
talk of baptism, Providence, sin and hell-fire. For Huck's stay at the
Widow's and Miss Watson's was not completely wasted. Far from it.
They taught him 'all about the bad place' and 'the good place' and
prayer and Providence and 'spiritual gifts'. Twain is deeply involved
in the humour of these early chapters. For this is his own education.
This is his own mother speaking. In Huck's final crisis, in confronting
his duty to report Jim's whereabouts to Miss Watson, he instinctively
resorts to her vocabulary. More than resorts, he *thinks* in it; he submits
unconditionally, if momentarily, to what (in the king's mouth) he had
scorned as 'soul-butter and hogwash' (132/213):

> here was the plain hand of Providence slapping me in the face and

letting me know my wickedness was being watched all the time
from up there in heaven, whilst I was stealing a poor old woman's
nigger that hadn't ever done me no harm, and now was showing me
there's One that's always on the lookout, and ain't agoing to allow
no such miserable doings to go only just so fur and no further, I
most dropped in my tracks I was so scared . . . So I kneeled down.
But the words wouldn't come. Why wouldn't they? It warn't no use
to try and hide it from Him. Nor from *me*, neither. I knowed very
well why they wouldn't come. It was because my heart warn't right;
it was because I warn't square; it was because I was playing double.
I was letting *on* to give up sin, but away inside of me I was holding
on to the biggest one of all. I was trying to make my mouth *say* I
would do the right thing and the clean thing . . .[4]

Huck is caught between a vision of 'everlasting fire' and of laundry.
For once he feels 'good and all washed clean of sin'.[5] For heaven was
watching; and God was his supervisor, 'One that's always on the
lookout'. The very language of the Sunday school can be overheard in
that periphrasis. Slip and slither as he might, God will catch him. For
Huck had broken the Seventh Commandment: 'THOU SHALT NOT
STEAL.' What is worse, he had helped steal a 'nigger'; he had helped a
hunted slave. The battle in Twain's soul between his church
upbringing and his Mugwump politics continued to rage mercilessly.

Twain recalled his own 'kind-hearted and compassionate' mother:
'she was not conscious that slavery was a bald, grotesque and
unwarrantable usurpation. She had never heard it assailed in any
pulpit but had heard it defended and sanctified in a thousand . . .'[6]
That was to be published posthumously in his autobiography. More
privately, in recollecting the villagers of his youth, Twain set down
this portrait of another compassionate lady of Hannibal:

Mrs Sexton (*she* pronounced it *Saxton* to make it finer, the nice,
kind-hearted, smirky, smily dear Christian creature – Methodist.)[7]

A lifetime's disdain for Christian snobbery and humbug is condensed
into that withering verdict. But neither the 60-year-old nor the 14-
year-old, neither Twain nor Huck, could escape that smily indoctrination. They could repudiate it (in their heart), but not expunge it
(from their conscience).

Add to this the Southern addiction to 'style' and no wonder Huck is besotted with Tom Sawyer. By the end of chapter 3 he contemptuously dismisses Tom's Gang:

> So then I judged that all that stuff was only just one of Tom
> Sawyer's lies. I reckoned he believed in the A-rabs and the
> elephants, but as for me I think different. It had all the marks of a
> Sunday school.[8]

But Tom's ultimate influence merely reinforces a permanently latent strain. Despite that resounding verdict, despite his self-elimination by 'murder', despite his friendship with Jim, despite his flight downriver, despite all the protean changes and permutations of his roles, Huck had by no means finished with Tom.

As Richard Poirier recognized: 'Huck is cultivating an imaginative association with Tom (and therefore society) all the way from Chapter 3 to Chapter 15.'[9] Beyond that even. Tom remains, throughout, Huck's authority; his model for adventures; his guarantee for the possibility of adventures; his source of the very typology of what constitutes an adventure. For Tom is a leader. Tom has heroic visions, for ever intent on transforming boys' games into triumphant quests, whether to return (like Odysseus) from the dead, or (with Jim) from the mouth of the Mississippi. Huck himself is no hero; he may blend the role of trickster and bard in the Odyssean fashion, but he is no Odysseus. Jim is positively saint-like in renouncing his freedom for the sake of Tom, as the doctor at length attests:

> I never see a nigger that was a better nuss or faithfuller, and yet he
> was resking his freedom to do it, and was all tired out, too, and I
> see plain enough he'd been worked main hard, lately. I liked the
> nigger for that; I tell you, gentlemen, a nigger like that is worth a
> thousand dollars – and kind treatment, too.[10]

But Jim is no hero. Thus Tom's exasperation all along: 'Now I want to ask you – if you got any reasonableness in you at all – what kind of a show would *that* give him to be a hero?' (192/304) That is how Tom aimed to translate him, at the head of torchlight procession, into a 'hero':

> And he said, what he had planned in his head, from the start, if we
> got Jim out all safe, was for us to run him down the river, on the

raft, and have adventures plumb to the mouth of the river, and then
tell him about his being free, and take him back up home on a
steamboat, in style, and pay him for his lost time, and write word
ahead and get out all the niggers around, and have them waltz him
into town with a torchlight procession and a brass band, and then
he would be a hero, and so would we.[11]

It is too such epic visions that Huck wistfully, fitfully, all too
conscious of his own inadequacies, aspires.

For it is to Tom's image, consistently throughout his *Adventures*,
that Huck turns. It is always Tom's image, never Jim's (except at
times of temptation), that he evokes. Even on planning his own
'murder' and flight from Pap's cabin, he sighs: 'I did wish Tom
Sawyer was there, I knowed he would take an interest in this kind of
business, and throw in the fancy touches. Nobody could spread
himself like Tom Sawyer in such a thing as that' (31/41). The
escapade on the *Walter Scott* is heavily rubbed in at Jim's expense. 'Do
you reckon Tom Sawyer would ever go by this thing?' he mocks:

> Not for pie, he wouldn't. He'd call it an adventure – that's what
> he'd call it; and he'd land on that wreck if it was his last act. And
> wouldn't he throw style into it? – wouldn't he spread himself, nor
> nothing? Why, you'd think it was Christopher C'lumbus discover-
> ing Kingdom-Come.[12]

For Huck grasps the nature of heroic quests; he has glimpsed the
Columbus dream. It is just that he feels incompetent, alone, to see one
through. He misses Tom. Thus the final sigh: 'I wish Tom Sawyer
was here.'

For all his affection Jim is no substitute for a boy-companion like
Tom. The white child and black man are hopelessly at odds. Jim is
scared out of his wits at the risks involved in boarding a foundering
steamboat:

> He said that when I went into the texas and he crawled back to get
> on the raft and found her gone, he nearly died; because he judged it
> was all up with *him*, anyway it could be fixed; for if he didn't get
> saved he would get drownded; and if he did get saved, whoever
> saved him would send him back home so as to get the reward, and
> then Miss Watson would sell him South, sure.[13]

In retrospect Huck agrees, though he still insists that 'these kinds of things was adventures'. Even if Jim 'didn't want no more adventures'. That his buddy is a hunted man, that he lives on borrowed time, that he survives on a knife's edge, Huck (feeding off Tom's vocabulary) seems simply unable to grasp.

What follows, in chapter 14, is the 'King Sollermun' debate which proved one of Twain's most popular turns on his reading tour. But, as Poirier astutely realized, it is also 'a preparatory and comic version of Chapter 15' (Huck's trick on Jim after their separation in the fog).[14] Now Huck even starts to *talk* like Tom by citing the Widow's authority and adopting a quixotic literary stance against Jim's decent, puzzled realism. Almost our first introduction to Huck, after all, had been his claim that he 'don't take no stock in dead people' (on the Moses question in chapter 1). But now it is Jim who 'doan' take no stock' in dead authority. Jim tenaciously insists on practical consequences: 'I want to ast you: what's de use er dat half a bill? – can't buy noth'n wid it. En what use is a half a chile? I would'n give a dern for a million un um.' Now it is Huck, like Tom, who gives up on the 'numbskull' with: 'But hang it, Jim, you've clean missed the point – blame it, you've missed it a thousand mile' (66/95).

Poirier continues:

> Huck's imitation and assumption of Tom's role at this point prepares us for the crucial scene about to take place. In the next chapter, after the separation in the fog, Huck continues the tricks begun by Tom in Chapter 2. He tries to convince Jim that he has merely been dreaming, that what he believed were naturally stimulated feelings of loss and love were the result rather of fantasy.

It strikes us as a peculiarly chilling and callow trick to imitate Tom Sawyer at this overwhelming (and overwhelmingly *real*) crisis. But Huck is capable – when shamed, after sulking for quarter of an hour – of humiliating himself before the runaway slave; which is inconceivable of Tom. Yet he never actually loses sight of Tom. Even at the Wilkses', when successfully outwitting the king and duke, he summons up his familiar:

> I felt very good; I judged I had done it pretty neat – I reckoned Tom Sawyer couldn't a done it no neater himself. Of course he would a throwed more style into it, but I can't do that very handy, not being brung up to it.[15]

Until finally and fittingly he *becomes* Tom Sawyer, when given that name – and so that role – extempore by Aunt Sally. It is his dearest and most abject wish. No wonder it felt 'like being born again'.

For heroic aspirations were confused, at the profoundest level, with social aspirations; and social aspirations with the moral imagination. Huck apparently did not realize that his own sympathies flowed altogether more readily than Tom's. Even his curse of his 'yaller dog' conscience needed Tom's seconding; 'Tom Sawyer he says the same' was the clincher. Even Jim, Tom's most blatant victim, in the end defers to Tom as the touchstone of chivalry:

> Well, den, dis is de way it looks to me, Huck. Ef it wuz *him* dat 'uz bein' sot free, en one er de boys wuz to git shot, would he say, 'Go on en save me, nemmine 'bout a doctor f'r to save dis one?' Is dat like Mars Tom Sawyer? Would he say dat? You *bet* he wouldn't![16]

So infatuated is Huck that the phoniness of this appeal quite escapes him. He merely reflects: 'I knowed he was white inside'; and, buoyed by that delusion, runs off to fetch a doctor. The Tom Sawyer mystique, as a private cult, is Huck's own peculiar version of Southern myth. For Tom is a fake as his historical fictions are fake and his name (Sid) is fake and his romantic 'evasion' is fake. The extent of his humbug can readily be gauged by that of two other more genial and equally assertive fakes, the king and duke. All three are bumptious; all three are outrageous; all three are frauds; and Twain clearly draws the parallel between them.

The king and duke are simply crooks. This couple of jeans-clad, anonymous charlatans claim between them to have been actors, journeymen-printers, patent-medicine salesmen, mesmerists, phrenologists, singing teachers, dancing masters, elocutionists, lecturers, doctors ('Layin' on o' hands' for cancer and paralysis), fortune-tellers, preachers – just about every quick-witted trade, needing no capital outlay, they can devise.[17] All is grist to their mill. The 30-year-old duke is certainly an ex-printer; and he *may* have been on the stage with his banter of 'the unities' and 'the histrionic boards'. The king's stock-in-trade is temperance revivals and camp-meetings – just 'missionaryin' around'. In their roles of minister (alias the Reverend Elexander Blodgett) and strolling players (alias David Garrick and Edmund Kean), they haunt the banks of the Mississippi, exploiting the ignorance and poverty of farming folk and their credulous thirst for news, drama and stylish salvation.

These two quick-change artists, with bulging carpet-bags, are ditinguishable by age (30+ and 70+) but hardly by function. It seems yet another case of Twain's propensity for twinning, or splitting, identity. The 30-year-old piles on more of the romantic agony ('Misfortune has broken my once haughty spirit'); the 70-year-old turns out to be more of a wag and a sot. But they merrily double-cross each other, or plan to double-cross each other, or suspect each other of double-crossing each other (as after the Wilks fiasco) with mutual chicanery:

'Mf! And we reckoned the *niggers* stole it!'
That made me squirm!
'Yes,' says the duke, kinder slow, and deliberate, and sarcastic, '*We* did.'
After about a half a minute, the king drawls out:
'Leastways – *I* did.'
The duke says, the same way:
'On the contrary – *I* did.'
The king kind of ruffles up, and says:
'Looky here, Bilgewater, what'r you referrin' to?'
The duke says, pretty brisk:
'When it comes to that, maybe you'll let me ask, what was *you* referring to?'[18]

But soon enough these duplicates get drunk together, and maudlin together, and fall asleep together 'snoring in each other's arms'.

They make a versatile duo and together they present a kind of boisterous, irreverent *kōmos*, or orgiastic rout of the old Southwest: 'I say orgies, not because it's the common term, because it ain't,' observes the king. 'Orgies is better, because it means the thing you're after, more exact' (135/217–8). The phallic clowning of 'The Royal Nonesuch', with its capering energy, reaches back to Dionysiac rites and Aristophanic comedy as well as to the prancing satyrs and Sileni of the tragic stage. This rollicking Rabelaisian pair do more than corrupt, however; they batten on to corruption. They feed off what they see. They are the very mirror-image of the culture that bred them. With their disdain for humble humanity and their greed, they parody (in aristocratic guise) the exploitation common to official Mississippi culture with its titles, its grandiloquence, its theatrical swagger.

It is to this itinerant pair that Huck, in his turn, attaches himself.

He seems almost to cherish these interlopers – these parasites – as if he instinctively recognizes more experienced, more versatile con-men than himself. 'Oh, this is the boss dodge,' crows the king, 'ther' ain't no mistake 'bout it' (134/215); and Huck goes along with him all the way. He speaks of the 'Shaksperean Revival' as 'our show': 'We struck it mighty lucky,' he says; 'we went around and stuck up our bills'; 'Then we went loafing around the town' (112/180–1). But *'our show'* fell flat, which is hardly surprising; after the Sherburn shoot-out, the 'Broad-sword conflict' from *Richard III* was a distinct let-down. So they try 'The Royal Nonesuch'; and even on the second night Huck joins wholeheartedly in the fraud. 'House was jammed again', he notes, 'and we sold this crowd the same way' (122/197).

Only at the Wilkses', where helpless girls are to be betrayed, does Huck detach himself. He begins to call them the 'bummers', 'the beats', 'our dead-beats'. He begins to withdraw. Up to this point he had been their stooge. Not that he had been conned exactly, as he was conned by the ring-master and acrobat-as-clown: 'It didn't take me long to make up my mind that these liars warn't no kings nor dukes, at all, but just low-down humbugs and frauds' (102/165). He sees through these two poseurs quickly enough as he never saw through the circus team's joint contrivance. Eventually he even outwits them, as we saw. Still, they outwit him in the end, since Huck misreads their fatal, final moves. When the king announces his intention to scout Pikesville for tell-tale rumours of 'The Royal Nonesuch', Huck comments: 'House to rob, you *mean*, and when you get through robbing it you'll come back here . . .' (166/266). So he quite misses the point of the confidential huddles in the wigwam ('two or three hours at a time') and fails to realize that their appointment at midday is the signal for Jim's capture. At this crisis of mutual betrayal it is the elders' double act that easily confounds and trumps the little con-man.

Jim, too, of course, sees through the royal couple. 'But, Huck, dese kings o' ourn is reglar rapscallions; dat's jist what dey is; dey's reglar rapscallions' (123/199) is his verdict; which was just what Huck had called the crooks on the *Walter Scott*. Perhaps Jim does not fully understand about European titles, and certainly Huck patronizes him: 'it warn't no use to tell Jim, so I didn't tell him' (102/165). But Jim can spot a rogue; and it is through Jim that the swindlers are caught. They had long been suspicious of 'niggers' as a group; the duke even has a flash of misgiving about Jim: 'Do you reckon that nigger would blow on us? We'd skin him if he done that!'[19] But it is already too late. It is through Jim that the two rogues are ultimately outwitted; the con-men hoaxed; the hoaxers double-crossed. For Jim does, in the end, 'blow on' them. 'The Royal Nonesuch' sinks them. In Uncle Silas's words: 'the runaway nigger told Burton and me all about that scandalous show . . .' (182/289).

Tom Sawyer alone is never outwitted, never trumped, never conned. No one ever tars and feathers him. No one rides him out of town on a rail. To the contrary, he is the pride and joy of his local community, the apple of their eye. Great things are predicted for this orphan lad, the ward of poor Aunt Polly ('my own dead sister's boy'). Judge Thatcher, in *Tom Sawyer*, called him 'no commonplace boy', promising to send him to West Point and later to 'the best law school in the country'. Yet his interventions in *Huckleberry Finn* are as fraudulent, as calculating and as ruthless as the king and duke's. More lethal, too.

Of course he is still just a boy, and his boyish characteristics, at first sight, seem far removed from the king and duke's. They were out for cash; Tom is out for 'fun'. From his first entry, when he wants 'to tie Jim to the tree for fun', to his re-entry at the Phelps farm, where he discovers Jim chained to a bed, it is always fun Tom is after, never mind at whose expense. Fun apart, he is obsessed by 'rules'. He is bureaucratically rule-bound. He must do everything by the 'authorities', by the book:

> Don't I tell you it's in the books? Do you want to go to doing different from what's in the books, and get things all muddled up? . . . Don't you reckon that the people that made the books knows what's the correct thing to do? Do you reckon *you* can learn 'em anything?[20]

Far from rule-bound, the king and duke are lords of misrule. It is clearly not here that the similarity lies. It is at the level of feeling, rather, that Tom's hidden identity with the king and duke begins to emerge. Tom's tricks, like theirs, writes Richard Poirier,

> are designed to exploit human feeling, while their own feelings are called forth only by artificial stimulation. The King and the Duke can slobber over Shakespeare and their own fabricated melodrama, knowing that their audience will do the same, and Tom can make up epitaphs for Jim ('*Here a captive heart busted*') and be so carried

away by his own version of phrases scrawled on prison walls by such heroes as the Count of Monte Cristo that his 'voice trembled, whilst he was reading them, and he most broke down'.[21]

The duke makes up pseudo-Tennysonian verse ('Yes, crush, cold world, this breaking heart') and sets it up ready to print, just as Tom makes up pseudo-historical graffiti and copies them out on paper.[22] Tom, the duke, the king, all swell over these mawkish productions. As Daniel G. Hoffman was the first to note: 'These two strains in Tom – his shrewdness and self-pitying romanticism – are run to seed in them.'[23]

Shrewd they certainly are. But, if the tricksters are shrewd, so is Tom. His very first trick, on his first entry in *Tom Sawyer*, had been the famous whitewashing ruse. Here, just as deliberately and systematically, he sets out to deceive Huck. When Huck reveals that he is trying to steal a slave out of slavery:

> '– and his name is *Jim* – old Miss Watson's Jim.'
> He says:
> 'What! Why Jim is—'
> He stopped and went to studying. I says:
> '*I* know what you'll say. You'll say it's dirty low-down business; but what if it is? – *I*'m low down; and I'm agoing to steal him, and I want you to keep mum and not let on. Will you?'
> His eyes lit up, and he says:
> 'I'll *help* you steal him!'[24]

At that stroke Tom's hoax is born and he furthers it mercilessly without a thought of what Huck might feel or what Huck might think, should he hear of Miss Watson's will, let alone what Jim might think or feel. It is a ruthless exercise of power. What is at issue really is Tom's will, not Miss Watson's will; and, as with all wills, it is an exploitation of power by a secret withheld.

But in other ways, too, he makes a trio with the king and duke. All three are enamoured of titles. All three rehearse quixotic dreams of royal and noble outcasts: Henri IV, Louis XVII, the Duke of Bridgewater.[25] All three are stagestruck: the king and duke as professionals; Tom as amateur. He is the born impresario, with dreams of torchlight processions and brass bands, always on the lookout for an audience. 'Why, Huck,' he exclaims on hearing his plan for stealing Jim from the Phelps farm, 'it wouldn't make no more talk than breaking into a soap factory' (184/292). Both the king and Tom are fascinated by pirates. At the Pokeville camp-meeting the king confesses – of all things – to actually being an ocean pirate, just as Tom's favourite pastime is to play at pirates.[26] Both the duke and Tom are fascinated by Arabs. Just as Jim is transformed into a '*Sick Arab*' by the duke, so a Sunday-school picnic is transformed into 'rich A-rabs' by Tom. But more specific still is the number that chinks so ominously throughout the text. Tom's compensation for his gross deception of an emancipated slave is 'forty dollars' (228/360), just as the king's price-tag for selling a runaway slave had been 'forty dollars' (167/268), just as the slave-hunters had paid forty dollars conscience money to Huck for their desertion. It is the repetition of the sum that confirms the symbolic reckoning. It is a Judas sum for an intimate betrayal. First for the king; then from Tom. But Tom, by combining Southern histrionics with Southern treachery, is the ultimate Judas.

NOTES

1 *Huckleberry Finn*, ch. 8, p. 39/52–3.
2 See above, Ch. 1, n. 2.
3 Working notes, Group C (1883), in Bernard DeVoto, *Mark Twain at Work* (Cambridge, Mass.: Harvard University Press, 1942), p. 77.
4 *Huckleberry Finn*, ch. 31, pp. 168–9/268–9.
5 cf. the preacher at the camp-meeting: '"come, black with sin! (*amen!*) come, sick and sore! (*amen!*) . . . come in your rags and sin and dirt! the waters that cleanse is free, the door of heaven stands open – oh, enter in and be at rest!" (*a-a-men! glory, glory, halleluya!*)' (ch. 20, p. 107/172).
6 See above, Ch. 1, n. 14.
7 'Villagers of 1840–3', in Walter Blair (ed.), *Mark Twain's Hannibal, Huck & Tom* (Berkeley, Calif.: University of California Press, 1969), p. 34.
8 *Huckleberry Finn*, ch. 3, p. 17/17.
9 Richard Poirier, *A World Elsewhere: The Place of Style in American Literature* (New York: Oxford University Press, 1966), pp. 189–90.
10 *Huckleberry Finn*, ch. 42, p. 223/353.
11 ibid., 'Chapter the Last', p. 228/360. But why should Jim of all people be 'pleased most to death' when his wife and children are still slaves? Why, asks Michael Patrick Hearn, 'would the entire town of St Petersburg come out to greet a pair of phony "nigger stealers" and the former runaway?': *The Annotated Huckleberry Finn* (New York: Clarkson N. Potter, 1982), p. 361. Yet Twain persisted. That is how *Tom Sawyer Abroad* (1894) was to begin:

> You see, when we three came back up the river in glory, as you may say, from that long travel, and the village received us with a torchlight procession and speeches, and everybody hurrah'd and shouted, it made us heroes, and that was what Tom Sawyer had always been hankering to be.

12 *Huckleberry Finn*, ch. 12, p. 57/81.
13 ibid., ch. 14, p. 64/93.
14 Poirier, *A World Elsewhere*, p. 191. But if the chapter reaches forward it also reaches back. The whole discussion turns on the issue of rival claimants for a single child and so returns to the initial premiss of *Huckleberry Finn*, the Widow's adoption of Huck against Pap's wishes.
15 *Huckleberry Finn*, ch. 28, p. 154/128.
16 ibid., ch. 40, p. 216/340–1.
17 As Dr Newton, the mind-healer, had cured Sam's wife, Olivia Langdon, of paralysis: 'Now we will sit up, my child'; 'now we will walk a few steps, my child'.
18 *Huckleberry Finn*, ch. 30, p. 164/262.
19 ibid., ch. 31, p. 171/273; cf. the duke: 'Don't ever tell *me* any more that a nigger ain't got any histrionic talent. Why, the way they played that thing, it would fool *anybody*. In my opinion there's a fortune in 'em. If I had capital and a theatre, I wouldn't want a better lay out than that' (ch. 27, p. 147/236).
20 *Huckleberry Finn*, ch. 2, p. 13/11.
21 Poirier, *A World Elsewhere*, pp. 203–4.
22 cf. Tennyson, 'Break, break, break,/On thy cold gray stones, O Sea!' (1842).
23 Daniel G. Hoffman, *Form and Fable in American Fiction* (New York: Oxford University Press, 1961), ch. 15, pp. 328–9.
24 *Huckleberry Finn*, ch. 33, p. 178/284. If this opens the deception *of* Huck, it equally opens a deception *by* Huck-as-narrator. For the narrator, of course, is well aware of Tom's suppression; and he suppresses his awareness of that suppression. This is true of other well-kept secrets: Pap's death, for example. There must be a distinction between the past, when the events of the narrative occurred, and the present, in which Huck writes of them. As Gérard Genette puts it, 'The narrator almost always "knows" more than the hero, even if he himself is the hero': *Narrative Discourse*, trans. Jane E. Lewin (Oxford: Basil Blackwell, 1980), ch. 4, p. 194. See also Watson Branch, 'Hard-hearted Huck: "no time to be sentimentering"', *Studies in American Fiction*, vol. 6 (Autumn 1978), pp. 212–18.
25 There was no lack of claimants to the throne of Louis XVII; the careers of seven of them are discussed by Horace W. Fuller in *Noted French Trials: Impostors and Adventurers* (Boston, Mass., 1882), a book owned by Twain. See especially 'The false dauphins', pp. 110–42. Such rumours naturally spread up-river from Louisiana and New Orleans. Eleazer the Iroquois, the most celebrated of these 'dauphins', was authenticated by Monsieur le Prince de Joinville on the Mississippi in 1841. A half-breed Mohawk from Caughnawaga, Eleazer Williams (like the king) was a missionary preacher.

The duke claims to be the rightful fifth Duke of Bridgewater, in a collateral line senior to the bachelor third and last Duke, Francis Egerton (1736–1803), reputed to be the richest man in the world.
26 *Tom Sawyer*, ch. 8. Rather closer to home, and home truths, was John A. Murrell, the land pirate of the Mississippi Valley. It was on his gang that 'Tom Sawyer's Gang' was most probably based. See *Tom Sawyer*, ch. 26, and *Life on the Mississippi*, ch. 29. See also Twain's working notes (Group A): 'Let some old liar of a keel-boatman on a raft tell about the earthquake of 1811 . . . & Murrell's gang (darkly hint he belonged to it)' (DeVoto, *Mark Twain at Work*, p. 65).

CHAPTER 10

Huck as Writer

. . . if I'd a knowed what a trouble it was to make a book I
wouldn't a tackled it and ain't agoing to no more ('Chapter the
Last')

Huck's one wholly inexplicable action is this: *Why does he write his
book?* Writing, for sure, is not a matter of passive or providential drift.
Nor can this have been a fortuitous act of self-indulgence. It seems an
altogether gratuitous gesture, an act of energetic and untypical self-
dramatization which, as a literary performance, finally far outstrips
and outsoars all Tom Sawyer's performances.[1]

We know, of course, that he can write. He writes a letter to Miss
Watson and even attempts a verse 'tribute' to poor Emmeline. But he
is hardly a fluent writer, nor had he mastered, it seems, a cursive
hand. Huck's original manuscript, presumably, was written in block
letters. For asked by Sophia Grangerford if he 'could read writing', he
replied, 'no, only coarse-hand': that is to say, printing. And his
orthography must have been appalling. Even 'George Jackson', his
assumed name, floors him. Not only can he not remember it, he
cannot begin to spell it. He has to trick Buck Grangerford into jotting
it down:

'G-o-r-g-e J-a-x-o-n – there now,' he says.
'Well,' says I, 'you done it, but I didn't think you could. It ain't
no slouch of a name to spell – right off without studying.'
I set it down, private, because somebody might want *me* to spell
it, next, and so I wanted to be handy with it and rattle it off like I
was used to it.[2]

Jackson's Island presumably, before Mr Mark Twain got hold of it,
was spelt 'Jaxon's Island'.

All this is distinctly mysterious and unsuitable for close inquiry.

Somehow, we are to understand, Huck could turn his impromptu oral fictions – unlike Pap or Jim – into written testimony. But the *moment* of composition is clear enough. *Adventures* was written at the Phelps farm, near Pikesville, while Tom was recovering from his wound, in the weeks immediately following the 'evasion'. Far from Wordsworthian emotion recollected in tranquillity, this is a blow-by-blow action replay, a breathless monologue like one enormous journal entry, ending in the writer's present: 'Tom's most well, now . . . so there ain't nothing more to write about' (229/362). Peace has been restored to the Phelps farm. Aunt Sally is bustling in the kitchen; Uncle Silas still pottering around. 'He was a mighty nice old man. And always is,' adds Huck, scribbling away (200/316).

So it is written after the revelation that Pap is dead; and Miss Watson is dead; while the king and duke are either permanently missing or dead. All four main characters who had once terrorized him have passed away. Only lost friends still haunt him: plucky Buck Grangerford and sweet Mary Jane. These alone he recalls as a writer in the act of writing. That is all we know of Huck, during his weeks of composition, after the resolution of his narrative.

Of Buck's death he records:

> The boys jumped for the river – both of them hurt – and as they swum down the current the men run along the bank shooting at them and singing out, 'Kill them, kill them!' It made me so sick I most fell out of the tree. I ain't agoing to tell *all* that happened – it would make me sick again if I was to do that. I wished I hadn't ever come ashore that night, to see such things. I ain't ever going to get shut of them – lots of times I dream about them.[3]

Of red-haired Mary Jane:

> I hain't ever seen her since that time that I see her go out of that door; no, I hain't ever seen her since, but I reckon I've thought of her a many and a many a million times, and of her saying she would pray for me . . .[4]

While Tom is physically recuperating in his 'sick-room', Huck, too, is psychologically on the mend. In effect he writes, George C. Carrington, Jr, argues, 'to get shut' of his bad dreams. It is no self-analytic couch. But Huck's feelings are still all pent up. They had never been properly released. At the time he had cried just 'a little' over Buck's corpse. Now he could relive and retrace those hectic months. The whole book, on this reading, thus turns into a long-drawn-out and puzzled requiem for Buck. The recording of his *Adventures* becomes Huck's stay against nightmares.

For the trauma of Buck's death touched on traumas of his own. Young Huck had survived at least nine attempts on his life. Within less than six months it had been threatened: by Pap with his clasp-knife; by the *Walter Scott* gang; by the steamship pilot who slices through the raft; by the Grangerfords when they first discover him; by the gun-happy Shepherdsons; by the blustering Boggs; by the mob at Peter Wilks's grave; by the king, who reckoned he'd drown him; and by the posse at the Phelps farm that shoots Tom. The Mississippi is awash with corpses. On his journey downstream Huck had encountered some thirteen.

Tom may be dangerously wounded, but Huck nurses a far deeper, more festering wound. Their very dreams are different. Tom is infatuated with his bookish dreams and enacts them. Jim is troubled by his dreams and fantastically decodes them. Huck alone has nightmares. That is why Huck can speak Tom's epitaph – which is really Twain's epitaph over the fallen South and the whole extravagance of the Civil War from Fort Summer to Appomattox. Huck is fetching the doctor, concocting some fib about camping

on a piece of a raft we found, and about midnight he must a kicked his gun in his dreams, for it went off and shot him in the leg . . .

'Who is your folks?' he says.

'The Phelpses, down yonder.'

'Oh,' he says. And after a minute, he says: 'How'd you say he got shot?'

'He had a dream,' I says, 'and it shot him.'

'Singular dream,' he says.[5]

Only through Huck could Twain find such comic expression for such suicidal longings. Not that Huck could ever have used such a phrase. Quite the strongest word for deranged feelings in his vocabulary is 'sick'. Sometimes – in tandem with 'scared', for example – it can denote extreme physical shock. When the rope gives and the raft disappears into the fog, Huck says:

I see the fog closing down, and it made me so sick and scared I couldn't budge for most a half a minute it seemed to me – and then there warn't no raft in sight; you couldn't see twenty yards.[6]

But 'sick' on its own connotes a profound psychological shock. Only four times is 'sick' used as a solo adjective; and on each occasion Huck's deepest fraternal instincts are undermined (from within or without), his instincts of good fellowship and ultimate human solidarity. He uses it, after Jim's final appeal, when he is off in the canoe to reconnoitre Cairo:

'Dah you goes, de ole true Huck; de on'y white genlman dat ever kep' his promise to ole Jim.'
Well, I just felt sick.[7]

He uses it again on watching the murder of the Grangerford boys:

It made me so sick I most fell out of the tree. I ain't agoing to tell *all* that happened – it would make me sick again if I was to do that.

He uses it a third time when the king and duke are ridden out of Pikesville on a rail: 'Well, it made me sick to see it' (182/290). He uses it for the fourth and last time when he sees the fifteen farmers sitting with their guns in the Phelps parlour: 'I was most powerful sick, and slunk to a chair and set down' (213/336). All those corpses may be gruesome. But this is the real horror Huck has to write out of his system.
But how? And for whom? Since he had to tell someone. Now the secret he had bottled up so long could at last be shared. Twice he had been tempted to 'tell': first by paddling ashore; then by writing. But his oath ('Honest *injun*') had been not to tell on Jim. The whole voyage had revolved round this problem of *not telling*. Even to Mary Jane he could only hint: 'there'd be another person that you don't know about who'd be in big trouble. Well, we got to save *him* . . . (149/240). That is why the separation of the Wilks slaves, by forced sale, still so moves him:

I can't ever get it out of my memory, the sight of them poor miserable girls and niggers hanging around each other's necks and crying; and I reckon I couldn't a stood it all but would a had to bust out and tell on our gang . . .[8]

This was the fate from which he had been desperately protecting Jim. It was yet another hidden bond between him and his sweetheart.

Now, at last, he is free to 'blow'. He is free to tell all. Once Huck had found an audience for his *Adventures*, the psychological block lifts and the words come tumbling out. He has an overpowering urge to tell. 'You don't know about me': the very opening words reveal him as an 'I' who has found a second person, 'you'. Throughout his narrative he is consciously aware of himself as narrator: 'and the way I lit out and shinned for the road in the dark, there ain't nobody can tell' (161/258). From time to time he acknowledges this audience, without deferring to it: 'You may say what you want to, but in my opinion . . .' (152/244). Or self-consciously he insists on his veracity: '. . . and laid him down on the ground to bleed – I say ground, because it *was* ground' (31/40). But who is this audience whom he courts, this secret sharer of Huck's dream? Who is this 'you' so familiarly addressed: 'on a raft or a scow, you know'; 'that was the town, you know'; 'no use to anybody, being gone, you see'? It is you. It is me. It is anyone who bothers to peruse his text. We are all what is called his 'implied readers'. But that seems a very cool, remote relationship. More than Tom even, Huck is in desperate need of an audience. His performance as a writer is *dependent* on 'you', his reader.

While Huck daydreams about Mary Jane and has his nightmares at the Phelps farm, Twain must have been busily looking over his shoulder. For as the moment of composition is clear so, oddly enough, is much of its chronology. Oddly enough, because Huck himself, as we saw, has only the dimmest sense of the passage of time. Hours, days, weeks drift by in vague clusters. Everything just happens as it happens 'by-and-by'. But the Phelps farm text re-creates a pretty precise three months' adventure in the course of which 'two months ago' old Miss Watson died.[9] Huck is writing his *Adventures* in October, it turns out, over half a year after he had been abducted from the Widow.

Twain kept an exceedingly tight grip on at least the first part of the journey. The chart (locating fictional place-names on the map of the Mississippi) and log (clocking the raft's nightly progress), included here, are the work of Michael G. Miller, who not only recalculated David M. Wells's earlier figures but also correlated all river distances with a mid-century edition of *The Western Pilot*.[10] What his tabulation makes strikingly clear is the diversity of fictional and non-fictional

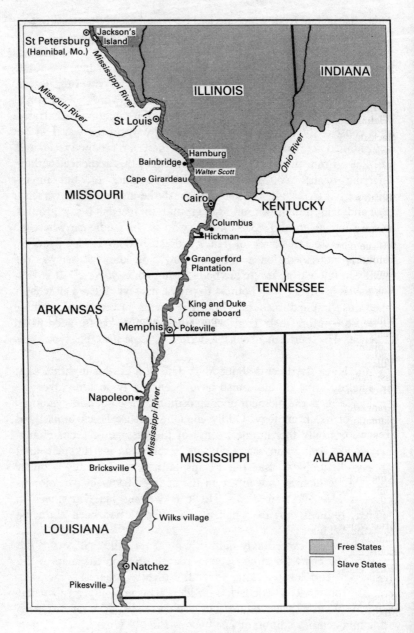

Figure 1 *Mississippi River Valley, c.1840.*

Location or episode (actual counterpart in parentheses)	Mileage from foot of Jackson's Island (mileage on actual river in parentheses)	Mileage from previous location	Travel time from previous location	Elapsed time of journey
St Petersburg (Hannibal, Mo.)				
Jackson's Island (Glasscock's I.)	0	0		
St Louis, Mo.	139½ (139½)	139½	31 hrs	4 days
Booth's Landing (Bainbridge, Mo.)	267½ (263½)	128	28½ hrs	8 days
Walter Scott	269½	2	½ hr	8 days
Village on west bank (Cape Girardeau, Mo.)	277½ (273½)	8	2 hrs	8 days
Cairo, Ill.	322½ (314+)	approx. 45	approx. 10 hrs	10 days
Village on east bank (Columbus, Ky)	384½ (334)	approx. 62	approx. 14 hrs	12 days
Village on hill on east bank (Hickman, Ky)	404½ (354)	approx. 20	approx. 4 hrs	13 days
Grangerford plantation (Tennessee)	434½	approx. 30	approx. 6 hrs	14 days (Grangerford interlude uncertain; perhaps 3 weeks)
King and duke come aboard	approx. 550	100–130	3–4 days	
Pokeville	approx. 590	34	1 day	
Bricksville, Ark. (almost certainly Louisiana)			at least 4 days and nights	
Wilks village (Miss.)			1 day and night	
Pikesville (La or Miss.)			'days and days'	

Figure 2   *The Raft's Log*

locations. They are of at least four types. There are the real names for
real places passed, or mentioned, in the course of the narrative: like St
Louis, Cairo, Memphis or New Orleans. There are fictional names for
identifiable places: like St Petersburg for Hannibal, Missouri;
Jackson's Island for Glasscock's Island; Booth's Landing for Bainbridge, Missouri; or (supposedly) Bricksville, Arkansas, for Napoleon,
Arkansas. There are identifiable locations for fictional episodes: like
that of the *Walter Scott*, north of Cape Girardeau, and various
anonymous Kentucky villages south of Cairo. Finally there are ever
vaguer locations for major episodes after chapter 17 – such as the
camp-meeting at Pokeville, the village of the Wilks funeral, or
Pikesville – which have no verifiable counterpart on the real map. The
Grangerford plantation, by Miller's reckoning, is no longer in
Kentucky but pushed deep into Tennessee.[11] Bricksville, Arkansas, is
almost certainly displaced into Louisiana.[12]

 That this slippage into a fictional geography begins only after Cairo
seems doubly odd. Not only was Twain an ex-pilot with a fabled recall
for every twist and turn of the great river, but previous to completing
Huckleberry Finn in 1883 he had also revisited the Mississippi, sailing
from St Louis to New Orleans and back upstream to Hannibal.
Having refreshed his memories, that is, he made no use of them at all.
To the contrary, he seems deliberately to have blurred them. Why?
Because he had to. That is the plain answer. There was no other way of
covering his tracks. From the very start, Jim's flight had bordered on
the absurd. Back in 1876 it had brought him to a full stop. An
insoluble problem overwhelmed him, as we saw, now that Huck was
helping a runaway slave plunge further and further into slave
territory. If, three years later, he had begun to resolve that problem,
the resolution was on wholly fictive terms; the old absurdity remained.
On resuming his manuscript in 1879–80, therefore, Twain allowed the
geography to lapse into vaguer and vaguer forms. The river – from
bluff to bluff, island to island – was precisely what he knew. But now
that Jim's flight for freedom had become impractical, Twain simply
suppressed his own practical knowledge of the river. His actual return
in 1882 became irrelevant.

 It must have hurt, though. Twain was a stickler for facts. Especially
facts about the Mississippi. Twain notoriously attacked James
Fenimore Cooper for his muzzy handling of facts in 'Fenimore
Cooper's Literary Offenses'. Twain harped on authentic, consistent
detail; and *Huckleberry Finn is* accurately detailed, with all Twain's

pilot cunning, as far as Cairo – or, at most, the Grangerford plantation. To that point, his fugitives had a goal and needed to pay close attention to their surroundings. After that their need to pinpoint landmarks disappears. After that mileage, chronology, geography, all blur.

Yet the whole span of the book is clear enough. It opens in late March or early April (say) to finish six months later in early October. That is what Twain was busy supervising over Huck's shoulder. The flight from Jackson's Island, chronologically speaking, occurs at the exact mid-point of the book. The first part of the *Adventures*, leading up to that departure, takes three months; the second part (the river journey and the Phelps finale) another three months. Huck had six frantic months to catch up on.

Pap kidnaps Huck 'one day in the spring' (24/29) and they live on the Illinois side 'two months or more': to early June, say. For Huck makes his escape from Pap at the beginning of the June rise: 'I noticed some pieces of limbs and such things floating down, and a sprinkling of bark; so I knowed the river had begun to rise' (29/37). The exact time of the June rise can vary – by as much as three weeks – but this must have been before the summer solstice (21 June). For, floating in the canoe from Pap's cabin to Jackson's Island, Huck overhears a St Petersburg ferryman remark: 'it was getting towards the long days and the short nights, now' (33/42). So call it the first week in June. Huck spends five days on Jackson's Island until he finds Jim; and after one more night they watch the river rise 'for ten or twelve days, till at last it was over the banks' (44/60). That is, either sixteen or eighteen days (between two and three weeks) for the river to crest. Call it the fourth week in June. Then an unspecified period elapses: 'It was Tuesday that we had that talk. Well, after dinner Friday . . .' (46/63-4); 'Jim was laid up for four days and nights' (47/65); 'Well, the days went along, and the river went down between its banks again' (47/65). That must be at least ten days; and ten days to a fortnight, it seems, is the average time for the June rise to fall. All in all, then, Huck lived on Jackson's Island for (say) eighteen days plus fourteen days, or exactly a month. Since he arrived in early June, that means Huck and Jim must leave in early July, or in the first week of July, maybe even on the Fourth of July. But *Huckleberry Finn* is no *Walden*. Twain does not rub in this symbolic conjunction of the American calendar with that raft on which black and white make their bid for freedom together. He may have had doubts from the start about the exact value of this Independence Day.

The voyage begins at 1 a.m. at the foot of Jackson's Island, six miles downstream from St Petersburg. It proceeds, as we saw, at around 4½ miles per hour and they sail from darkness to dawn for around 7½ hours each night.[13] Miller has shown how precisely this brought the raft past St Louis at 2 a.m. ('like the whole world lit up'), after thirty-one hours' travel, on the fifth night; and to Booth's Landing and the *Walter Scott* after eight nights; and past Cairo in the fog two nights later.[14] He identifies various villages on the east bank (Columbus and Hickman, Kentucky), before locating the collision with that blazing inferno (of a steamboat) and Huck's resurrection (at the Grangerfords') exactly two weeks after departure.[15]

The length of the Grangerford interlude is quite uncertain. Miller estimates a possible three weeks. This means four to five weeks have elapsed by the time Huck and Jim continue their journey. Shortly afterwards the king and duke come aboard. That is the exact halfway point, by Miller's reckoning, in what Aunt Polly claims is the 'eleven hundred mile' distance between St Petersburg and Pikesville: approximately 550 miles from the foot of Jackson's Island. But this is where a wholly fictional geography and fictional chronology take over. For 1,100 miles from Hannibal, according to *The Western Pilot*, would take a traveller about as far as Natchez, Mississippi. The Phelps farm, as we already realize, must then be in either Mississippi or Louisiana, despite Twain's assertions that he had hijacked his uncle's Missouri farm down to the state of Arkansas.[16]

If the geography becomes spurious, the log-book becomes useless. After Pokeville, because of the duke's handbill advertising Jim as a runaway, the raft can travel both night and day. An estimate of a further three weeks (say) for the journey from Pokeville to Bricksville, and from Bricksville to the Wilks village (including their stay there), would bring the raft into the deep South, past trees hanging with Spanish moss, by early September. But since Pikesville is simply Pike County, Missouri, by another name, rather than any place on a map, it really makes no difference. For the book has come full circle.

NOTES

1 See George C. Carrington, Jr, *The Dramatic Unity of 'Huckleberry Finn'* (Columbus, Ohio: Ohio State University Press, 1976), ch. 2, p. 98.
2 *Huckleberry Finn*, ch. 17, p. 82/136.
3 ibid., ch. 18, p. 94/153.
4 ibid., ch. 28, p. 152/244.

5 ibid., ch. 41, p. 217/343.
6 ibid., ch. 15, p. 68/99.
7 ibid., ch. 16, p. 74/125.
8 ibid., ch. 27, p. 146/234.
9 In fact, she must have died within days of Jim's escape. Miss Watson has had a poor press. She has been much maligned by the commentators. She was tempted, it is true, but she never sold Jim down to New Orleans. She resisted the temptation. Jim overheard a discussion about the $800 deal between the sisters, but 'never waited to hear de res'' (39/53). That was wise maybe. But the fact is that Miss Watson did *not* sell Jim. Nor did she separate him from his wife and family. Nor could she have set his wife free incidentally since she 'was owned on a farm close to where Miss Watson lived' (74/124). Perhaps the Widow talked her out of it. Or perhaps she saw the light at the camp-meeting which the two sisters attended on the fatal day of Jim's escape. At any rate she must have promptly changed her will. For she died within days.

If this is ironical, even more ironical is the corollary that not only had Huck been free of Pap, but also (more important) Jim had been a free man for the whole length of their precarious journey from Jackson's Island to Pikesville.

There is only one snag about this reconstitution of Miss Watson's final days. Jim went missing the very night Huck was 'killed'. In Judith Loftus's words: 'Well, next day they found out the nigger was gone; they found out he hadn't ben seen sence ten o' clock the night the murder was done' (49/69). There was a $300 reward on his head. 'Yet, we are now to believe', Julius Lester observes, 'that an old white lady would free a black slave suspected of murdering a white child. White people might want to believe such fairy tales about themselves, but blacks know better': 'Morality and *Adventures of Huckleberry Finn*', *Mark Twain Journal*, vol. 22 (Fall 1984), p. 45.
10 Michael G. Miller, 'Geography and structure in *Huckleberry Finn*', *Studies in the Novel*, vol. 12 (Fall 1980), pp. 192–209. This article revises David M. Wells's compilations in 'More on the geography of *Huckleberry Finn*', *South Atlantic Bulletin*, vol. 38 (November 1973), pp. 82–6. Both the chart (somewhat revised) and the log are reproduced by kind permission of the author.

Samuel Cumings's *The Western Pilot* (Cincinnati, Ohio) was published in ten editions from 1822 to 1854.
11 See above, Ch. 5, n. 12. Miller writes: 'I do not believe Twain located the Grangerford–Shepherdson feud where he wished, for from consideration of internal evidence in *Huckleberry Finn* alone, the Grangerford plantation is well into Tennessee and not, as is widely believed, in Kentucky', or on the Kentucky–Tennessee border, site of the Darnell–Watson feud. See 'Geography and structure in *Huckleberry Finn*', pp. 200–1.
12 Miller writes: 'it should be noted that because Pokeville is no more than twenty miles north of the Tennessee–Mississippi border, and perhaps below it, Bricksville is well south of that border'. Yet the vanished town of Napoleon, Arkansas, is Twain's acknowledged source for Bricksville: ibid., pp. 202–3.
13 See above, Ch. 5, pp. 63–64. The hours were from dark to dawn: 'we run nights, and laid up and hid day-times; soon as night was most gone, we stopped navigating and tied up' (ch. 19, p. 96/156). cf. The first night's journey from 1 a.m. to 'the first streak of day' (54/77). Miller adds: 'At the latitude of St Louis, the period from sunset to sunrise for July 4 is nine and one-quarter hours. Darkness to dawn is seven and one-half hours', from 8.20 p.m. to 3.50 a.m. 'Geography and structure in *Huckleberry Finn*', p. 195.
14 The *Walter Scott* is grounded on a rock in a 'big straight' stretch of the river with 'high rocky bluffs on both sides' (56/80). This stretch between St Louis and Cairo

has the only hazardous rock formation on the entire length of the Mississippi. Miller explains in detail just how accurate Twain's topography is. After escaping from the wreck, Huck and Jim pursue the raft 'a long time'; then they see the light of a village 'away down to the right . . . up on a hillside' (61/88). Huck rows to the village landing and his conversation with the ferryman reveals that the town just above the wrecked steamboat (Booth's Landing) must lie directly opposite another settlement on the east bank. The village on a hill is Cape Girardeau, Missouri, exactly 134 miles below St Louis on the west bank. Ten miles above Cape Girardeau, facing each other across the Mississippi, are the towns of Bainbridge, Missouri, and Hamburg, Illinois.

15 It was in Hickman, Kentucky, that Twain had intended to stop 'and ask about old feuds' (see above, Ch. 2, n. 16). In *Life on the Mississippi*, however, he only makes passing mention of Columbus, Kentucky, and Hickman, 'a pretty town perched on a handsome hill'.

16 See above, Ch. 4, n. 4.

Part Three

CHAPTER 11

The Writer as Huck

'. . . it was because I was playing double.' (ch. 31)

Like the real Mississippi, Huck Finn's Mississippi, too, had simply doubled on itself and changed its course. The voyage had become a fraud. As Southern society was a fraud. As fiction itself was a fraud. If there was one thing Twain cherished, after all, it was a confidence trick; it there was one thing he understood, it was confidence men. Such as his own appearances on the public stage. Like another P. T. Barnum, he fed the national greed for plugs and impostures. His very entrances and exits were part of the performance: coming on with a sidelong, awkward stride or a funny little shuffle and often hippity-hopping off the stage. His verbal mannerisms became a trademark: impassive, diffident, drawling, even bumbling. He developed a deadpan style, punctured by mock perplexity at the laughter which it evoked. He openly confessed that he plotted a 'little finely acted stumbling and stammering for a word'. He delighted in telling reporters about his ploys, aware that audiences would cheerfully gather for 'something they suspected might be an exaggeration or even a masquerade'.[1]

Such damping of his natural ebullience was in artful contrast to the florid oratory then current. He manipulated his audiences and let them share in the knowledge of their own manipulation. He had manipulated them from the start in publishing his books by means of door-to-door advance subscriptions. There was a ruthless aggression in all this. The very mark of his style, since *The Innocents Abroad*, had been an irreverent and impudent undermining of decorum. As he himself was to put it in *Is Shakespeare Dead?*: 'I cannot call to mind a single instance where I have ever been irreverent, except toward the things which were sacred to other people.'

That was the paradox. He was 'a consummate actor' (in Louis J. Budd's phrase) 'so professionally good at openness'. His sly and genial act – itself a parody of Victorian sincerity – was used for the exposing of sham and debunking of humbug. He struck a phoney posture, in other words, to attack phoney posturing. As he told a Yale audience in 1888, on accepting the honorary degree of Master of Arts: it was the humorist's calling to deride all shams and 'nobilities, and privileges and all kindred swindles'. Twain was always the double man, the duplicit man, speaking with dual voice. His *nom de plume*, whatever its origins, exposed this split personality.

Huck's opening disclaimer, therefore, is to be ignored. The deadpan humorist lurks inside Huck's own text. He is the secret sharer of that text. He is Huck's twin (as implied narrator) as much as Tom's (as reader). He is a whole nestful of Russian dolls: inside Huck, Mark; inside Mark, Sam. This allows for the constant play of irony either at Huck's expense (over the top of his head) or at the reader's (over the top of his). Take the description of Pap:

> He was most fifty, and he looked it. His hair was long and tangled and greasy, and hung down, and you could see his eyes shining through like he was behind vines. It was all black, no gray; so was his long, mixed-up whiskers. There warn't no color in his face, where his face showed; it was white; not like another man's white, but a white to make a body sick, a white to make a body's flesh crawl – a tree-toad white, a fish-belly white.[2]

That is Huck's idiom, all right, and Huck's cool eye. He can spot a natural sign. He knows dead fish always float belly up. But the range and intense multiplication of metaphors must surely be Mark's: those 'vines' entangling both a 'tree-toad' and a fish. Still more lies half-concealed. Old Finn is *all* black and white. Six times the colour white is hammered in. Before uttering a word even, Pap is shown as a deadly white, a sickening white, a living corpse. From his very first appearance he prefigures the corpse that will haunt his runaway son down the length of the entire Mississippi. This cannot be Huck's contrivance; nor ultimately Mark's. It runs too deep. Such all-controlling symbolism, which is both racial and metaphysical, can only be ascribed to Sam.

This is an extraordinary achievement, and it is hardly surprising that it does not always come off. Sometimes Mark simply takes over. Sometimes he rides Huck too hard. The description of the Bricksville tobacco-chewers, for instance, is a touch too pedantic for Huck:

Store tobacco is flat black plug, but these fellows mostly chaws the
natural leaf twisted. When they borrow a chaw, they don't generly
cut it off with a knife, but they set the plug in between their teeth,
and gnaw with their teeth and tug at the plug with their hands till
they get it in two.[3]

Why is Huck telling us all this? What does *he* care? And why does he
run on so about 'Saxon heptarchies' and the 'Doomesday Book'
(124/199)? Heptarchies? Huck? The exact tilt of imagery is an even
more delicate affair. Those vines entangling Pap seem a natural
enough image for Huck. Or are they too artfully framed perhaps? On
occasion Twain lets us overhear too much. Sometimes it is the
Victorian man of letters: 'where the light sifted down through the
leaves' (34/45). Sometimes the club bore: 'anybody but a lot of
prejudiced chuckleheads would a *seen* that . . .' (157–8/252). Sometimes the commuting stockbroker:

'What did you speculate in, Jim?'
'Well, fust I tackled stock.'
'What kind of stock?'
'Why, live stock. Cattle, you know.'[4]

Sometimes the Mugwump even: 'both of them going it at once, like a
cat-convention' (226/356).

This sly, possibly middle-aged, gentleman pops up here and there to
peer through the text. He is the same omniscient joker who was given
his head when Twain revised the captions for Kemble's illustrations.
Twain's wit, that is, unrestrained by Huck, merely patronizes the
text, imposing jokes for his bourgeois readers who were (by definition)
fond parents, paid evening calls, travelled by rail, invested in stock,
attended conventions and staunchly upheld a floating exchange rate.[5]
This tendency increased with that burst of energy in the summer of
1883 which allowed Twain to finish the book. He was feeling skittish
and stopped fussing 'over a lot of gold-leaf distinctions' (191/303), to
borrow Huck's phrase. But why was it Huck's phrase? What did *he*
know of gilt illumination? The equilibrium was always wobbly; yet
Twain, amazingly, always managed to retrieve his balance.

Even back in 1879, when beginning on the Grangerford feud, he
had trouble setting a scene entirely through Huck's eyes. Especially
when women were involved. They lean 'pensive', holding a 'reticule'

(84/137), or look 'like the most loveliest parasol' (119/192). This seems both too knowing for Huck and too ornate. At the camp-meeting he even starts sorting out the materials of their frocks: the 'linsey-woolsey' from the 'gingham' and the 'calico' from children's 'tow-linen' shirts, as if he really were Sarah Mary Williams. But most obviously Twain takes over in the great set speeches, such as Pap's anti-government diatribe whose parodic energies double back to mock the speaker out of his own mouth as a 'prowling, thieving, infernal' free White. Here we must assume an age-old convention of first-person narrative: that Huck has total verbatim recall. He can repeat the duke's Shakespearian farrago word for word just as he can do the voices of the Brothers and Sisters clackity-clacking at the Phelpses'. His *pièce de résistance* is Colonel Sherburn's lofty and withering address which bypasses his own inflection altogether. That piece of *oratio recta* is an undiluted blast of Twain at his most vitriolic. Huck neither summarizes it nor mediates it in any way. If this seems a unique case of authorial intrusion, it may be because Huck's recall is out of all proporion to his inherent involvement. For at other times Huck offers some kind of self-conscious explanation. The duke's speech he had learnt 'easy enough' (111/179); but the counter-claimant's speech in the Wilks case is too much even for him. 'I can't give the old gent's words, nor I can't imitate him; but he . . . says, about like this' (155/249) is the best he can do.

Much of this is over the top of Huck's head; that's the joke. More interesting, though, are the many passages which entangle Huck himself in their ironies. They are the very essence of his style. To the humour of this double voice I shall return. Here it is enough to recall Huck at the circus, gazing at clothes 'that cost millions', the ring-master and drunken clown. Or, again, take Huck prowling around the Grangerford parlour. We have already noted how he scrutinizes and tests each object, yet is nevertheless taken in. For he is overawed. He thinks it's all grand. But as for us (in Huck's own phrase) we 'think different' (17/17). Twain levers us into this gap between Huck's perception and his incomprehension, his total illiteracy when up against cultural signs. We, too, see 'Dr Gunn's Family Medicine' among those books perfectly piled on a corner of the table (83/137). We may, or may not, know that this was a popular medical encyclopaedia, first published in 1830 under the title *Domestic Medicine or Poor Man's Friend, in the Hours of Affliction, Pain and Sickness*.[6] But what is unlikely to escape us, as it escapes Huck, is that for this family (with their guns) even the family doctor is eponymously called Dr Gunn. Huck, who cannot manage riddles, of course cannot spot a pun. Just as he cannot fathom the Grangerford clock:

> There was a clock on the middle of the mantel-piece . . . It was beautiful to hear that clock tick; and sometimes when one of these peddlers had been along and scoured her up and got her in good shape, she would start in and strike a hundred and fifty before she got tuckered out. They wouldn't took any money for her.[7]

For time stood still in the South, as Faulkner was to explore and Carson McCullers to express in her very title, *Clock without Hands*. But Huck cannot *hear* 'the sound and the fury'. His hands cannot explore it. Only we are meant to grasp this symbolic montage of the South as a gun-happy, fraudulent, sentimental, hypocritical time-warp. Twain returns to it in the final image of the book, Tom's 'bullet around his neck on a watch-guard for a watch'; and he's 'always seeing what time it is', adds Huck. As well he might.[8]

So, despite his searching eye and exploring hand, Huck remains the stooge of his own text. He *sees* the tell-tale signs. He notes the artifice and fraudulence without grasping their significance – without pushing to the point of interpretation. That is Twain's game behind Huck's back. He pushes *us* to an act of interpretation.

The joke turns serious. But even more serious is the game played over the top of the reader's head, at the reader's own expense. This is the symbolic text which lurks behind even Twain's text, as it were, and belongs to Sam. We have already checked repeated sums of $40 (paid by the slave-hunters, by the king and finally by Tom) to a Judas account. We have rehearsed repeated rituals of death and resurrection; of baptism, too, as Huck dives into the Mississippi, or is washed overboard from the raft, until (as the Pokeville preacher had promised) he feels 'good and all washed clean of sin' (169/269).[9] We have pondered the parable of the son's pursuit of his prodigal father (now in *Life on the Mississippi*).[10] We have interpreted the black-and-white tangle of Pap's face. Huck's whole yarn is patterned in black and white: the blackness of sin, of hell, of slavery, of night. Black and white motifs pervade *Huckleberry Finn*; they are as commonplace here as in Melville's more radically subversive *Benito Cereno* and *Moby-Dick*. 'White' is everywhere suspect, whether in Pap's white face or the Grangerfords' white linen suits or whitewashed house. 'White', throughout *Huckleberry Finn*, spells a whited sepulchre, concealing and sanctifying corruption.

The whole text, then, is layered like an archaeological mound. Every paragraph, every sentence presents a complex site of multiple, interpenetrating levels. The astonishing fact, I repeat, is that Twain could keep the performance going for the length of a whole book. As T. S. Eliot observed:

> This is a style which at the period, whether in America or in England, was an innovation, a new discovery in the English language. Other authors had achieved natural speech in relation to particular characters – Scott with characters talking Lowland Scots, Dickens with cockneys: but no one else had kept it up through the whole of a book.[11]

To the nature of Huck's 'natural speech' I shall turn in the following chapters. It is the interpenetration that concerns me here, not only with that authorial voice and its ironic symbolism but also with bookish parodies. Many of the literary allusions, of course, are due to Tom. 'Why, hain't you ever read any books at all?' he asks indignant, ' – Baron Trenck, nor Casanova, nor Benvenuto Chelleeny, nor Henri IV, nor none of them heroes?' (188/299). It is Tom who introduces *Don Quixote* (his favourite sourcebook),[12] *The Arabian Nights*,[13] even Sir Walter Scott with bits jumbled from *The Lady of the Lake* and *The Lay of the Last Minstrel*.[14] He is a prime victim of the 'Sir Walter disease', in love 'with dreams and phantoms'.[15] He seems to have read a whole library of prison and prison-escape literature, including Charles Dickens, *A Tale of Two Cities* (1859); Harrison Ainsworth, *The Tower of London* (1840); Alexandre Dumas, *The Count of Monte Cristo* (1844–5) and *The Man in the Iron Mask* (1851).[16] He is clearly a Dumas fan and an Ainsworth fan, keen on *The Tower of London* in particular for its gaudy detail: secret passages, executions, inscriptions on prison walls. In this sense Tom subverts *Huckleberry Finn*. While Twain (as Huck) was busy converting the matter of Hannibal into fiction, Twain (as Tom) was intent on translating fiction into street theatre. For Tom could only rewrite what he had read, as I argued earlier. So he rewrites the fiction of Jim's escape in terms of escapist fiction.

But even before Tom re-emerges, there are other signs of bookishness. It is Sam (as Twain) who names two wrecked steamboats the *Walter Scott* and *Lally Rook*. It is Sam who is acquainted with

Charles Reade; the trick for catching out a transvestite male is his.[17]
The allusions to Thomas Moore, Robert Burns and Thomas Carlyle
are his.[18] Carlyle's *History of the French Revolution* (1837) was a
constant favourite, frequently reread; his obsession with the
Dauphin – and royalty in general – was at least partly due to Carlyle.
A more devious influence was W. E. H. Lecky, *History of European
Morals from Augustus to Charlemagne* (2 vols, 1869); especially his
division of moralists into utilitarians and intuitive thinkers fascinated
Twain. He repeatedly studied and scored key passages. The whole
question of Huck's 'conscience' seems ultimately to have been shaped
by Lecky.[19]

Such a range of influences, for a book supposedly written by an
unbookish boy, is already vast. Yet these are relatively simple matters.
There are much deeper influences at work. There are whole passages
that seem to be engaged in parodying, or commenting on, other
literary texts. I am drawing a thin line here. But the main intertextual
areas (other than Tom's romantic fiction) are contemporary American
and the Bible.[20]

Parodies of Old Testament scenes and characters abound. Even
Huck's language is imbued with biblical lore. He calls the king in his
preacher's duds 'old Leviticus' (127/204). He can say of his father,
surprisingly: 'A body would a thought he was Adam, he was just all
mud' (26/33). There are jokes at Jim's expense, who tells the story of
'Balum's Ass' (42/56); who, like Esau, has faith in his hairy chest; and
who is bitten by a 'serpent in the wilderness'.[21] There is a subtle joke
at Uncle Silas's expense, who, in his absent-minded way, was studying
his namesake (the companion of Paul) 'in Acts Seventeen' (199/316).
But these are sideshows. The Christian cycle (of death and
resurrection) apart, three controlling myths pervade *Huckleberry Finn*:
that of Solomon; that of Moses; and that of Cain and Abel.

The judgement of Solomon (1 Kings 3: 16–27) I have already
discussed.[22] It is a central issue of chapter 14, but also of the entire
book; for it reflects the uneasy status of Huck, torn between Judge
Thatcher and the Widow on the one hand and Pap on the other.
There had already been a court case and it is now up for retrial. As
Jim puts it: 'De 'spute warn't 'bout a half a chile, de 'spute was 'bout
a whole chile' (66/95). His indignation over Solomon's decision reveals
him as a true father.

For Jim 'doan' take no stock' in *authority*. That had been Huck's
position from the start. At the Widow's he had had to listen to her
reading Exodus, 2: 1–10:

After supper she got out her book and learned me about Moses and the Bulrushers; and I was in a sweat to find out all about him but by-and-by she let it out that Moses had been dead a considerable long time; so then I didn't care no more about him; because I don't take no stock in dead people.[23]

But Huck would have been wiser to take stock. The story of 'Moses and the Bulrushers' was intended by the Widow as an exemplary story. In her mouth it became an allegory of her adoption of Huck: 'she took me for her son' (7/1). In this allegory, which Huck rightly and instinctively rejects, *she* figures as Pharaoh's daugher and *he* as baby Moses floating on the Nile.[24] In thus rejecting this biblical precedent, however, Huck rejects more than he quite knows. 'Goshen, child?' asks Mrs Loftus, astonished. 'This ain't Goshen. This is St Petersburg. Goshen's ten mile further up the river. Who told you this was Goshen?' (52/73) For it was in Goshen that the Hebrews were held captive in the land of Egypt. Huck is clearly no Moses. He is heading the wrong way. Or he is a confused and footloose Moses who has failed to grasp his role as deliverer leading a slave out of bondage. *That* parallel should have been clear enough. Moses had long been the looked-for archetype of a saviour among Blacks. 'Let my people go!' in the anguished words of the spiritual. Huck's journey even takes him past Cairo through the river valley which Abraham Lincoln was to call the 'Egypt of the West'.[25]

But Huck is a deliverer in the *dark*. 'Where was Moses when the candle went out?' Buck asked him; and, of course, Huck didn't know. 'Why he was in the *dark*!' (81/135) Huck heads for Goshen; he misses Cairo in a fog; he never reached the Promised Land. He cannot recognize his own Moses role on the Mississippi-Nile. As a naïve (or native) hero, Huck claims no prophetic kinship. He fulfils no scripture. He remains outside history. All this is as it should be, no doubt. The contextual elaboration of this paradigm is wholly authorial, setting up an ironic commentary and counterpoint of expectation that the text can only subvert. To the end Huck is no Moses; the Mississippi no Nile. The Egyptians are not evaded. The biblical promise of the land of Canaan is not fulfilled.

But, if Huck does not reach Canaan, he lands (after the collision) at the post-Mosaic court of Israel's first king. Saul Grangerford, like his namesake, is a troubled soul.[26] He has the blackest kind of cavernous eyes, filled with brooding *Angst*. There is no known reason for his

perpetuation of the feud, as there was no reason for the king's loathing
of David. Except that David, too, was the son of a shepherd. Twice
David refused to kill King Saul, just as Harney Shepherdson twice
flinches from killing Buck; and just as David married the king's
daughter and fled, so Harney elopes with Sophia Grangerford.[27]

But such details are peripheral; and they are interlaced with other
biblical texts. Saul's wife becomes Rachel 'weeping for her children . . . because they were not' (Jeremiah, 31: 15; Matthew, 2:
17–18). For the whole feud derives, at its remotest origin, from the
feud of Cain and Abel. 'A man has a quarrel with another man, and
kills him', as Buck formulates it. The Grangerfords are simply the
'grangers', or settled gardeners, descendants of Cain; the Shepherdsons are the shepherds, or wandering herders, descendants of Abel.
The whole conflict is archetypal in the sense that even the oldest
fighters 'don't know, now, what the row was about in the first place'
(89/146). Huck, who, to Buck's amazement, does not even know what
a feud is, reveals himself as a true Adamic innocent.[28] This myth is
the key to Twain's vision of mayhem on the banks of the Mississippi.

For Twain was himself part of this knockabout tradition – that of
the Old Southwest. True Easterners hardly deigned to call it literate.
As he recognized when reviewing a collection of George Washington
Harris's *Sut Lovingood Yarns* in 1867 for the *Alta California*: the
'Eastern people', he wrote, would 'call it coarse and possibly taboo it'.
Still, by mixing a high style and a low (oral, semi-literate and
journalistic), he had access to a wide range of sources: from old
newspaper buddies like Dan De Quille (William Wright) and Artemus
Ward (Charles F. Browne) to such accredited bestsellers as Edgar
Allan Poe and Harriet Beecher Stowe. The *Territorial Enterprise* of
Virginia City, Nevada, had been his Yale College and his Harvard. He
still could not resist a wisecrack or a spoof, even of such sitting targets
as Bloodgood H. Cutter (the 'Poet Lariat') or Julia A. Moore (the
'Sweet Singer of Michigan'). A rhymster who could begin

> Come all good people far and near,
> Oh, come and see what you can hear

was clearly beyond parody.[29] But Twain could also pay tribute to such
an exemplary Southern hoaxer as Poe, when renaming the king's
caperings of 'The Burning Shame', 'The King's Camelopard';[30]
perhaps even to Stowe's *Uncle Tom's Cabin* which had also brought a

white child (Little Eva) and a black (Uncle Tom) downstream to the mouth of the Mississippi. It is as if Twain needed to turn Stowe's tragic conclusion inside out for his own comic purposes.

Twain revelled in his box-office successes as comic lecturer and burlesque journalist. The marvel of his career was that he could lift himself beyond such publications as *Artemus Ward, His Book* (1862) or even *The Life of P. T. Barnum, Written by Himself* (1855). It was the tradition of Western and Southwestern humour that had nurtured him from his earliest days in Missouri. He began as a comic pseudonym on a par with Dan De Quille and Petroleum V. Nasby; and, though he outsoared them, he never forgot his origins. Between 1879 and 1882, in the very years that *Huckleberry Finn* was incubating, Twain was compiling a collection of American and British humour. He had finished his initial selection of some 93,000 words by March 1882. On his own shelves sat works by Augustus Baldwin Longstreet, Joseph M. Field, William Tappan Thompson, George Washington Harris, Johnson Jones Hooper and Joseph G. Baldwin, and he included most of these in *Mark Twain's Library of Humor* (1888).[31]

This is not the place for unravelling Twain's debt to this tradition. He had already made use of Longstreet's *Georgia Scenes* (1835) for *Tom Sawyer*. The 'Child of Calamity' owes something to Thomas Bangs Thorpe's sketches of the keelboatman, Mike Fink (1842). The camp-meeting in *Huckleberry Finn* (ch. 20) is a cleaned-up version of Hooper's 'The Captain Attends a Camp-Meeting' in *Some Adventures of Captain Simon Suggs* (1845). Of the key topics of Southwestern humour (including hunts and fights and electioneering and weddings) Twain used only four, it is true; and the development of three (the camp-meeting, the circus and the 'Royal Nonesuch' swindle) is brief.[32] But he vastly extended that of confidence tricksters, in the shape of the king and duke; so much so that it threatens to take over the narrative and become the central issue of *Huckleberry Finn*.

Twain's key predecessor was George Washington Harris. His *Sut Lovingood Yarns* for the first time brought an adolescent outsider to speak in his own voice centre-stage; but the whole debate on Twain's relationship to Harris and the evolving Southwestern tradition is a complex one.[33] It has to do with shifts of tone between the genteel and the vulgar. In earlier Southwestern fiction a gentleman always framed the story. The story was full of vivid, violent, brawling folk; the gentleman stood outside as commentator and guide. The coarse events were framed by his more elevated discourse. It was all a matter of balance; and the balance could be tipped either way.[34] In Longstreet the gentlemanly narrator clearly represents a superior moral judgement. But was he inevitably superior? Was he more feeling, more manly, in the last resort more *free*? Throughout the Jackson years and after there was a swing away from gentlemanly forms and conventions to an instinctive morality and the vernacular. Twain revolutionized this tradition by eliminating – or, at least, seeming to eliminate – this double focus. In the opening paragraph the gentlemanly narrator, 'Mr Mark Twain', bows out *in propria persona*. Huck is left on stage alone to fuse, in Kenneth Lynn's expression, 'the Gentleman and the Clown'.[35] Furthermore Twain changed the language of his narrator by soft-pedalling on his dialect. For if dialect was to be used not only as an accessory, for dialogue, but as a medium to characterize a whole personality, then it had to be transformed into something more akin to vernacular. Twain was, of course, brilliant at dialect and immensely proud, as is explained in the preliminary note, of his deployment of three main dialects: 'to wit: the Missouri negro dialect; the extremest form of the backwoods South-Western dialect; the ordinary "Pike-County" dialect'. He loved Joel Chandler Harris's *Uncle Remus Stories* (1883); and his 'negro dialect' and Arkansas gossips (of chapter 41) owe much to Harris's example. But among the many dialects of *Huckleberry Finn* Huck's own is the *least* like the speech employed by the traditional Southwestern humorists.[36]

The achievement of *Huckleberry Finn*, then, can hardly be grasped outside this native tradition. That adolescent voice is both the culmination of one strand of American humour and the origin of a modern American prose style. For it is a voice capable of sustaining a comic dialectic within itself, as Huck had internalized the joker Twain, who had cocooned within himself the gentlemanly Mr Clemens of Hartford, Connecticut. Not only were the geography, chronology, bookish allusions and biblical parodies well beyond Huck's range, but also Huck himself, it turns out, is a creation of the very tradition in which he wrote. Huck is not even an author so much as an embodiment – a construct – of that tradition. He is not so much a character as the voice of the text. Here at least structuralists can be vindicated: the text created Huck; not Huck the text. For the real author all along, of course, was Twain, who controlled that dual voice as much as the narrative strategy of the whole book.

I have already quoted Robert Tracy on the organization of *Tom Sawyer* as dependent in large part on a kind of thematic resonance or echo: a myth, a superstition, or an incident from romance is evoked, and this is followed by a sudden startling realization of that myth or romance.[37]

The strategy of *Huckleberry Finn* stands *Tom Sawyer* on its head. Now, instead of games being a rehearsal for the affairs of the real world, that world is reflected back in games. Instead of play being resolved in moral action, action is dissolved in aesthetic play. Instead of myth being penetrated by experience, experience is continually undermined by dreams. The reversal of sequence could not be more absolute or complete: rehearsal inevitably *follows* action as a farcical coda or burlesque. It is this limping progress, inescapable by the finale, that has dismayed so many critics.[38]

At the opening of *Huckleberry Finn*, as in *Tom Sawyer*, what is at stake is the testing of gratuitous fictions by a sinister, violent, even tragic reality. But the opening moves detach Huck from Tom's gang and remove him from St Petersburg. Abandoned with Jim, he still has painfully to learn the use and abuse of play-acting: of tricks and games and lies. It was this moral education of Huck – this insistence on imaginative responsibility and restraint in a treacherous world – that exhausted the first rush of Twain's inspiration. It took him to near the end of chapter 16. There the 'tank ran dry'.

When he felt able to begin again, it was no longer the testing of fictions by uncompromising reality that concerned him. He was a comic writer, after all; *Huckleberry Finn* was to be a comedy. What was at stake was the diffusion – the ironic reconstitution, as it were – of such threatening reality. Serious and comic scenes now alternate. Mirroring and commenting on each other, they usually appear in tandem. A whole cluster of chapters (from 17 to 24), at the exact mid-point of the narrative, is involuted and duplicated in just this way. Alternating tragedy and burlesque, they are paradigmatic of Twain's method. The horror of the Grangerford–Shepherdson shoot-out is followed by a rehearsal for the 'Broad-sword conflict' in *Richard III*; the elopement of Sophia Grangerford with Harney Shepherdson by the *Romeo and Juliet* 'Balcony Scene'; a real drunk by a fake drunk; Boggs's fatal horseback ride by the clown's comic horseback ride in the circus. (No wonder Huck was scared: 'It warn't funny to me, though.') Jim's anguished tale of his 'deef en dumb' daughter is partnered by the duke's goo-gooing 'deef and dumb' act. It is an inexorable inversion. A feud on the Mississippi is mirrored both by the feuding Montagues and Capulets and by the warring houses of Lancaster and York, just as the drunken Pap prefigured the drunken Boggs or Jim's verdict on Solomon complemented the judge's verdict on Huck.[39]

The narrative concludes with two further long episodic blocks, in which each again comments on the other. The king and duke's fradulent takeover of the Wilks household is mirrored by Tom's equally aristocratic, equally fraudulent stratagems to befuddle the Phelpses (another warm-hearted, all-too-trusting Southern family). But the evasion, as it progresses, picks up wider echoes: Jim as prisoner, as we saw, is a burlesque version of Huck as prisoner;[40] the shooting of Tom a repetition (as farce) of the shooting of Buck Grangerford. Tom's exercise in extended fantasy becomes the ultimate burlesque which transforms Huck's narrative – the whole echo-chamber of his *Adventures* – into *art*. For Tom is the final replica of that anonymous Uncle Sam in the white fur hat who stands at the symbolic centre of the whole book:

> One long lanky man, with long hair and a big white fur stove-pipe hat on the back of his head, and a crooked-handled cane, marked out the places on the ground where Boggs stood, and where Sherburn stood, and the people following him around from one place to t'other and watching everything he done, and bobbing their heads to show they understood, and stooping a little and resting their hands on their thighs to watch him mark the places on the ground with his cane; and then he stood up straight and stiff where Sherburn had stood, frowning and having his hat-brim down over his eyes, and sung out, 'Boggs!' and then fetched his cane down slow to a level, and says 'Bang!' again, and fell down flat on his back. The people that had seen the thing said he done it perfect; said it was just exactly the way it all happened. Then as much as a dozen people got out their bottles and treated him.[41]

What began as a melodramatic farce, with a sassy drunk 'weaving about in his saddle', ends with this impromptu rehearsal. What opened as a mock-Western (a proto-*Darkness at Noon*) collapses into action replay. This is Hollywood on location before Hollywood. This is documentary drama, as we now know it, before television. And the message is grim. The South will not, and cannot, confront its own tragedy. For the South there is no reality but fiction; fiction is its only reality; the South can only be transcribed as fiction and in terms of fiction. That is the enchanted penalty of the 'Sir Walter disease'. (The scene is immediately followed by the pusillanimous lynch mob and a second drunken charade at the circus.)

Tom is the supreme play-actor. Tom, enacting his gratuitous duplications, is Twain's own twin within the narrative. That is why he both loved him and despised him and ultimately could not do without him. For he is his own spokesman as an authority (stickler for precedents) and author (contriver of fictions).

NOTES

1 See Louis J. Budd, *Our Mark Twain: The Making of His Public Personality* (Philadelphia, Pa: University of Pennsylvania Press, 1983).
2 *Huckleberry Finn*, ch. 5, p. 20/23.
3 ibid., ch. 21, p. 113/182.
4 ibid., ch. 8, p. 41/55.
5 See above, Ch. 2, nn. 24 and 25.
6 Dr Gunn's *Domestic* (later *Family*) *Medicine*, published in Knoxville, Tennessee, had reached its 213th edition by 1885. Not only physical but also psychological advice was tendered. Dr Gunn was a kind of nineteenth-century Dr Spock for the lovelorn. The long section 'Of the passions' might have proved helpful for Emmeline. 'When the passions run counter to reason and religion,' writes Dr Gunn, '*nationally* and *individually*, they produce the most frightful catastrophes.'
7 *Huckleberry Finn*, ch. 17, p. 83/136.
8 As Tom keeps his bullet, Jim keeps Tom's 'five-center piece around his neck' (11/8). For another of Twain's chimes, see Captain Sellers's 'clock which never came within fifteen strokes of striking the right time, and whose hands always hitched together at twenty-two minutes past anything and traveled in company the rest of the way home' (*The Gilded Age*, 1873, ch. 7).
9 cf. Aunt Sally's mortified 'Babtist' on another shipwreck of Southern romance, the steamship *Lally Rook* (175/279).
10 See above, Ch. 7, pp. 85–86.
11 T. S. Eliot, introduction to *The Adventures of Huckleberry Finn* (London: Cresset Press, 1950), p. x.
12 Claiming that 'hundreds of soldiers' had been turned into an 'infant Sunday school' outing (16/16), just as an army of knights in *Don Quixote* were turned into sheep (pt 1, ch. 18).
13 Called the *Arabian Nights' Entertainments* in the first English translation of 1838–41. Obviously Huck rubbing 'an old tin lamp' in the woods (17/17) parodies the 'History of Aladdin', but Pap's 'Angel of Death' (28/36) also derives from *The Arabian Nights*.
14 By sending 'a boy to run about town with a blazing stick, which he called a slogan' (16/14), Tom confuses the fiery cross from *The Lady of the Lake* (canto 3) with a battlecry from *The Lay of the Last Minstrel* (canto 4, stanza 27).
15 Twain runs on: 'with the sillinesses and emptinesses, sham grandeurs, sham gauds,

and sham chivalries of a brainless and worthless long-vanished society' (*Life on the Mississippi*, ch. 46).

16 See *Huckleberry Finn*, chs 35, 38 and 39. *The Man in the Iron Mask* is the English title for *Le Vicomte de Bragelonne* (1848–50). Tom's double-edged 'evasion' no doubt derives from another Dumas title, *L'Evasion du duc de Beaufort*, extracted from *Vingt ans après, suite des Trois Mousquetaires* (1845). 'When a prisoner of style escapes,' says Tom, 'it's called an evasion' (211/333). These were, of course, all long-standing preoccupations of Twain's. He had specially hired a sailing boat in Marseilles to visit the 'Castle Deef', as Tom calls it, or Château d'If:

> The walls of these dungeons are as thick as some bed-chambers at home are wide – fifteen feet. We saw the damp, dismal cells in which two of Dumas's heroes passed their confinement – heroes of *Monte Cristo*. It was here that the brave Abbé wrote a book with his own blood; with a pen made of a piece of iron hoop, and by the light of a lamp made out of shreds of cloth soaked in grease obtained from his food; and then dug through the thick wall with some trifling instrument which he wrought himself out of a stray piece of iron or table cutlery . . . It was a pity that so many weeks of dreary labor should have come to naught at last. (*The Innocents Abroad, or The New Pilgrim's Progress*, 1869, ch. 11)

17 Twain had met Charles Reade in England in 1872 and was fond of *The Cloister and the Hearth* (1861); cf. 'Tis a man, or a boy. A woman still parteth her knees to catch the nuts the surer in her apron, but a man closeth his for fear they should fall between his hose' (vol. 2, ch. 14) with Mrs Loftus in ch. 11: 'And mind you, when a girl tries to catch anything in her lap, she throws her knees apart; she don't clap them together, the way you did when you catched the lump of lead.'

18 The *Lally Rook* is named after the emperor's daughter in Thomas Moore's *Lalla Rookh* (1817). Huck recognizes the pictures on the Grangerford walls ('mainly Washingtons and Lafayettes . . . and Highland Marys'), but not of course the parallel between Emmeline's deathbed tributes and Burns's elegies for Mary Campbell: 'Highland Mary' and 'To Mary in Heaven'. It seems unlikely that Tom had read Carlyle, but his cry, at the climax of the evasion – 'Boys, we done it elegant! – 'deed we did. I wish *we'd* a had the handling of Louis XVI, there wouldn't a been no "Son of Saint Louis, ascend to heaven!" wrote down in *his* biography' (216) – incorporates a direct quotation from *The French Revolution*, Vol. 3, bk 2, ch. 8.

19 For a full discussion, see Walter Blair, *Mark Twain & 'Huck Finn'* (Berkeley, Calif.: University of California Press, 1960), ch. 10, pp. 131–45.

20 The story of Bill, Packard and Turner aboard the *Walter Scott* (chs 12–13) ultimately derives from Chaucer; but there are no formal references to 'The Pardoner's Tale'. The elopement of Harney Shepherdson with Sophia Grangerford (ch. 18), however, clearly parodies *Romeo and Juliet*, with Huck playing the part of Juliet's nurse. In Twain's version, note, the two lovers 'got across the river and was safe' (94/153).

21 So exuberantly invoked by the preacher at the camp-meeting: 'It's the brazen serpent in the wilderness! Look upon it and live!' (107/172). For Balaam, see Numbers, 22:21–34. For the brazen serpent, see Numbers, 21:8: the Lord said to Moses, 'Make thee a fiery serpent, and set it upon a pole: and it shall come to pass, that everyone that is bitten, when he looketh upon it, shall live'.

22 See above, Ch. 9, p. 109.

23 *Huckleberry Finn*, ch. 1, p. 8/2.

24 As the baby Charles William Albright, whose persona Huck briefly adopts, is found floating on the Mississippi.

25 See Daniel Barnes, 'Twain's *The Adventures of Huckleberry Finn*, ch. 1', *The Explicator*, vol. 23, no. 8 (April 1965), item 62; and Billy G. Collins, 'Huckleberry Finn: a Mississippi Moses', *Journal of Narrative Technique*, vol. 5 (May 1975), pp. 86–104.

26 An 'evil spirit from God troubleth thee'; 1 Samuel, 16: 15. For the Saul–David story, see 1 Samuel, chs 16–31.

27 'The woods warn't thick, so I looked over my shoulder, to dodge the bullet, and twice I seen Harney cover Buck with his gun; and then he rode away the way he come' (88/145).

28 See James F. Hoy, 'The Grangerford–Shepherdson feud in *Huckleberry Finn*', *Mark Twain Journal*, vol. 18 (Winter 1975), pp. 19–20; and Dale R. Billingsley, '"Standard authors" in *Huckleberry Finn*', *Journal of Narrative Technique*, vol. 9 (Spring 1979), pp. 126–31.

29 Julia A. Moore, 'William Upson', *The Sentimental Song Book* (Cleveland, Ohio, 1877). She was Emmeline Grangerford's principal model.

30 This is a bit of a wild shot. But there does seem to be more than a nodding reference to Poe's 'Four Beasts in One; or The Homocameleopard' (in *Tales of the Grotesque and Arabesque*, 1845) where a king (Antiochus Epiphanes), who worships a baboon deity, prances in triumph.

31 Twain's personal copies of Southwestern humorists are listed in Alan Gribben, *Mark Twain's Library: A Reconstruction*, 2 vols (Boston, Mass.: G. K. Hall, 1980); for the plans for *Mark Twain's Library of Humor*, see *Mark Twain's Notebooks & Journals*, Vol. 2 *(1877–1883)*, ed. Frederick Anderson, Lin Salamo and Bernard L. Stein (Berkeley, Calif.: University of California Press, 1975), notebook 19, pp. 361–5.

32 See Hennig Cohen and William B. Dillingham (eds), *Humor of the Old Southwest* (Athens, Ga: University of Georgia Press, 1975), p. xvii.

33 Collected in 1867. The first 'Sut Lovingood Yarn' was published in 1854.

34 See Walter Blair, *Native American Humor* (New York: American Book Co., 1937), pp. 90–2, and Kenneth S. Lynn, *Mark Twain and Southwestern Humor* (Boston, Mass.: Little, Brown, 1959), passim. For alternative views on this political transaction, cf. Louis J. Budd, 'Gentlemanly humorists of the old South', *Southern Folklore Quarterly*, vol. 17 (1953), pp. 232–40, and James M. Cox, 'Humor of the old Southwest', in *The Comic Imagination in America*, ed. Louis D. Rubin, Jr (New Brunswick, NJ: Rutgers University Press, 1973), pp. 101–12. For a wider range of perspectives, see M. Thomas Inge (ed.), *The Frontier Humorists: Critical Views* (Hamden, Conn.: Archon, 1975). For Mark Twain's relation to Southwestern humour, see also Pascal Covici, Jr, *Mark Twain's Humor: The Image of a World* (Dallas, Tex.: Southern Methodist University Press, 1962).

35 Lynn, *Mark Twain and Southwestern Humor*, p. 148.

36 See David Carkeet, 'The dialects in *Huckleberry Finn*', *American Literature*, vol. 51 (November 1979), pp. 315–32. To this important article I return in Chapter 12.

37 See above, Ch. 4, n.21.

38 Much of this argument was anticipated by Virginia Wexman, 'The role of structure in *Tom Sawyer* and *Huckleberry Finn*', *American Literary Realism*, vol. 6 (Winter 1973), pp. 1–11.

39 One might add that since the two American lovers are almost the sole survivors, their story is also an exact inversion of *Romeo and Juliet*. Pap and Boggs both come to a violent end: the one shot off-stage, the other centre-stage; the one in the back, the other in the front; the one unattended by his 14-year-old son, the other attended by his 16-year-old daughter.

An odd exception which proves the rule, is the burlesque attempt, by 'firing cannon', to retrieve Huck's 'carcass' (34/46) which *precedes* by ten chapters Huck's retrieval of Buck's corpse and Joe's corpse from the Mississippi.

40 See above, Ch. 7, p. 84; cf. also *Huckleberry Finn*, chs 2 and 40: first there is talk of tying up Jim, then of untying him; but in neither case, in the dark, do the boys quite *touch* him (10/7 and 214/338).

41 *Huckleberry Finn*, ch. 21, p. 117/187–9; cf. how the site of Huck's supposed 'murder' becomes the immediate object for local sightseers. In Jim's words: 'Dese las' skifts wuz full o' ladies an genlmen agoin' over for to see de place' (39/53).

CHAPTER 12

Soul-Butter and Hogwash

'. . . and it warn't often that we laughed, only a little kind of a low chuckle.' (ch.12)

The fictions, then, are extraordinarily involuted and contrived. It is time to draw closer and watch their contrivance in action. For *Huckleberry Finn* is, above all, a rhetorical performance. It speaks simultaneously, as it were, with many tongues. It is not merely an intertextual but an interlingual *tour de force*.

Here I wish to acknowledge an astute article by Janet Holmgren McKay.[1] I shall use the same key passage for discussion. It occurs on the arrival of the king, duke and Huck at the Wilkses'. After bursting into tears, the men kneel down on either side of the coffin as if in prayer. This sets off a storm of sobbing among the women from which Huck holds himself contemptuously aloof. Four times he repeats the phrase: 'I never see two men leak . . .'; 'I never see anything like it'; 'you never see anything like it'; 'I never see anything so disgusting'. The preterite form of 'I see' in Huck's mouth, though never 'I saw', is usually 'I seen', as in his fifth sentence: 'I never seen anybody but lied, one time or another' (7/1). So this truncated form already suggests a drift or shift in time, until with a final shove on the verb 'give' the whole construction is moved from the past into the historic present:

> and every woman, nearly, went up to the girls . . . and kissed them . . . and then put their hand on their head, and looked up towards the sky . . . and then busted out and went off sobbing and swabbing, and give the next woman a show. I never see anything so disgusting.
>
> Well, by-and-by the king he gets up and comes forward . . .[2]

As soon as the king has finished speaking, Huck drops back into the preterite – until the king starts up again.

This ebb and flow of tenses was, no doubt, instinctive. What Twain found harder going was the actual speech over the coffin. Here it is in its final, printed version:

> Well, by-and-by the king he gets up and comes forward a little, and works himself up and slobbers out a speech, all full of tears and flapdoodle about its being a sore trial for him and his poor brother to lose the diseased, and to miss seeing diseased alive, after the long journey of four thousand mile, but its a trial that's sweetened and sanctified to us by this dear sympathy and these holy tears, and so he thanks them out of his heart and out of his brother's heart, because out of their mouths they can't, words being too weak and cold, and all that kind of rot and slush, till it was just sickening; and then he blubbers out a pious goody-goody Amen, and turns himself loose and goes to crying fit to bust.

The speech has a six-ply complexity. It is by (1) an anonymous huckster, (2) who imposes on Huck as King 'Looy the Seventeen', (3) who imposes on the Wilks family as an English preacher (Harvey Wilks, long-lost and grieving brother of the late Peter Wilks), (4) whose speech is rendered by Huck Finn, (5) who is the mouthpiece of Mark Twain, (6) which is the comic mask of Samuel L. Clemens. Originally, like Colonel Sherburn's harangue to the lynch mob, the speech was written in *oratio recta* as follows:

> 'Friends – good friends of the diseased, and ourn too, I trust – it's indeed a sore trial to lose him, and a sore trial to miss seeing of him alive, after the wearisome long journey of four thousand mile; but it's a trial that's sweetened and sanctified to us by this dear sympathy and these holy tears; and so, out of our hearts we thank you, for out of our mouths we cannot, words being too weak and cold. May you find such friends and such sympathy yourselves, when your own time of trial comes, and may this affliction be softened to you as ourn is to-day, by the soothing ba'm of earthly love and the healing of heavenly grace. Amen.'[3]

Two things became apparent once Twain decided to recast this speech in indirect speech. The last third (from 'May you find' to 'heavenly grace') had to be cut altogether. It must have exceeded Huck's threshold of even mimic tolerance and is dismissed in a single phrase: 'and all that kind of rot and slush'. But, if part of the speech had to go, one sentence from the first draft could be transferred wholesale, Twain thought, into Huck's version: 'but it's a trial that's sweetened and sanctified to us by this dear sympathy and these holy tears'. Huck might, as it were, quote that. So Twain lopped and pruned. But he did more.

Compare Huck's treatment of the king's pseudo-terminology with a real Sunday-morning service. It is the sermon delivered to a congregation of Grangerfords and Shepherdsons and the discussion it prompted among the Grangerfords on their way home. This time no manuscript version is available, so that we do not know if there was a first version in direct speech. All we have is Huck's précis:

> It was pretty ornery preaching – all about brotherly love, and such-like tiresomeness; but everybody said it was a good sermon, and they all talked it over going home, and had such a powerful lot to say about faith, and good works, and free grace, and prefore-ordestination, and I don't know what all, that it did seem to me to be one of the roughest Sundays I had run across yet.[4]

Here is a comparable, but more compact, interpenetration of Huck's diction and church diction. Huck presents first a Presbyterian sermon on 'brotherly love'; then the Grangerford discussion of that sermon in terms of 'faith, and good works'. But the discussion at once collapses under the piled-up weight of verbiage: pleonastic 'free grace' capped by the hybrid 'preforeordestination', conflating two cardinal doctrines of Presbyterianism, predestination and foreordination. Twain, of course, is deliberately undermining such theological jargon. The whole context is absurd, so he can riddle it with his contempt. But such is the ambiguity of this style that Huck seems quite unconscious of the deflation. For his recollection of the sermon and the Grangerford Sunday prattle is consciously orchestrated by his own devastatingly *mild* judgements: 'pretty ornery'; 'such-like tiresomeness'; 'one of the roughest Sundays I had run across yet'.

The invasion of the king's speech by Huck's speech results in the same log-jam of inflation and deflation, of thrust and counter-thrust, except that this time Huck is quite conscious of what he is doing. For he is not aiming at high-flown Presbyterian talk (for which he feels residual respect), but at the king's waffle. It is the king who parodies biblical cadences with strings of adjectival supplements: 'a *sore* trial for him *and* his *poor* brother . . . after the *long* journey . . . but . . . sweetened *and* sanctified . . . by this *dear* sympathy *and* these *holy* tears . . . words being too *weak and cold* . . .' (my emphasis). It is this pleonasm, rhetorically speaking, that outrages Huck. What Huck goes for is casual, unpretentious precision, not these unctuous repetitions: 'a sore trial . . . but its a trial . . . out of his heart and out of his brother's heart'; nor such inversions into the passive as 'its a trial that's sweetened and sanctified to us by . . .'.

His manoeuvre again is to deflate such formal diction by his own colloquialisms: first by adding yet further tautological constructions: 'the king he'; 'all full of'. Then by framing the quotations with his own caustic doublings and repetitions: a final 'blubbers' to echo 'slobbers'; 'rot and slush' to supplement 'flapdoodle', before nose-diving to 'soul-butter and hogwash'. It is a collision of languages, jamming 'brotherly' up against 'ornery', transforming 'tears' to 'slush'. But a collision that is also an active collusion, an imperson-ation within an impersonation; and *both* are self-consciously histrionic. The bathos of 'sickening' is as rhetorical an artefact as the king's bombast. The very subject here is that of rhetorical fraud; and Twain's virtuoso performance continually splays and splinters the text as one set of vocabulary undermines and cancels another. So in revising to indirect discourse he could even leave one quotation verbatim. Huck simply runs on, co-ordinating his clauses with barely a hint of subordination, in a continual narrative present. The whole paragraph, almost, consists of a single run-on sentence.

The structure, as Janet Holmgren McKay observed, is perfectly symmetrical, unfolding towards that impromptu quotation and immediately retracting from it:

HUCK: 'Well, by-and-by the king he gets up . . . tears and flapdoodle'
HUCK/KING: 'about its being a sore trial . . . after the long journey of four thousand mile'
KING: 'but its a trial . . . sanctified to us . . . these holy tears'
HUCK/KING: 'and so he thanks them . . . words being too weak and cold'
HUCK: 'and all that kind of rot . . . crying fit to bust.'[5]

What opens with Huck's solo eventually merges Huck's voice and the king's voice until for a moment the king's voice detaches itself and sounds solo only to capitulate again to Huck's duo that finally tapers to Huck's solo where he began.

The backstage joker, behind these branchings and derailments, of course is Twain; and he, too, shows his hand. The twice-repeated homophonic spelling of 'diseased' for 'deceased' could be either a malapropism of the king's or of Huck's. Since the king is capable of confusing 'orgies' with 'obsequies', Huck may be accurately reporting another muddle here. (The first draft, in *oratio recta*, had also read 'diseased'.) On the other hand, Huck himself uses 'diseased' a few pages on and may be introducing a misapprehension of his own. In *either* case the implied author irradiates the text, drawing attention to the implications of his versatility. Whether intended as a patronizing smile at Huck, or to mock the pseudo-preacher behind his back, the author of the joke can only be the ultimate author.[6] Even the clincher of the paragraph, reinforcing 'goody-goody', seems a giveaway touch. For 'pious' is just a meaningless duplication. It sounds more like Twain's vocabulary; far too genteel for Huck.

In spite of the invisible hand, though, Huck is thoroughly in control. He knows exactly where he stands. He knows what he thinks of Presbyterian theology. He knows what he thinks of this corny tear-jerker. But he is easily entangled in ironies. Such self-entanglement, as we saw earlier, is the very essence of his style. It is also the very essence of Twain's humour.[7] Broadly it comes to this: Twain is *always* the humorist; never Huck. Huck may combine, in Kenneth Lynn's phrase, 'the Gentleman and the Clown'.[8] But it does not follow that 'Mr Mark Twain' is the Gentleman and Huckleberry Finn the Clown. To the contrary, it is one of the amazing paradoxes of *Huckleberry Finn* that it is the other way round; that inevitably it is Huck who is the Gentleman and Twain who is the Clown.

Huck laughs with Jim on the raft. 'The Royal Nonesuch' he finds 'awful funny'. But, on the whole, Huck is humourless. He plays things straight. He is, in fact, Twain's straight man, or fall guy, never a funny fellow in his own right.[9] He never cracks a joke. At the circus Huck is astonished at 'the clown cracking jokes', especially at the pace of his repartee:

The ring-master couldn't ever say a word to him but he was back at him quick as a wink with the funniest things a body ever said; and how he ever *could* think of so many of them, and so sudden and so pat, was what I couldn't noway understand. Why, I couldn't a thought of them in a year.[10]

Jim laughs *at* Huck when he is washed overboard. He roars with laughter. 'It most killed Jim a-laughing,' rubs in the injured boy. 'He was the easiest nigger to laugh that ever was, anyway' (104/168). But what else they find to laugh at – especially laugh at *together* – we are never told. It wasn't often, Huck says at one point, and then 'only a little kind of a low chuckle' (55/78). After Jim is gone, of course, he wraps it all in a golden haze: '. . . and we a floating along, talking, and singing, and laughing' (169/270).

It is this straight man who is Twain's stooge; this chump, washed overboard, who becomes Twain's mask. It is a deadpan mask from behind which he can launch some of his finest jokes. This was essential for Twain. Not to seem to realize his own jokes was, for him, the essence of the joker's art. He praised his mother's 'ability to say a humorous thing with the perfect air of not knowing it to be humorous'.[11] His platform manner, as lecturer or after-dinner speaker, was notoriously sly. His drawling mannerisms became a trademark.[12] 'The humorous story is told gravely,' he explained in 'How to Tell a Story':

the teller does his best to conceal the fact that he even dimly suspects that there is anything funny about it . . . Very often, of course, the rambling and disjointed humorous story finishes with a nub, point, snapper, or whatever you like to call it. Then the listener must be alert, for in many cases the teller will divert attention from that nub by dropping it in a carefully casual and indifferent way, with the pretense that he does not know it is a nub.[13]

Huck Finn, then, was the comedian's screen. That was the astonishing inversion. Instead of a punctilious, poker-faced, gentle-manly narrative mask (traditional to Southwestern humour) for heightening the irruptions of laughter, Twain chose a 14-year-old boy. Instead of puncturing the complacencies of middle age, Twain bounces his subtlest effects off Huck's anxious and preoccupied head. We expect youth to be giggly, to see the funny side of things; but Huck, even at the circus, is under a constant watchful strain. Those

strained and anxious eyes turned out to be the most effective of all
Twain's masks. The gravity, which would seem pompous in middle
age, becomes a lovable trait in Huck. His naïvety is wholly
understandable and forgivable once he is caught up in the fraught and
dramatic adventure which sweeps him down the Mississippi.

So Twain perfected his double act: that of the grave simpleton. So
his humorous stage presence, in all its perturbed and stumbling
confusion, was conferred on Huck. So the bright-eyed joker donned
an impassive mask of boyish seriousness.[14] Huck, the Nietzschean
man of disguises and metamorphoses, was himself nothing but a
mask.[15] That is why he was such a quick-change artist. That is why
he could adopt such a variety of further masks for the shifting needs
of his shifting roles.

But is there no 'ole true Huck'? No authentic voice? No real mode
of expression, however momentary, beyond this duplicit and com-
ically deadpan mask? Take his lyrical description of a sunrise (ch. 19)
or his abasement before Jim (ch. 15). That apology, above all,
prompts expectations of a moral development which Twain's text
cannot begin to honour. Articulate feelings occasionally transcend the
double entendres, marvellously suspending them, but such occasions
cannot possibly be sustained. Dissembling, imposture, trickery and
deception lie at the very roots of Twain's charade. The whole comic
brio – not merely that of the 'evasion' at the Phelpses' – turns out to
be elaborately theatrical.

Alan Trachtenberg has put this even more intransigently:

> Mark Twain's own needs, perhaps for some revenge against
> Southern river society, seemed to require a Huck Finn who is
> ignorant, half-deformed and permanently humorless. To put the
> case strongly, we might say that Huck's character is stunted by his
> creator's need for him to serve as a technical device. The same
> devices of irony which liberate the reader by instructing him about
> civilization and human nature also repress Huck by using him; they
> prevent his coming into his own.[16]

So Huck is not merely a stooge but the victim of Twain's aggressive
drive. That is certainly too strong. Huck is not 'half-deformed' so
much as barely half-formed. What he is allowed, in generous measure,
are his sensibility, his perception, his easy-going gentlemanly style. I
do not mean 'genteel', of course. Huck is simply one of nature's

gentlemen. That, I suspect, is what is meant by those who call his speech a 'natural style'. Twain, we have already seen, deliberately neutralized that style so that Huck's speech is the least like that employed by traditional Southwestern humorists. Even misspelling was considerably modified. Huck's unorthodox spellings are almost wholly confined to phonetic effects, and even these are severely limited. 'In the entire first chapter, totaling about 1,400 words,' writes Robert J. Lowenherz, 'one finds only thirteen words whose spellings reflect Huck's pronunciation. This restriction of dialect spelling to less than one per cent of Huck's narrative speech is maintained quite consistently throughout the novel.'[17] Huck's quoted speech in conversation, as might be expected, more or less doubles the dialect spellings to a little over 2 per cent.

Twain liked to flourish these dialect masks as if he could don and doff them with consummate ease. But one consequence of speaking with many voices, many tongues, was the need to *eliminate* misspellings for comic effect. There was no room for quirky orthography in the manner of Artemus Ward: 'I want you should rite me a letter, sayin how is the show bizniss in your place.' Nor the visual aberrations which became Petroleum V. Nasby's trademark:

All wuz peace with me, for after bein buffetted about the world for three skore years, at last it seemed to me ez tho forchune, tired uv persekootin a unforchnit bein, hed taken me into favor.[18]

In revising, it is true, Twain not only regularized but also judiciously introduced phonetic variants.[19] He juggled the demands of his ear and his eye and his mastery of deviant diction. In *Huckleberry Finn*, nevertheless, visual decorum is the rule; it is not, and was never intended to be, an oral obstacle course.[20]

Exceptions that prove the rule usually make an ironic point. After their *Richard III* rehearsal, the duke talks correctly of 'encores'. 'What's onkores, Bilgewater?' asks the king. Since this is phonetically sound, why misspell the word? To mock his ignorance, perhaps. There are many such oddities. Twain had opened a hornets' nest. In any case he was careless. Scholars still disagree about his merit, let alone his consistency, as a dialect writer. Take the word 'deficit' which tacks through the king and duke's quarrel at the end of chapter 30. It is spelt 'deffisit' (133/215) on its first appearance in the duke's mouth, and 'deffesit' (165/264) on its second for some reason. But when the king timidly picks up the word as 'deffersit', the duke promptly pounces on his pronounciation: 'don't you deffersit *me* no more deffersits'.

Such are the pitfalls of dialect writing. *Huckleberry Finn*, 'THE AUTHOR' boasts, uses seven different dialects. This pride in the discrimination of dialects cannot possibly be Huck's, of course. It is always and consistently Twain's. The illusion of oral realism serves to sustain Huck's reality, while Huck, *in propria persona*, is the first to admit of the Wilks claimant's English-English as of the king's fake English-English: 'he tried to talk like an Englishman; and he done it pretty well too, for a slouch. I can't imitate him, and so I ain't agoing to try to; but he really done it pretty good.'[21] Huck can only just differentiate between them. But what Huck can't do, Twain can. He is a master of discriminations, listing the Missouri 'negro dialect', 'the extremest form of the backwoods South-Western dialect', the ordinary 'Pike-County' dialect 'and four modified varieties of this last'. The Missouri 'negro dialect' is clearly what Jim speaks, and what four other minor black characters speak. But the identification of the six white dialects and the relationship between them has sparked off a long debate among linguists. I follow a recent, highly convincing article by David Carkeet.[22]

Carkeet, by close linguistic analysis, identifies nine white dialects. These are, in order of appearance:

(1) Huck's dialect
(2) Pap's
(3) Judith Loftus (on the Illinois shore)
(4) The thieves on the *Walter Scott*
(5) The Raftsmen (deleted from chapter 16)
(6) The king
(7) The Bricksville loafers
(8) Sally and Silas Phelps
(9) The Arkansas gossips (Sisters Hotchkiss, Damrell, etc., of chapter 41).

If Huck's dialect is taken as the norm, then listed in order of divergence from Huck they run:

(1) Huck
(2) Mrs Loftus

(3) Pap
(4) Thieves on the *Walter Scott*
(5) The Raftsmen
(6) Sally and Silas Phelps
(7) The Bricksville loafers
(8) The king
(9) The Arkansas gossips.

The 'extremest form of the backwoods South-Western dialect', it is generally agreed, must be that of the Arkansas gossips (with their 's'I' and 's'e' and 'sh'shee'). 'Pike-County' is a Missouri county to the south of Hannibal as well as an Illinois county across the river. Twain put St Petersburg, however, in Pike County. So for him speakers of 'the ordinary "Pike-County" dialect' are likely to have included Huck, Tom, Aunt Polly, Ben Rogers, as well as (with slight variations) Mrs Loftus and Pap. Huck tells the king that he is from 'Pike County, in Missouri' (103/166). But 'the Pike', in common parlance, also included a broad band of Westerners from Illinois to Arkansas who wandered further west in search of gold. This fabled 'Pike' is reflected in the few names Twain drops among the southernmost river towns: Pokeville and Pikesville.

If the home group (Huck, Tom, Pap, etc.), then, are to be identified, as Carkeet argues, with 'the ordinary "Pike-County" dialect', and if the Raftsmen are eliminated (as deleted, with Twain's endorsement, from the published text), this leaves exactly four groups for the modified variants of Pike speech. In order of divergence from Huck's idiolect:

(1) The thieves on the *Walter Scott*
(2) Sally and Silas Phelps
(3) The Bricksville loafers
(4) The king.

So Twain was not exaggerating. He was being, as he said, 'explanatory'. *Huckleberry Finn* was published at the 'high tide' of 'the greatest flood of dialect literature that America has ever known'.[23] From New England, Harriet Beecher Stowe published *Old Town Folks* (1869) and *Sam Lawson's Fireside Stories* (1871); from Indiana, Edward Eggleston *The Hoosier Schoolmaster* (1871); from Nevada and California, Bret Harte *The Luck of Roaring Camp and Other Sketches*

(1870). Such writers came collectively to be known as the 'local color' school. *Recherches du temps perdu* were very much in vogue after the catastrophe of the Civil War; and Twain, like them, was quite capable of sustaining idyllic evocations of the past, of childhood, of rural America. In *Tom Sawyer*, for example. But not in *Huckleberry Finn*. However idyllic about nature (in a handful of pages), that book is consistently sardonic and mocking about society. Its multiplicity of dialect renderings can by no stretch of the imagination be called 'local color'. Yet even Huck, of course, is cleaned up. He, too, is idealized. He, too, is bowdlerized. Above all, as a poor White of that frontier region, he is depoliticized. In subverting Huck's voice from *within* by his gentlemanly presence, Twain defused any hint of social radicalism and derailed the Southwestern tradition from its populist – that is, mock-political – origins. If, as I argued in Chapter 11, Twain successfully revolutionized that tradition, he also gutted it.

NOTES

1 Janet Holmgren McKay, '"Tears and flapdoodle": point of view and style in *The Adventures of Huckleberry Finn*', *Style*, vol. 10 (Winter 1976), pp. 41–50.
2 *Huckleberry Finn*, ch. 25, pp. 131–2/212.
3 Buffalo and Erie County Library manuscript, pp. 241–2; in the Gale Research edition (Detroit, Mich., 1983), Vol. 1, pp. 149–50.
4 *Huckleberry Finn*, ch. 18, p. 90/147.
5 McKay, '"Tears and flapdoodle"', p. 44.
6 cf. 'just hawking and sp— Sh!' (65/94), where the punster, slithering from (medieval) hawking to spitting, is all too clearly Twain.
7 See above, Ch. 11, pp. 131–136.
8 See above, Ch. 11, n. 35.
9 cf. Louis D. Rubin, Jr: 'Part of the time Huck Finn is a "straight man" for Tom Sawyer, much of the time for the author' (*The Teller in the Tale* (Seattle, Wash.: University of Washington Press, 1967), ch. 3, p. 57).
10 *Huckleberry Finn*, ch. 22, p. 120/192.
11 'Jane Lampton Clemens', in Walter Blair (ed.), *Mark Twain's Hannibal, Huck & Tom* (Berkeley, Calif.: University of California Press, 1969), p. 52.
12 'He speaks slowly, lazily, and wearily, as of a man dropping off to sleep'; London *Sketch*, vol. 12 (27 November 1895).
13 Youth's Companion (1894), reprinted in Justin Kaplan (ed.), *Great Short Works of Mark Twain* (New York: Harper & Row, 1967), pp. 182–7. See above, Ch. 4, pp. 50–51.
14 What Andrew Lang called 'the profound and candid seriousness of boyhood': 'The art of Mark Twain', *Illustrated London News*, vol. 98 (14 February 1891), p. 222.
15 See above, Ch. 7, nn. 17 and 18.
16 Alan Trachtenberg, 'The form of freedom in *Adventures of Huckleberry Finn*', *Southern Review*, new series vol. 6 (October 1970), p. 969.
17 Robert J. Lowenherz, 'The beginning of "Huckleberry Finn"', *American Speech*, vol. 38 (October 1963), p. 197. The thirteen words are: *sivilize, warn't* (used three

times), *most* (for 'almost', used twice), *Bulrushers, somewheres, whippowill, amongst, a-bothering, a-shaking* and *a-stirring*.

18 *Artemus Ward, His Book* (New York, 1862), p. 17, and Petroleum V. Nasby, *Swinging Round the Cirkle* (Boston, Mass., 1867), p. 13, both quoted by Lowenherz, 'Beginning of "Huckleberry Finn"', p. 196.
19 See above, Ch. 2, n.18.
20 See Sydney J. Krause, 'Twain's method and theory of composition', *Modern Philology*, vol. 56 (February 1959), p. 176.
21 *Huckleberry Finn*, ch. 24, p. 130/208; cf. ch. 29, p. 155/249.
22 See above Ch. 11, n.36.
23 Professor Pattee, quoted by Walter Blair, *Native American Humor* (New York: American Book Co., 1937), p. 25.

CHAPTER 13

Mississippi Style

'You know what I mean – I don't know the words to put it in.'
(ch. 7)

I called Huck's an easy-going, gentlemanly style. But it is not
gentlemanly in the decorous, hierarchical, European mode. It just
saunters like a gentleman. It is open to all occasions, all encounters,
all comers. It has time to spare and curiosity to spare for all
adventures along the common highway of life. In this sense the very
concept of gentleman in bustling democratic America was transformed
to that of bum. Loafing, as Huck (and his contemporary Whitman)
calls it. Huck's style loafs. It drifts as he drifts. It is his verbal
raft – his only raft we can ever hope to experience for ourselves.

Many passages already quoted could illustrate this drafting syntax.
The 'long lanky man' rehearsing Boggs's murder is one. But I shall
quote another from nearer the opening of that chapter, the arrival in
Bricksville:

> Then we went loafing around the town. The stores and houses was
> most all old shackly dried-up frame concerns that hadn't ever been
> painted; they was set up three or four foot above ground on stilts,
> so as to be out of reach of the water when the river was overflowed.
> The houses had little gardens around them, but they didn't seem to
> raise hardly anything in them but jimpson weeds, and sunflowers,
> and ash-piles, and old curled-up boots and shoes, and pieces of
> bottles, and rags, and played-out tin-ware. The fences was made of
> different kinds of boards, nailed on at different times; and they
> leaned every which-way, and had gates that didn't generly have but
> one hinge – a leather one. Some of the fences had been white-
> washed, some time or another, but the duke said it was in
> Clumbus's time, like enough. There was generly hogs in the
> garden, and people driving them out.[1]

Conjunction is Huck's favourite device. Unit is simply juxtaposed to unit without subordination. That is the key to Huck's style, to his experience, to his vision of the world: x + x + x + x + x. Just one damned, or amazing, thing after another. In mathematics, it is called addition. Rhetorically speaking, this paratactic structure of words, of phrases, of sentences, of whole episodes, is either controlled by asyndeton (without connectives) or by polysyndeton (the repetition of the same connective, usually the copula 'and'): jimpson weeds, *and* sunflowers, *and* ash-piles, *and* old curled-up boots *and* shoes, *and* pieces of bottles, *and* rags, *and* played-out tin-ware. In that final sentence the visual equilibrium achieves a kind of moral equilibrium (not that Huck underscores it) that feeds back into the entire passage: 'hogs in the garden' *and* 'people driving them out' are as impartially balanced as weights in a pan.

If Twain can use Huck's vision in this instance for social satire, he can also use it for purely aesthetic purposes. As in Huck's celebrated description of a sunrise which he records, moment by moment, with Ruskinian accuracy. But it is just his normal mode of sequential operation by means of his usual watchfulness:

It was a monstrous big river down there – sometimes a mile and a half wide; we run nights, and laid up and hid day-times; soon as night was most gone, we stopped navigating and tied up – nearly always in the dead water under a tow-head; and then cut young cottonwoods and willows and hid the raft with them. Then we set out the lines. Next we slid into the river and had a swim, so as to freshen up and cool off; then we set down on the sandy bottom where the water was about knee deep, and watched the daylight come. Not a sound, anywheres – perfectly still – just like the whole world was asleep, only sometimes the bull-frogs a-cluttering, maybe. The first thing to see, looking away over the water, was a kind of dull line – that was the woods on t'other side – you couldn't make nothing else out; then a pale place in the sky; then more paleness, spreading around; then the river softened up, away off, and warn't black any more, but gray; you could see little dark spots drifting along, ever so far away – trading scows, and such things; and long black streaks – rafts; sometimes you could hear a sweep screaking; or jumbled up voices, it was so still, and sounds come so far; and by-and-by you could see a streak on the water which you know by the look of the streak that there's a snag there in a swift

current which breaks on it and makes that streak look that way; and
you see the mist curl up off of the water, and the east reddens up,
and the river, and you make out a log cabin in the edge of the
woods, away on the bank on t'other side of the river, being a wood-
yard, likely, and piled by them cheats so you can throw a dog
through it anywheres; then the nice breeze springs up, and comes
fanning you from over there, so cool and fresh, and sweet to smell,
on account of the woods and the flowers; but sometimes not that
way, because they've left dead fish laying around, gars, and such,
and they do get pretty rank; and next you've got the full day, and
everything smiling in the sun, and the song-birds just going it!²

Huck deals with his affairs in practical, ship-shape fashion: 'we run
nights, *and* laid up *and* hid day-times . . . we stopped navigating *and*
tied up . . . *and then* cut young cottonwoods *and* willows *and* hid the
raft . . . *Then* we set out . . . *Next* we slid into . . . *then* we set
down . . .'. The sunrise is given much the same treatment: '*The first*
thing to see . . . *then* a pale place . . . *then* more paleness . . . *then* the
river softened . . . *and by-and-by* you could see . . . *and* you see the
mist . . . *and* the east . . . *and* the river, *and* you make out a log
cabin . . .' His paratactic sequences are *all* like sunrises. They are
ignorant of hierarchy. They resist classification. They are unsubordin-
ated and unclassified. Each unit, passing on the verbal conveyor-belt
before our gaze, demands an equal scrutiny, an equal share of our
attention. Be it boots or tin-ware. Each momentarily fills an entire
frame. Until the next unit, the next frame, takes its place. Next, next,
next. Parataxis is wholly egalitarian. No favouritism, no élitism. It is
simply a queue. This refusal to impose any rational or causal logic on
a chain of events is also thoroughly undidactic. Huck deduces almost
nothing from his experience.

The description of the sunrise, however, differs from that of the
stroll through Bricksville. The one in a unique event and recounts
Huck's first impressions of that event; the other is a synthetic, or
composite, account of many sunrises. It is a rare instance in
Huckleberry Finn of what Gérard Genette has labelled 'iterative
narrative'.³ One night by that stage of the trip (despite the
Grangerford interlude) was much like another. They had established
their routine: tying up, hiding the raft, setting out fish-lines, taking a
dip. But no sunrise is ever routine. So Huck offers variants, mainly of
sounds and smells. Only once, though, does he embroider the facts.

The 'log cabin', he thinks, *may* be a wood-yard, where logs *may* be unscrupulously piled. That Huck cannot even mention an imaginary wood-yard without introducing imaginary 'cheats' seems typical. But only two or three days earlier, in sight of a log store, he had witnessed the ghastly shoot-out near a 'wood-rank' where Buck and his 19-year-old cousin were desperately holding out. Mental blocks and blackouts are equally typical of his text. Parataxis, as a narrative mode, cannot cope with complexities.

Under intense emotional stress, though, even Huck's style buckles. In agonizing over Jim's loss and the king's treachery, subordinate clauses *do* build up:

> I thought till I wore my head sore, but I couldn't see no way out of the trouble. After all this long journey, and after all we'd done for them scoundrels, here was it all come to nothing, everything all busted up and ruined, because they could have the heart to serve Jim such a trick as that . . .[4]

For once the moral indignation breaks the paratactic pattern, and the twists of memory are reflected in the unusually distorted, inverted syntax.

Parataxis, then, naturally entails repetition, just as x + x entails the equation x = x. For any x must ultimately be interchangeable, as substitute, with any other x. That is the essence of egalitarianism. Its rhetorical name is tautology. It is the second key feature of Huck's style. His whole narrative is a vast syntagmatic structure stringing episode to episode without much distinction of weight and function; yet these paratactic units (the feud, the 'Shaksperean Revival', cheating the Wilkses, cheating the Phelpses) also reflect and distort each other, as if each addition were merely another thematic iteration. For pleonasm operates not merely on the grammatical or micro-level: 'a monstrous big river'; the mist curling 'up off of the water'; 'the king he gets up'.[5] The whole narrative is one vast tautological construction duplicating gang warfare and crises of conscience, death and resurrection.

Parataxis and tautology, though, are respectable rhetorical modes. Huck's grammatical habits are less respectable. The most noticeable is his implacable use of the double negative. The very opening sentence contains two: 'You don't know about me, without you have read a book by the name of "The Adventures of Tom Sawyer", but that ain't no matter.' From there on the count is endless. Another habit is a persistent confusion of verb tense shifting (as we saw in the last chapter) from the past into the historic present and back again to the past. This is no venal fault. My own text is equally guilty of such meanderings. But, taken collectively, Huck's avoidance of passive constructions, his confusion of tenses and misuse of the double negative do suggest a final insight into his character. From his verb use alone one is aware of an active enough boy, though with a somewhat unco-ordinated, displaced sense of time. That repeated habit of double negation, however, begins to conjure up a wary, dour, even sour and prematurely aged manikin. 'The moment we begin listening attentively to the way Huck talks', Jonathan Raban notes, 'we hear the voice . . . of a bitter and premature resignation.'[6]

Taken all in all, Huck's inveterate use of addition (by parataxis) and repetition (by tautology), together with his displacement in time, evoke a random, unpredictable, aleatory sense at one with his haunted, fatalistic, occult world. Huck is at home in that world; and his random lists (like those of Emerson and Whitman) mime an impressionism – a shifting perception of 'jimpson weeds, and sunflowers, and ash-piles' item by independent item – controlled only by the passage of time. For it is temporal sequence alone that links these fragmentary sense-data to a narrative cohesion. Huck is only conscious of the contingent. His imagination, being so literal, just strings together these independent clauses, sentences and episodes without seeking for a motive, a pattern, a reiterated theme, an argument, a generalization, or an explanation.

His style, therefore, is diametrically opposed to such hierarchically controlled, absolutist or totalitarian styles as those developed by James and Mann, Proust and Musil (among others) at the turn of the century. Huck resists such luxuriance, such baroque intensities. That is why he could be recovered by Ring Lardner and Sherwood Anderson and Hemingway as a proto-modern. His is a peculiarly American pragmatic and democratic style: a riot of specific and insubordinate units, unenforced by any overarching, syntactically supreme, governing principle. It bears the very hallmarks of the American constitution.

Huck himself, of course, is resolutely non-political. His democratic outlook is wholly *moral*. Based on neither political nor legal nor religious rights, his casual morality can only be expressed, it seems, in terms of 'swapping'. Huck approves of 'swapping'. All life to him is a matter of give and take – in rituals of random, easy-going exchange – called 'swapping'. It is nature's sign, and he can spot it anywhere. As in the terror of the fog: 'it was worse than chasing a Jack-o-lantern. You never knowed a sound dodge around so, and swap places so quick and so much' (69/101). But usually it is more benign. As he says, at the Widow's, of her 'victuals':

there warn't really anything the matter with them. That is, nothing only everything was cooked by itself. In a barrel of odds and ends it is different; things get mixed up, and the juice kind of swaps around, and the things go better.[7]

Or as he says of woodland shadows:

There was freckled places on the ground where the light sifted down through the leaves, and the freckled places swapped about a little, showing there was a little breeze up there.[8]

Swapping for Huck means open sharing – a volatile exchange of separate elements and an amalgamation of such elements in a constant state of realignment, in fusion and confusion and rediffusion – which is the seething and acceptable chaos of life at play: both of physical life (of tow-heads and snags and the collapsing banks of the Mississippi) and of social life, in the family tradition of borrowing ('Pap always said, take a chicken when you get a chance, because if you don't want him yourself you can easy find somebody that does'). But certainly not in the conceptual terms of Presbyterian sermons 'all about brotherly love, and such-like tiresomeness'. Swapping is opposed to all rational systems or regulations or notions of decorum or sets of rules which impose a rigid discrimination (culinary or racial), or hierarchical distinction (from aristocracy to trash), or segregation.

Huck, of course, would never have said all that. Yet, whether he knew it or not, he belonged to a much wider American tradition than that of the Widow or Judge Thatcher or Colonel Grangerford in which he was trapped. He stands at a point – and it is an extraordinary point – where the tradition of the Southwestern humorists and New England Transcendentalists meet. It was Emerson who taught Americans 'the worth of the vulgar'. His was a radical vision for a revolutionary republic. The same movement, he wrote, which effected the elevation of what was called the lowest class in the state, assumed in literature a very marked and as benign an aspect. Instead of the sublime and beautiful, the near, the low, the common, was explored and poetized. That which had been negligently trodden under foot by those who were harnessing and provisioning themselves for long journeys into far countries, is suddenly found to be richer than all foreign parts. The literature of the poor, the feelings of the child, the philosophy of the street, the meaning of household life, are the topics of the time. It is a great stride. It is a sign – is it not? of new vigor when the extremities are made active, when currents of warm life run into the hands and the feet. I ask not for the great, the remote, the romantic; what is doing in Italy or Arabia; what is Greek art, or Provençal minstrelsy; I embrace the common, I explore and sit at the feet of the familiar, the low. Give me insight into today, and you may have the antique and future worlds. What would we really know the meaning of? The meal in the firkin; the milk in the pan; the ballad in the street; the news of the boat; the glance of the eye; the form and the gait of the body – show me the ultimate reason of these matters; show me the sublime presence of the highest spiritual cause lurking, as always it does lurk, in these suburbs and extremities of nature; let me see every trifle bristling with the polarity that ranges it instantly on an eternal law; and the shop, the plough, and the ledger referred to the like cause by which light undulates and poets sing – and the world lies no longer a dull miscellany and lumber-room, but has form and order; there is no trifle, there is no puzzle, but one design unites and animates the farthest pinnacle and the lowest trench.[9]

Forget about ultimate reasons and eternal laws, pinnacles and trenches; they are nothing to Huck. But he *is* 'low', as he repeatedly insists. He *is* 'familiar'. He *embraces* 'the common'. It is Tom who longs for 'the great, the remote, the romantic'; and it is Tom's dreams that Emerson rejects.

A New World, not yet venerable (like Europe) with history, needed a venerating eye that could note all its prosaic, isolated, random, radiant, everyday details. *That* was Emerson's lesson. 'We are a poor people,' he wrote. 'It is the poor who make America and its institutions.' What he himself could not supply, but thundered in prophecy from Concord, Massachusetts, was an egalitarian eye for an egalitarian society; a rejection of history in favour of the everlasting

NOW; the need for a vernacular strategy; by simple, untutored man; in self-celebration; whose language, as he once put it, is 'fossil poetry'. Emerson preferred, he said, those not 'subdued by the drill of school education'. 'Do you think the porter and the cook', he asked, 'have no anecdotes, no experiences, no wonders for you? . . . The walls of crude minds are scawled over with facts, with thoughts.' This is high-flown stuff. But Huck, more than Thoreau or Whitman, fulfilled this prophecy. It is Huck who rejects school and Sunday school and Bible indoctrination. It is Huck who, in Emerson's phrase, accepts 'the potluck of the day'; sets up 'a strong present tense'; and makes 'friends with matter'. Even smut became part of Emerson's lofty vision: 'What would be base, or even obscene, to the obscene, becomes illustrious, spoken in a new connection of thought.'

Huck's vision, though, unlike Whitman's or Thoreau's, hardly expressed a new connection of *thought*. But it *is* a vision. That description of the sunrise, seen by Huck as he squats in the Mississippi like a frog with only his head out of water, is the very embodiment of Emerson's famous dictum: 'I am become a transparent eyeball; I am nothing; I see all.' Huck is not an observer merely, but steeped in the very element which he transmits: 'then we set down on the sandy bottom . . . and *watched* the daylight come . . . The first thing to *see, looking away* over the water . . . you could *see* little dark spots . . . you could *see* a streak . . . you could *see* the mist . . . you *make out* a log cabin . . .' The whole passage is structured on sight, on scrutiny, on identifying with the intensity of the near-blind a 'dull line' (woods), 'dark spots' (trading scows), 'long black streaks' (rafts), an indefinably different kind of streak (snags). But not only on sight. Every sense is involved. Sounds travel clearly across water: bull-frogs, an oar, jumbled voices, song-birds. Huck records touch (cool water, a fanning breeze) and smell (woods, flowers, dead fish). He does everything except *taste* the sunrise.

So, too, with catalogues. Emerson compiled a catalogue (the meal, the milk, the ballad, the news, the eye, the body) of just six items. Huck can do much better. From the Bricksville gardens he clocks up a list of eight. The haul off the floating house (an old tin lantern, a butcher's knife, a brand-new Barlow knife, etc.) piles up to as many as eighteen. Everything is scrutinized, noted, accounted for. That really was 'the potluck of the day'. But Emerson never anticipated quite this disciple. Huck was both too unscrupulous and too unintellectual; and he lacked what Emerson prized above all, self-reliance.

The self-reliant man, wrote Emerson, 'must sit solidly at home, and not suffer himself to be bullied by kings or empires, but know that he is greater than all the geography and all the government of the world'. Huck knows no such thing. Stuck in his room, he soon feels lonesome and blue. He is too easily cowed by dukes and kings. Huck's world *remains* a 'miscellany and lumber-room'. For he remains incapable (without Tom) of rising to more general concepts, let alone such a universal and unifying vision.

Far from self-reliant, Huck is overawed by Mississippi grandeur, Mississippi style. He is the dupe of any sham or meretricious ploy. There is a gaudy streak in Huck that has nothing in common with Emerson's austere, egalitarian programme. The only two set-speeches he records (those of Colonel Sherburn and Pap) are filled with an overwhelming, aggressive contempt which elevates them above a (visible or invisible) mob of niggers or fellow-Whites. Such was the politics of a slave society. But Huck's readiness to adopt new masks, new theatrical roles, suggests his own ready identification with the theatrical South of Grangerfords and Sawyers: the South where every gentleman was 'a Major or a Colonel, or a General or a Judge, before the war'; and, after it, of such chivalric-sounding vigilante groups as Knights of the White Camellia, Knights of the White Rose, Knights of the Black Cross, or the White Brotherhood.[10] This is the South of inflated rhetoric, inflated emotions, inflated titles, inflated promises and dreams:

> There's a hand that was the hand of a hog; but it ain't so no more; it's the hand of a man that's started in on a new life, and 'll die before he'll go back . . .

> Oh, come to the mourners' bench! come, black with sin! (*amen!*) come, sick and sore! (*amen!*) come, lame and halt, and blind! (*amen!*) come, pore and needy, sunk in shame! (*a-a-men!*) come all that's worn, and soiled, and suffering!

> Cler the track, thar. I'm on the waw-path, and the price uv coffins is a gwyne to raise.

> 'Tis my fate to be always ground into the mire under the iron heel of oppression. Misfortune has broken my once haughty spirit; I yield, I submit; 'tis my fate. I am alone in the world – let me suffer; I can bear it.

. . . but its a trial that's sweetened and sanctified to us by this dear
sympathy and these holy tears . . .[11]

This is the South that re-creates every occasion of life and death as
show.

The duke knew what he was about. 'He said he could size their
style' (121/194). But Huck is nowhere near so adroit, nor so sure. He
resists and rejects the pervasive rhetoric, but is invariably drawn to it.
He admires Emmeline Grangerford's doggerel tributes. He admires
the duke's Byronic self-dramatization as poet and exile. There is more
than a literary joke here at Huck's expense. He is riddled with self-
doubt. In moral terms this is not funny at all. He speaks, as we have
seen all along, with a dual voice. Which is also Twain's voice. But it
was Twain's genius to resolve that rhetorical conflict in comic terms.
By manipulating Huck from within the mask, he created that
inimitable 'voice capable of sustaining a comic dialectic within itself'
(p. 141, above). It was not just a trick or spurt of colloquial gusto. It
was a performance so complex that Twain was never able to repeat it
himself. Yet it continues to exert an inexhaustible influence on later
generations of American prose writers. As T. S. Eliot remarked:
'Twain, at least in *Huckleberry Finn*, reveals himself to be one of those
writers of whom there are not a great many in any literature, who have
discovered a new way of writing, valid not only for themselves, but for
others.'[12]

His most obvious heirs I have already mentioned: Lardner,
Anderson, Hemingway. Their experiments with adolescent voices
reached a glorious culmination in J. D. Salinger's *The Catcher in the
Rye* (1951). But Twain was the dominant influence on a whole
generation of comic prose writers (S. J. Perelman, Damon Runyon,
James Thurber) and their successors up to Woody Allen today. Listen
to the opening of Anita Loos's *Gentlemen Prefer Blondes* (1925) where
Huck's often laboriously thoughtful manner is transformed into that
of a poker-faced, peroxyde blonde:

March 16th:
   A gentleman friend and I were dining at the Ritz last evening and
he said that if I took a pencil and a paper and put down all of my
thoughts it would make a book. This almost made me smile as what
it would really make would be a whole row of encyclopediacs. I
mean I seem to be thinking practically all of the time. I mean it is

my favorite recreation and sometimes I sit for hours and do not seem to do anything else but think. So this gentleman said a girl with brains ought to do something else with them besides think.[13]

The debt here is not just the confident, confiding tone. It is the vernacular mask that is Twain's.

Most of Twain's heirs after the First World War were Midwesterners like him, born in Ohio, Michigan, Illinois, Kansas – with the exception of urban Jewish wits like Perelman.[14] Most were newspapermen, or had escaped the advertising and business world like Anderson, who used vernacular as a comic affront to an increasingly suburbanized commuter public.[15] Huck was metamorphosed into Lardner's professional sportsmen and Runyon's petty crooks, into Loos's gold-diggers and Anderson's adolescents – all marginal, often semi-criminal types, drop-outs from mainstream society. Even Thurber's whimsical innocents, adrift in America's sexual and technical revolution, were lateral descendants of Huck.

But Twain also exercised a major influence on the South, especially on William Faulkner; and through Faulkner on most contemporary Southern writers. But Blacks? Have black writers benefited from Twain? Certainly not from Jim, who, with the best will in the world, remains a stumbling-block today.[16] Missouri-born Langston Hughes wrote fine dialect poems and dialogues.[17] But black dialect fiction, in autobiographical form, is a very recent phenomenon, confined so far mainly to women. The runaway bestseller has been Alice Walker's *The Color Purple* (1982).[18] Huck's protean and continuing versatility in masquerade can be gauged by the success of *Gentlemen Prefer Blondes* in 1925 and *The Color Purple* in 1982.

But what about Jim? Is he wholly a lost cause? At this point I shall attempt a paradox. I shall attempt to recoup the narrative from Jim's point of view, even if this entails occasionally recrossing familiar trails. For the shift of viewpoint may clarify the limitations of a traditional white reader's inevitable identification with Huck.[19]

NOTES

1 *Huckleberry Finn*, ch. 21, pp. 112–13/181.
2 ibid., ch. 19, p. 96/156–7.
3 Gérard Genette: 'This type of narrative, where a single narrative utterance takes upon itself several occurrences together of the same event . . . we will call *iterative* narrative' (*Narrative Discourse*, trans. Jane E. Lewin (Oxford: Basil Blackwell, 1980), ch. 3, p. 116).

4 *Huckleberry Finn*, ch. 31, p. 168/268.
5 Huck will also repeat a single word as a kind of refrain through several phrases or sentences. On Jackson's Island he found 'green summer-grapes, and green razberries; and the green blackberries was just beginning to show' (36/48). Or, at the end of ch. 18, just prior to the description of the sunrise: 'We said there warn't no home like a raft, after all. Other places do seem so cramped up and smothery, but a raft don't. You feel mighty free and easy and comfortable on a raft.' This was to prove Huck's most enduring legacy to American prose style.
6 Jonathan Raban, *Mark Twain: Huckleberry Finn* (London: Edward Arnold, 1968), ch. 1, p. 18. For Huck's bad speech habits, see Sydney J. Krause, 'Twain's method and theory of composition', *Modern Philology*, vol. 56 (February 1959), p. 176. Apart from the double negative, the break of verb tense and pleonasm, Krause lists the use of past participles for finite forms ('they done' for 'they did'), the use of non-standard forms ('catched' for 'caught', 'brung up' for 'brought up'), and the use of adjectival forms for adverbs ('awful mixed' for 'awfully mixed').
7 *Huckleberry Finn*, ch. 1, p. 7/2.
8 ibid., ch. 8, p. 34/45.
9 Emerson, 'The American Scholar' (1837). See also *Complete Works* (Boston/New York: Houghton Mifflin, 1903), Vol. 1, p. 10, Vol. 2, p. 330, and Vol. 3, pp. 17 and 22. The Final quotation on self-reliance is from his essay on 'History'.
10 *Life on the Mississippi*, ch. 46.
11 *Huckleberry Finn*, ch. 5, p. 23/27; ch. 20, pp. 103–4/167 and 107/172; ch. 21, p. 115/184; and ch. 25, p. 132/213.
12 T. S. Eliot, 'American literature and the American language', *Washington University Studies in Language and Literature*, new series vol. 23 (St Louis, Mo., 1953), pp. 16–17.
13 *Gentleman Prefer Blondes* originally ran for six monthly instalments in *Harper's Bazaar* (1925).
14 Sherwood Anderson and James Thurber were born in Ohio; Ring Lardner in Michigan; Ernest Hemingway in Illinois; Damon Runyon in Kansas.
15 Lardner was a newspaperman in South Bend, Indiana, and St Louis; his 'Jack Keefe' letters appeared in the *Chicago Tribune*. Hemingway was a Paris correspondent for the Hearst Press; Runyon, too, wrote for Hearst; Thurber for the *New Yorker*. Anita Loos became a Hollywood screenplay-writer; Perelman gag-writer for the Marx Brothers.
16 In Ralph Ellison's words: 'Jim's friendship for Huck comes across as that of a boy for another boy rather than as the friendship of an adult for a junior; thus there is implicit in it not only a violation of the manners sanctioned by society for relations between Negroes and whites, there is a violation of our conception of adult maleness.' See Ellison, 'Change the joke and slip the yoke', *Partisan Review*, vol. 25 (Spring 1958), pp. 212–22; reprinted in *Shadow and Act* (New York: Random House, 1964), p. 51. For the whole question of the black reception of *Huckleberry Finn*, see the *Mark Twain Journal*, vol. 22 (Fall 1984), a special issue by black writers; in particular Arnold Rampersad, '*Adventures of Huckleberry Finn* and Afro-American literature', pp. 47–52.
17 There was almost no dialect fiction among Harlem Renaissance writers. From 1943 on Hughes contributed his Jessie B. Semple, or 'Simple', dialogues to the *Chicago Defender*, published as *Simple Speaks His Mind*, *Simple Takes a Wife*, *Simple Stakes a Claim*, *Simple's USA* (1950–65).
18 Whose heroine, Arnold Rampersad declares, 'whether or not Walker herself would like the notion, is definitely a black country cousin of Huck Finn' ('*Adventures of Huckleberry Finn* and Afro-American literature', p. 48). Recent black dialect fiction, conceived as adolescent autobiography, includes: Alice Childress, *A Hero*

Ain't Nothing but a Sandwich (1973), and Al Young, *Sitting Pretty* (1976).

19 See Harold Beaver, 'Run, nigger, run: *Adventures of Huckleberry Finn* as a fugitive slave narrative', *Journal of American Studies*, vol. 8 (December 1974), pp. 339–61.

CHAPTER 14

Run, Nigger, Run

'Ain't them old crippled picks and things in there good enough to dig a nigger out with?' (ch. 35)

Say, an abolitionist *had* taken an interest in Jim's story. It was strange enough, after all, in its flight downstream into cotton territory, protected by a 14-year-old boy. The account might have been published under some such title as 'The Narrative of James Watson of Missouri, Formerly a Slave'.[1] What would such a narrative have revealed?

At the end of *Adventures of Huckleberry Finn*, Jim is a free man. 'Chapter the Last' Huck calls that final chapter. But for Jim, of course, it was only a beginning. Jim was now free to purchase his wife from off that neighbouring plantation, as he had planned all along, 'saying how the first thing he would do when he got to a free State he would go to saving up money and never spend a single cent' (73/124). But cash might have proved the least of his problems. As a 'free Negro' he was barred from re-entering Missouri.[2] In any case he did not yet have his freedom papers. Should he boldly risk a return, he would be in constant danger from 'the pater-rollers' as well as bloody-minded busybodies like Old Finn. A sworn statement by any predatory White would '*prove*' ownership; and he'd be clapped back in chains. Huck and Tom could afford to ignore all this. But it was clear enough to Jim. That is why even attempting to *buy* his wife and two children was no easy matter. Their master might refuse to sell. He might (as he foolishly let slip) have to 'get an Ab'litionist to go and steal them'. Or sneak back himself on the Underground Railway. If Harriet Tubman could do it, why not Jim?

The answer depends on a much wider question. Was Jim capable of taking *any* decisive action? Or was he merely the tool of white men's machinations, a passive focus for others rather than the controlling factor of his own escape? To what extent was Twain, in other words, aware of the social and intellectual identity of the black man whose career his hero had so ambiguously espoused? To what extent was he aware that his link between black man and white boy was rather less than idyllic? Certainly, if it *was* less idyllic, those final chapters on the Phelps farm might seem less of a betrayal. Since it is Huck's story, not Jim's, among all other rebounding ironies this question of Jim's truth, as revealed by Huck's self-centred and often self-deluding monologue, needs very careful scrutiny.

Jim enters the drama ready-made. Despite his 'Missouri negro dialect', that is, he is wholly stereotyped, a walking cliché, what Elizabethans might have called a 'humour'.[3] So the point for Twain, as for Marlowe or Shakespeare, can hardly have been the stereotype in itself so much as how that stereotype is handled and developed in the context of the drama. Furthermore the stereotype is highly selective. It is deliberately detached from that of the idle chatterbox in *Tom Sawyer*.[4] To use the cant phrases of the period, Jim is neither 'fervent' exactly, nor 'gossipy', nor 'vain', nor 'dishonest', nor 'idle', nor 'lying'. He fulfils none of those truisms once dear to a Southern heart: that a Negro lacks mental energy; that a Negro loves finery; that a Negro has a distaste for bodily labour; that a Negro is prey to transient passions; that a Negro is overpowered by animal lust. He is detached, too, from the nigger minstrel tradition. For, though he is recalled as 'singing', none of his songs is quoted; he merely carries around a jew's harp.

Jim is the good nigger: 'good-humoured', 'simple' (with the king and duke), 'improvident' (with his financial investments), 'kind-hearted' (to Huck), displaying a 'contented African patience' with a physical endurance that might have 'proved fatal to anyone except an African'.[5] The stress throughout is not on his trances or voodoo potency so much as on his ability to preserve an equilibrium between 'true Negro optimism', as a Southerner would have put it, and 'African fatalism'.[6] So much Huck could observe. The inherent shrewdness was not so conspicuous. For Jim rarely speaks out.

He must be 30 years old at least and a giant of a man with 'hairy arms en a hairy breas''. Weigh him down with chains and he can still wheel a grindstone 'along like nothing'! Tall and muscular, he was a field-hand, a cattle-herder, going 'off wid de cattle 'bout daylight', and not returning 'tell arter dark'.[7] On all questions of field-lore – such as bee-keeping, or chickens, or laying out fish-lines – he holds forth like an expert; and he is practical, too, building a wigwam on the raft as readily as a raised fireplace. He must have grown up on a farm; like any rural Black, he sleeps with 'a blanket around his head, and his head . . . nearly in the fire' (37/50).[8] He is illiterate, of course. Superstitions and ritual knowledge are, by their very nature, oral: how *not* to cook dinners, or shake out tablecloths, or touch snakeskins, or look at a new moon over one's left shoulder. 'Jim knowed all kinds of signs. He said he knowed most everything.' He even has a smattering of Bible knowledge – however garbled – picked up no doubt at the Widow's and Miss Watson's evening prayers when 'they fetched the niggers in'. In his wife's cabin he clearly played boss, shouting orders at his 4-year-old daughter and sending her sprawling. A *kind* of family man, then, and a *kind* of Christian, too – but closer at heart to some atavistic African rites, a religion of the dead – his whole person, as he well realized, represented a guaranteed emotional and economic and psychological investment for Whites (with interest paid), while valueless for his own black needs.

This is the presence for which Huck opts. But Jim as decisively opts for Huck. He was certainly glad of his company after that snake bite. Now he had a buddy who supplied him with whiskey. He was looked after until the fever abated and the swelling went down. That the accident was no *accident* he never realized. He never suspected a thing. Huck just tossed both snakes into the bushes and never confessed. Even when the guilt weighs heavier and heavier on him, all he can blurt out is: 'I wish I'd never seen that snake-skin, Jim – I do wish I'd never laid eyes on it.' To which Jim, in all innocence, replies: 'It ain't yo' fault, Huck; you didn' know. Don't you blame yo'self 'bout it' (77/129).

But, if Huck nurses a dirty secret, so does Jim. If Huck can keep mum, so can Jim. There was a wall of reticence – of truths suppressed and secrets withheld – by now between them. For Jim had immediately recognized that corpse in the floating house:

'It's a dead man. Yes, indeedy; naked, too. He's ben shot in de back. I reck'n he's ben dead two er three days. Come in, Huck, but doan' look at his face – it's too gashly.'
I didn't look at him at all. Jim throwed some old rags over him, but he needn't done it; I didn't want to see him.[9]

He had covered that face instinctively, no doubt, to spare Huck's feelings. But, quick as a flash, it struck him: what if the white boy ditched him? What was to prevent him, once he knew his father was dead, from sloping off to his friends (and cash deposit) in St Petersburg? 'Well, he was right', as Huck more than once was to observe; 'he was most always right; he had an uncommon level head, for a nigger' (64/93).

Postwar critics now seem astonishingly naïve. James M. Cox wholeheartedly cherished the mammy image. It is Jim, he explains, 'who, knowing secretly that Huck's Pap is dead forever, takes Huck to his own bosom to nourish him through the ordeal of being lost'.[10] Daniel G. Hoffman is equally sentimental: 'But now it is Jim who comprehends the degradation of Pap's death and protects Huck from that cruel knowledge. Jim is now free to take the place that Pap was never worthy to hold as Huck's spiritual father.'[11] Jim *free*? How blinkered could one be! Jim was on the run. He was a fugitive slave. Now at last he held a trump card and he kept it face down. It was a ruthless exercise of power. Huck was now his unconscious hostage. Throughout the length of that 1,100-mile-long journey he clung to that image.

It was not until 1967 that it first dawned on critics that Jim, too, might be capable of double-dealing. 'Should not Jim have told him that?' Louis D. Rubin wondered. 'Is not the fact that he did not tell him partly attributable to the fact that Jim knows that he will need Huck's help if he is ever to make his way to freedom?'[12] Spencer Brown forthrightly answered these questions: 'Huck is really free (free of his father, and thus no longer in danger, he can go back home, or wherever he pleases); but Jim needs Huck for his flight to freedom.'[13] So White and Black, from the start, were mutual pawns, utilizing each other, manipulating each other as *objects* of romance or *tools* of escape. Affection – human needs – intervened, but in a slave-holding republic, where human labour was bought and sold, human relations, too, were inevitably turned to strategic devices and men to things. Only Jim's final words reveal his infinite wariness: 'you k'n git yo' money when you wants it; kase dat wuz him'.

In the light of such power-play, it might be wise to look again at Jim's interventions elsewhere. His room for manoeuvre was slim. But this was his third decisive act. The first had been his escape. He was used to keeping his eyes open. He had noticed the slave-trader sniffing after him. He crept round the house at night. He snooped. He eavesdropped. He knew what was up. As soon as he heard Miss Watson he made a dash, hiding out for twenty-four hours by the river

until, on the second night, he plunged in. His plan did not come off.
But he had a plan. As Huck was soon to observe: 'Jim could most
always start a good plan when you wanted one.'[14]

> I'd made up my mine 'bout what I's agwyne to do. You see ef I kep'
> on tryin' to git away afoot, de dogs 'ud track me; ef I stole a skift to
> cross over, dey'd miss dat skift you see, en dey'd know 'bout whah
> I'd lan' on de yuther side en whah to pick up my track. So I says, a
> raff is what I's arter; it doan' *make* no track.[15]

He is a strong swimmer and makes it more than halfway across the
Mississippi, in the dark, dodging driftwood, struggling against the
current until a raft comes along. He can judge the exact speed of a
raft:

> De river wuz arisin' en dey wuz a good current; so I reck'n'd 'at by
> fo' in de mawnin' I'd be twenty-five mile down de river, en den I'd
> slip in, jis' b'fo' daylight, en swim asho' en take to de woods on de
> Illinoi side.

In five or six hours, that is, from around 10.30 p.m. to 4 a.m., at a
speed of 4½–5 miles per hour, he would be twenty-five miles
downstream. His maths, too, is pretty good; better than Huck's. But
luck was against him as it was to be throughout his bid for
freedom – what with snake bites and fog, a collision and finally
betrayal.

Still, he made it to Jackson's Island. That was Jim's first decisive
act. Next he accepted this white 14-year-old boy when he might easily
have throttled him. Huck was already 'killed' (as he knew) as far as St
Petersburg was concerned. So why not do away with this awkward
interloper and potential witness? But he decided to stick with him.
That was his second decisive act. The third was to make sure the boy
didn't run off, didn't leave him in the lurch, didn't turn the tables
against him by doubling back to St Petersburg. So he withheld Pap's
death. Quick-witted Huck, who can fool almost everybody, turns out
to be everybody's fool.

So their special relationship begins. Jim takes control in the privacy
of their cave; Huck must take over on the river, making 'Jim lay down
in the canoe and cover up with the quilt' (45/62). For a white boy is
free to come and go as he likes. It is Jim who is in hiding. It is Jim

who has committed his life to Huck. With the greatest reluctance he submits to boarding the *Walter Scott*. This gives rise to an appalling dilemma which Huck, even in retrospect, seems barely able to acknowledge. For once Jim speaks out. Usually he kept a tight rein on his tongue. But the closer they get to Cairo, the more he opens up. Until, exhausted after their separation in the fog, he momentarily drops his guard. On Huck's return he calls;

> 'It's too good for true, honey, it's too good for true. Lemme look at you, chile, lemme feel o' you. No, you ain' dead! you's back agin, 'live en soun', jis de same ole Huck – de same ole Huck, thanks to goodness!'[16]

But it is not the 'same ole Huck'. Suspiciously Jim starts backing off. But when the fog in his brain finally lifts and it dawns on him that Huck had been intent on making him look the traditional 'tangle-headed old fool', with a pack of cool lies about nigger drinking and nigger dreaming, he is furious. He is contemptuous, dismissing Huck as '*trash*'. He carries it off with dignity, but the scene should have been avoided. A black man should *never*, under any circumstances, tell a white man to his face exactly what he thinks. For this was not just another piece of tomfoolery, like boarding the *Walter Scott*. This was part of the emotionally distorted white psychology with which a Black must keep on chuckling good terms and somehow try to control for his own ends. It is exactly this head-on racial conflict – of Jim's dignified stand and Huck's abject surrender – that rouses the Southern conscience of caste loyalty in the Missouri boy.

Jim withdraws in a huff. But he had overreached himself; his candour almost proves his undoing. Every White, he well knew, was a potential sneak. Every White, however friendly, needed incessant homage as 'genlman' and 'boss'. Jim had momentarily stepped out of the masonic code of signs and double-talk. That was asking for trouble. As W. J. Cash observed, in 'common whites' virtually unlimited power

> bred a savage and ignoble hate for the Negro, which required only opportunity to break forth in relentless ferocity; for all their rage against the 'white-trash' epithet concentrated itself on him rather than on the planters.[17]

But Jim by now is beyond caring. He talks out loud of *buying* his wife, maybe *stealing* his children. He fidgets up and down, 'all over trembly and feverish to be so close to freedom'. Not a trace of the old Sambo about him. But even in his euphoria he remains alert. There's a change in the atmosphere: Huck gone curiously quiet suddenly, curiously aloof. Jim feels so vulnerable, so tense, that he senses it instantly. He doesn't let on, though. He gets the canoe ready and puts his old coat in the bottom for luck. Only at the very last minute, when Huck is already shoving off, does he say it:

'Jim won't ever forgit you, Huck; you's de bes' fren' Jim's ever had; en you's de *only* fren' ole Jim's got now.'

I was paddling off, all in a sweat to tell on him; but when he says this, it seemed to kind of take the tuck all out of me. I went along slow then, and I warn't right down certain whether I was glad I started or whether I warn't. When I was fifty yards off, Jim says:

'Dah you goes, de ole true Huck; de on'y white genlman dat ever kep' his promise to ole Jim.'[18]

In less than four pages he elevates Huck to 'white genlman' from white 'trash'. He successfully confuses and defuses him. That burst of flattery is Jim's fourth decisive act.[19] But it is already too late. They had passed Cairo, it turns out. A steamboat confirms Huck's vision of doom. Mechanical culture, that is, decisively splits them in two.

In a divided world colour alone was tell-tale. Only a White was free to masquerade; only Huck could always adopt a new role. At the Grangerfords', Young Finn is unquestioningly confirmed in his white status: allotted a personal nigger and addressed as 'Mars Jawge'. Jim is salvaged and hidden by his fellow-Blacks. Huck, alias George, is instinctively carried away by the escapades and elopements of the Big House; Jim alone looks after their *things*, patching the raft at night, buying pots and pans, laying in supplies (corn and buttermilk, pork and greens). Huck becomes the willing tool of this whole swashbuckling fiction as surely as he soon becomes the willing tool of the king and duke.

But from here on Jim's hands are tied – literally tied with a rope. He is degraded and can do nothing to fight his degradation. First he is reduced by the duke to a neutered madman in a 'long curtain-calico gown' (126/203); then Huck seconds the duke's triumph by dolling him up in Aunt Sally's calico gown. Against Tom, Jim is resourceless;

but *not* against the king and duke. It is his fifth decisive act. Once out of their clutches – once they have informed on him – he seizes the initiative. Jim, in his turn, informs on them. He betrays their shoddy swindle. In the duke's phrase, he blows on them. The lovable mask is dropped as soon as he feels secure in his revenge. Just this once Jim has the satisfaction of degrading his persecutors as *he* had been degraded. Huck predictably fails to ponder Jim's share in the event, but rushes off to alert the king and duke. For the white boy is the white men's natural ally; Huck *even now* has a soft spot for that ruthless couple.

But that is positively Jim's last intervention. As Huck truckles to Tom, so Tom dominates over Jim. He is totally at Tom's mercy. He simply has to accept the whole Messianic parody imposed on him, as Huck himself dimly seems to realize: 'and as for me, I wished I was in Jerusalem or somewheres' (199/315). But that is exactly where he is. For Pikesville read Jerusalem, with Huck taking the part of St Peter with his denials. 'Who nailed him? – Huck's own question – opens a long and tedious mock-Calvary. Matthew, 27:28–31, supplies the text:

> And they stripped him, and put on him a scarlet robe. And when they had platted a crown of thorns, they put it upon his head, and a reed in his right hand . . . And after that they had mocked him, they took the robe off from him and put his own raiment on him, and led him away to crucify him.[20]

With 'his hands tied behind him', *Ecce Homo*:

> They cussed Jim considerble . . . and give him a cuff or two, side the head, once in a while, but Jim never said nothing, and he never let on to know me, and they took him to the same cabin, and put his own clothes on him, and chained him again . . . to a big staple drove into the bottom log, and chained his hands, too, and both legs.[21]

The Gethsemane scene occurs at dawn on the banks of the Mississippi:

> then some men in a skiff come by, and as good luck would have it, the nigger was setting by the pallet with his head propped on his knees, sound asleep; so I motioned them in, quiet, and they slipped

up on him and grabbed him and tied him before he knowed what he
was about, and we never had no trouble . . . and the nigger never
made the least row nor said a word, from the start.[22]

To this Calvary Jim has to carry his own cross – rolling the
grindstone, hacking the hole with his pick, blessing his persecutors:

'You got any spiders in here, Jim?'
    'No, sah, thanks to goodness I hain't, Mars Tom.'
    'All right, we'll get you some.'
    'But bless you, honey, I doan' *want* none. I's afeard un um. I jis'
    's soon have rattlesnakes aroun'.'[23]

Until by sacrificing himself for his persecutor's sake Jim at last
achieves resurrection.

That resurrection, unlike Huck's, is a wholly contrived affair; and
the final horror is that the victim himself is cast as literary critic. It is
Jim's task, as he is well aware, to appreciate the whole fiasco as an
aesthetic production. 'It 'uz planned beautiful', he duly pronounces,
'en it 'uz *done* beautiful; en dey ain't *nobody* kin git up a plan dat's mo'
mixed-up en splendid den what dat one wuz' (215/340). Jim simply
had no choice. Even now he had to prove himself the Grateful Nigger,
cajoling the boys, flattering the boys, allowing they 'was white folks
and knowed better than him' (196/309). A White, he knew, must
always take the initiative. A White accepts a nigger's gratitude, that is,
as his due. Just as Huck had accepted Jim's gratitude as his due.[24]
That was the mark of the South's fatal, self-indulgent delusion.[25]

Jim was trapped. Even now he had to live with these Southerners.
Twain should surely be given some credit for drawing this close to
black strategies of survival. In the words of one recent study: 'the Jim
who emerges from our reading is nobody's simple companion. He is a
crafty, calculating student of human behavior, a confidence man with
an ability to deceive that equals Huck's or Tom's.'[26] Jim was trapped
from without; Twain remained trapped within, going round and
round in tortuous circles. For *Adventures of Huckleberry Finn* was
never intended, of course, as a fugitive-slave narrative. If anything, it
developed into a wide-ranging survey of this very trap closing in from
St Petersburg to Bricksville, Bricksville to Pikesville. The violent
South gives way to the sentimental South of the Wilks girls and their
niggers; the sentimental South to the paranoiac South of the Pikesville

vigilantes. But the drama comes to rest at the ambiguous heart of Huck's confusion: the smug South of the Phelps plantation, where 'Southern hospitality' for Whites is counterbalanced by kind looks and prayers for the Blacks. The doctor is 'kind' as old Silas is 'mighty nice' and both the Phelpses are 'kind as they could be' and 'where the people's all so kind and good'. For precisely here, on that 'little one-horse cotton plantation' (evoking memories of his uncle John Quarles's farm), the unresolved crux of Twain's own Southern heritage and education was painstakingly reached.

NOTES

1   Twain owned a copy of Charles Ball, *Slavery in the United States: A Narrative of the Life and Adventures of Charles Ball, A Black Man, Who Lived Forty Years In Maryland, South Carolina and Georgia, as a Slave* (1837, republished 1859), which he used as a source for *A Connecticut Yankee in King Arthur's Court*.

2   Increasingly stringent laws had been passed since 1835, and by 1847 free Negroes and mulattos were prohibited from entering Missouri under any conditions. To know the precise date between 1835 and 1845, in which the novel is so casually set, would be of crucial importance in determining Jim's legal position.

3   See Chadwick Hansen, 'The character of Jim and the ending of *Huckleberry Finn*', *Massachusetts Review*, vol. 5 (Autumn 1963), p. 55.

4   cf. his first entrance, *en route* to the town pump: 'Jim came skipping out at the gate with a tin pail, and singing "Buffalo Gals".' Though 'the pump was only a hundred and fifty yards off, Jim never got back with a bucket of water under an hour – and even then somebody generally had to go after him' (*Tom Sawyer*, ch. 2).

5   All adjectives and phrases in inverted commas are drawn from George R. Lamplugh's study of the *Atlantic Monthly, Harper's Monthly, Scribner's Monthly/The Century* and *Scribner's Magazine* in the closing decades of the nineteenth century: 'The image of the Negro in popular magazine fiction, 1875–1900', *Journal of Negro History*, vol. 57 (April 1972), pp. 177–89.

6   Daniel G. Hoffman has traced the European origins of all Jim's beliefs. Only his divination with the hairball from the stomach of an ox appears to be of voodoo origin. See 'Jim's magic: black or white?', *American Literature*, vol. 32 (March 1960), pp. 47–54.

7   Miss Watson was offered $800 to sell him down to New Orleans, which was close to the prime rate of $1,000 for a strong working male in his twenties; cf. the doctor: 'I tell you, gentlemen, a nigger like that is worth a thousand dollars – and kind treatment, too' (223/353).

8   Unlike Indians, who turn the bottom of their feet towards the blaze.

9   *Huckleberry Finn*, ch. 9, pp. 44–5/61. At this key moment Huck-as-narrator is as duplicitous as Jim. He withholds from the reader the same information withheld from him, in the narrative past, by Jim. The text is poker-faced. Twain deliberately rubs it in: 'After breakfast I wanted to talk about the dead man and guess out how he come to be killed, but Jim didn't want to . . .' (45/63). This enigma (as Roland Barthes would call it) remains dormant. The text is nowhere engaged in unravelling it. Even on the final page it is only partly resolved. See above, Ch. 9, n. 24.

10 James M. Cox, 'Remarks on the sad initiation of Huckleberry Finn', *Sewanee*

Review, vol 62 (Summer 1954), pp. 389–405.

11 Daniel G. Hoffman, 'Black magic – and white – in *Huckleberry Finn*', in his *Form and Fable in American Fiction* (New York: Oxford University Press, 1961), ch. 15, p. 333.

12 Louis D. Rubin, Jr, *The Teller in the Tale* (Seattle, Wash.: University of Washington Press, 1967), ch. 3, p. 65.

13 Spencer Brown, '*Huckleberry Finn* for our time', *Michigan Quarterly Review*, vol. 6 (Winter 1967), p. 45.

14 Opening of the Raftsmen's Passage, now *Life on the Mississippi*, ch. 3.

15 *Huckleberry Finn*, ch. 8, p. 40/53.

16 ibid., ch. 15, p. 70/103.

17 Cash, *The Mind of the South*, bk 1, ch. 3, sect. 9.

18 *Huckleberry Finn*, ch. 16, p. 74/125.

19 For a subtly different reading, see Neil Schmitz, 'The paradox of liberation in *Huckleberry Finn*', *Texas Studies in Literature and Language*, vol. 13 (Spring 1971), p. 133.

20 cf. also 'Acts Seventeen' (199/316), which Uncle Silas was studying before breakfast. It opens in the Thessalonika synagogue: 'alleging that Christ must needs have suffered, and risen again from the dead; and this Jesus, whom I preach unto you, is Christ' (Acts 17:3). It closes with Paul's sermon on the Areopagus: God 'hath made of one blood all nations of men for to dwell on all the face of the earth, and hath determined . . . the bounds of their habitation' (Acts, 17:26).

21 *Huckleberry Finn*, ch. 42, p. 223/352; cf. the spiritual: 'An' he never said a mumbalin' word'.

22 ibid., ch. 42, pp. 223–4/353–4.

23 ibid., ch. 38, pp. 205/324.

24 For Huck's involuntary transposition of memory, see above, Ch. 7, p. 89.

25 As Tom puts it: 'Every animal is grateful for kindness and petting, and they wouldn't *think* of hurting a person that pets them. Any book will tell you that' (205/325).

26 Thomas Weaver and Merline A. Williams, 'Mark Twain's Jim: identity as an index to cultural attitudes', *American Literary Realism*, vol. 13 (Spring 1980), pp. 19–30.

Part Four

CHAPTER 15

Liberrians and Crickits

'. . . and we just set there and "thunk", as Jim calls it.'
                                    Tom Sawyer Abroad, ch. 4

From *Huckleberry Finn* Twain dived straight into 'Huck Finn & Tom
Sawyer among the Indians', taking his comic trio along the Oregon
Trail from the Missouri across Nebraska to the Platte River and along
the Platte into Sioux Territory.[1] But he soon ran into trouble. He was
relying too heavily on secondary sources; and the rescue mission of an
angelic girl (on the model of Sophia Grangerford or Mary Jane Wilks)
from Indian captivity harped too insistently on the theme of rape.[2]
After nine chapters Twain abandoned the project. But he still could
not let go of Huck, Tom and Jim. For the rest of his life he turned
them over and over. This was partly for commercial reasons: could
Tom Sawyer be transferred to the stage? could it go on Broadway?[3]
After his bankruptcy, when he had to draw on every scrap of literary
capital, he dashed off *Tom Sawyer Abroad* (1894) and *Tom Sawyer
Detective* (1896). Like an epic bard he wanted to sing more and more
'lays' of his great matter. But what matter? He continued rumbling
this around in his head without finding a solution. There was some
intolerable secret in *Huckleberry Finn*, but Twain was no longer able
to sustain it or develop it.[4]

No wonder, then, that the critics have had trouble with *Huckleberry
Finn*. The debate, now over half a century old, shows no sign of
abating. It has centred, almost exclusively, around the last ten
chapters devoted to the rescue of Jim. Hemingway, in 1935, called it
'just cheating'. Bernard DeVoto, in 1942, shook his head over it,
groaning: 'in the whole reach of the English novel there is no more
abrupt or chilling descent'.[5] Contemporary critics, too, have dismissed
Tom's 'evasion' as just that: an evasion, 'a failure of nerve' (Leo
Marx), a 'travesty' (Neil Schmitz). The victims of Twain's reckless-
ness, or tiredness, or sheer pigheadedness (so the argument runs) were

Huck and Jim. Henry Nash Smith, echoing Leo Marx, gave the
majority verdict: that in the last ten chapters Huck was inferior to the
boy he had been during the voyage down the Mississippi; and that
Jim, too, became stunted, a mere caricature of himself.[6] In Walter
Blair's words: 'Jim, whom the reader and Huck have come to love and
admire, becomes a victim of meaningless torture, a cartoon. Huck,
who has fought against codes of civilization, follows one of the silliest
of them.'[7]

These so-called 'crimes against characterization' (Blair) revealed
another area of controversy. What exactly was the unblemished
character of Huck and Jim? Especially Jim. For everyone loved Huck
and, like the Widow, seemed to know exactly what was good for him.
But the issue centred squarely on the depiction of Jim. I have already
quoted Ralph Ellison and noted the vociferous and complex reaction
to Jim by black readers in recent years.[8] Thadious M. Davis sums it
up in her foreword to the *Mark Twain Journal*'s special number by
black writers on *Huckleberry Finn*: 'Huck and Twain have not told
Jim's story so that its true relevancy to Huck's own is evident. The
tragedy is that perhaps it could not have been – not in the 1840s or
50s by a Huckleberry and not in the 1880s by a Mr Mark Twain.'[9]
But, if black critics have increasingly distanced themselves from
Jim, white critics have always been fascinated by him. To them he
seemed something of a potent and primitive archetype. Huck and Jim,
Roger B. Salomon wrote,

> are related to the demigods of the river, to the barbarous
> primitivism of the Negro, and beyond that to the archetypal
> primitives of the Golden Age, instinctively good, uncorrupted by
> reason, living close to nature and more influenced by its portents
> than by the conventions of civilization.[10]

James Cox described Jim as 'the conscience of the novel, the spiritual
yardstick by which all men are measured . . . [the] great residue of
primitive, fertile force'.[11] For Walter Blair, Jim's 'soaring improvis-
ations prove his mastery of supernatural lore'.[12] Gladys Bellamy
conducts a positively Lawrentian love-affair, admiring Jim's 'manly
qualities' and the 'dark knowledge that lies in his blood and his nerve
ends'.[13]

The most intense development of this controversy was between
those who attempted a structural defence and those who charged back

with a moral counter-offensive. By now there is also a strong line of moral counter-counter-offensives to head off Bernard DeVoto, Leo Marx, Walter Blair – all the founding fathers of the feud:

> 'But it's kind of slow, and takes a long time.'
> 'Has this one been going on long, Buck?'
> 'Well I should *reckon*! it started thirty years ago, or som'ers along there. There was trouble 'bout something . . .'[14]

The trouble started between thirty and forty years ago when two of the most celebrated critics of their day supplied introductions to *Huckleberry Finn*. Lionel Trilling wrote:

> In form and style *Huckleberry Finn* is an almost perfect work. Only one mistake has ever been charged against it, that it concludes with Tom Sawyer's elaborate, too elaborate, game of Jim's escape. Certainly this episode is too long – in the original draft it was much longer – and certainly it is a falling-off, as almost anything would have to be, from the incidents of the river. Yet it has a certain formal aptness – like, say, that of the Turkish initiation which brings Molière's *Le Bourgeois Gentilhomme* to its close. It is a rather mechanical development of an idea, and yet some device is needed to permit Huck to return to his anonymity, to give up the role of hero, to fall into the background which he prefers, for he is modest in all things and could not well endure the attention and glamour which attend a hero at a book's end. For this purpose nothing could serve better than the mind of Tom Sawyer with its literary furnishings, its conscious romantic desire for experience and the hero's part, and its ingenious schematization of life to achieve that aim.[15]

T. S. Eliot, two years later, seconded Trilling:

> Readers sometimes deplore the fact that the story descends to the level of *Tom Sawyer* from the moment that Tom himself re-appears . . . But it is right that the mood of the end of the book should bring us back to that of the beginning. Or, if this was not the right ending for the book, what ending would have been right?

Then, dandling his own question:

For Huckleberry Finn, neither a tragic nor a happy ending would be suitable. No worldly success or social satisfaction, no domestic consummation would be worthy of him; a tragic end also would reduce him to the level of those whom we pity. Huck Finn must come from nowhere and be bound for nowhere . . . He has no beginning and no end. Hence, he can only disappear; and his disappearance can only be accomplished by bringing forward another performer to obscure the disappearance in a cloud of whimsicalities.[16]

Henry Nash Smith, for many years umpire of the great feud, accepted Eliot's 'neither a tragic/nor a happy' dilemma, arguing that Tom's re-entry enabled Twain to restate his primary concerns in another key:

The perplexing final sequence on the Phelps plantation is best regarded as a maneuver by which Mark Twain beats his way back from incipient tragedy to the comic resolution called for by the original conception of the story.[17]

But this formula did nothing, retrospectively, to blunt the counter-attack launched by Leo Marx. 'Structure', he insisted in 'Mr Eliot, Mr Trilling, and *Huckleberry Finn*', 'after all, is only one element – indeed, one of the more mechanical elements – of unity':

The return, in the end, to the mood of the beginning therefore means defeat – Huck's defeat; to return to that mood *joyously* is to portray defeat in the guise of victory.[18]

The premises of Marx's argument can be summarized as: (1) Huck, from the moment they run, is identified with Jim's flight; (2) this bond between Huck and Jim establishes the ideal society of the raft; (3) that such an ideal friendship is the prerequisite of an ideal society; (4) that this ideal (raft) society is diametrically opposed to the greed and complacency of real (shore) society from which they flee. QED: their quest in a real world can never succeed. 'Should Clemens have made Huck a tragic hero?' Marx asks in conclusion:

Both Mr Eliot and Mr Trilling argue that that would have been a mistake, and they are very probably correct. But between the ending as we have it and tragedy in the fullest sense, there was vast room for invention. Clemens might have contrived an action which left Jim's fate as much in doubt as Huck's. Such an ending would have allowed us to assume that the principals were defeated but alive, and the quest unsuccessful but not abandoned.

The original structuralists never rebutted these charges, though their case has recently been reformulated by George C. Carrington, Jr, in *The Dramatic Unity of 'Huckleberry Finn'*. On his reading the 'evasion' chapters become the logical resolution of a submerged drama (of physical and verbal gestures) by which Huck absorbed his experiences to become a writer. This French approach has not caught on.

But Marx did. His reading had a long and successful run, though challenged (only one year later) by James M. Cox. Cox tried to outflank Marx by shifting the battle to new ground. In 'Remarks on the sad initiation of Huckleberry Finn' he argued that the major theme of the novel – far from a quest – is adolescent growth through rituals of death and rebirth which become fully apparent *only* in the finale. Tom's domination in the final chapters is 'not only vital, but inevitable; it proves that Huck must go west because he knows that to be Huck Finn is to be outcast beyond paling fences'.[19] Twelve years later, in *Mark Twain: The Fate of Humor*, Cox further refined this approach. The true rebellion of *Huckleberry Finn* is an 'attack upon the conscience':

> The conscience, after all is said and done, is the real tyrant in the book. It is the relentless force which pursues Huckleberry Finn; it is the tyrant from which he seeks freedom. And it is not only the social conscience which threatens Huck, but *any* conscience. The social conscience, represented in the book by the slaveholding society of the Old South, is easily seen and exposed.

Marx's thesis, he charged, inverted the true dynamics of the book. Far from being a quest, Huck's journey is a flight:

> A quest is a positive journey, implying an effort, a struggle to reach a goal. But Huck is escaping. His journey is primarily a negation, a flight *from* tyranny, not a flight toward freedom.

Marx according to Cox was far too moral, too '*political*', for a boy who is neither political, not particularly moral even. Huck is governed by the pleasure principle. His whole flight down-river was an evasion – an evasion of conscience. For someone who likes to be comfortable, 'the conscience is *uncomfortable*':

> Indeed, comfort and satisfaction are the value terms in *Huckleberry Finn*. Freedom for Huck is not realized in terms of political liberty but in terms of pleasure . . . In almost every instance Huck projects the good life in terms of ease, satisfaction, comfort. A satirist would see it in terms of justice; a moralist would have it as a place of righteousness. But a humorist envisions it as a place of good feeling, where no pain or discomfort can enter.[20]

Richard Poirier came to Marx's rescue by building on his position refining it and extending it. Far from slavery being the central concern of the novel, he argued, for great stretches it was of no concern at all. From chapters 17 to 30 Jim is almost wholly ignored. What is at stake here is not black slavery but 'a more general enslavement – of feeling and intelligence within inadequate and restrictedly artificial modes of expression'. For all of society, as conceived here, is artificial, incapable of accommodating individual freedom. So Marx was right; the 'quest' or 'flight' (whatever you choose to call it) cannot succeed because society

> provides no opportunity, no language, for the transformation of individual consciousness into social drama. The provision is lacking because Mark Twain cannot imagine a society that offers alternatives to artificiality or that has in it, like Joyce's Dublin, evidences of an official culture that has historical dignity and value.[21]

For Poirier, then, the collapse began far, far earlier than the final 'evasion'. The culmination of Huck's imaginative apprenticeship – of his moral growth and detachment from Tom – is in chapters 15 and 16: the episode in the fog, followed by the smallpox hoax. Those are the crucial chapters. After that it is downhill all the way. The novel goes to 'pieces'.

Marx's essay, it becomes clear, occupies a classic status in the whole debate. His passionate moral defence of four-fifths of *Huckleberry Finn* against the formalist neutrality of Trilling and Eliot continues to draw flak, though both besiegers and defenders are falling back on more

and more sophisticated positions. The wiliest comic interlude was
provided by John Seelye, who literally accepted Marx's challenge that
'between the ending as we have it and tragedy in the fullest sense,
there was vast room for invention'. In 1970 he published *The True
Adventures of Huckleberry Finn* – Huck's own, final, summative
version:

> Well, it was kinder sad, in a way, with everything scattered about
> and people saying it was a good book they guessed, but it had
> terrible weaknesses, and nobody really able to enjoy it any more
> except children. So I thought to myself, if the book which Mr Mark
> Twain wrote warn't up to what these men wanted from a book, why
> not pick up the parts – the good ones – and put together one they
> *would* like? So I done it, the best I could anyways, only this time I
> told the story like it really happened, leaving in all the cuss words
> and the sex and the sadness . . .
>
> And I want you to understand that this is a different book from
> the one Mr Mark Twain wrote. It may look like *The Adventures of
> Huckleberry Finn* at first sight, but that don't mean a thing. Most of
> the parts was good ones, and I could use them. But Mark Twain's
> book is for children and such, whilst this one here is for crickits.
> And now that they've got *their* book, maybe they'll leave the other
> one alone.[22]

This was the decisive shift from Mark Twain (authorized version), as
it were, to Marx Twain (revised version). Except that Seelye opted for
the (probably incorrect) tragic ending.

What he does, in short, is to delete the more tedious-seeming,
wisecracking chapters (like the King Solomon debate in chapter 14).[23]
He inserts some sexual expletives and teenage innuendo; and restores
the wonderful 'Child of Calamity' passage that Twain had cast adrift
into *Life on the Mississippi*. But the twist of the whole performance lay
in the tail. This version, unlike Eliot's or Trilling's, is in no doubt
that Tom with his masquerades offers a futile anticlimax, a kind of
critical and moral and even spiritual surrender to the playboy code of
the chivalric imagination, undermining everything that the journey on
the raft had relentlessly exposed. So Twain's last twelve chapters are
cut entirely; and with them goes the description of the Phelps farm.
Since, in the Seelye version, Huck can naturally never enter the
Phelps world and become subject again to Tom, Tom, too, is excised.

What happened at the sawmill was this: the captured Jim escapes and all hell breaks loose with popping guns and dogs barking. Huck, out on the river in his canoe, sees Jim plunging wounded into the water 'when a crowd of men and dogs come busting out of the thicket, everybody yelling and howling at once, making powwow enough for a million. It was just like a bear-hunt, only Jim was the bear.'

The men shout to the white boy to 'Stop that nigger!'. And in a desperate, hypocritical manoeuvre Huck fumbles his oars – while Jim, loaded with chains, plunges on – incompetently loses one oar and hides the other so that his boat drifts round a point of land where he can wait for Jim. But when the trick succeeds and the guns are silenced;

> I couldn't see him nowheres, and my heart flopped up into my mouth. Next I stood up, bracing myself with the paddle I was a-shaking so, but it warn't no use. There was nothing on that whole broad river but me, and I knowed then there warn't no sense looking further for Jim, because he was somewhere deep down under, weighted by them goddamn heavy chains.

It is a fine ending and a fine performance. But it is not Mark Twain. This twentieth-century Huck ends on the river as he began on the river, lonesome and alone. Between grey water and grey sky hovers Huck on the wide, wide, wandering Mississippi. The adventure is over; life's journey barely begun. Of course he cannot turn back to the Widow and Tom and the childhood oasis of St Petersburg:

> Money warn't no problem, because I still had that yaller boy left in my pocket, and the canoe was worth ten dollars any day. I thought maybe I would go on down to Orleans and ship as a cabin boy on one of the big riverboats.[24]

As the Mississippi flows into the delta and so into the sea, Seelye has carried the moment of adolescence forward to adult vision. But Twain was eternally locked in his childhood pastoral. He could break through momentarily, but he could not escape. His great book is both linear and circular. Twain's ending *is* distressing. But there can be no revision. Huck's frustration is our frustration. His frustrated search for freedom becomes our frustrated search. He could never escape society; for the forces of the shore were constantly invading his raft, as

the play world of Tom (which is 'civilization') invades the ending.
Between Pap and Aunt Sally there was no 'Territory ahead'.

But, even worse, the invading forces were not social merely; they
were instinctive. 'Conscience', Twain wrote in his notebook, is
'mortal, not physical':

> It is merely a *thing*; the creature of *training*; it is whatever one's
> mother and Bible and comrades and laws and systems of
> government and habitat and heredities have made it . . . Inborn
> nature is Character, by itself in the brutes – the tiger, the dove, the
> fox, etc. Inborn nature *and* the modifying Conscience, working
> together make Character in man.

Or, again, brooding on slavery:

> It shows that that strange thing, the conscience – that unerring
> monitor – can be trained to approve any wild thing you *want* it to
> approve if you begin its education early & stick to it.

'Nature' might stage the odd insurrection against the occupation, but
those were rare, exceptional events. As Twain was to note, almost
twenty years later, of chapter 16 of *Huckleberry Finn*:

> Next, I should exploit the proposition that in a crucial moral
> emergency a sound heart is a safer guide than an ill-trained
> conscience. I sh'd support this doctrine with a chapter from a book
> of mine where a sound heart & a deformed conscience come into
> collision & conscience suffers defeat. Two persons figure in this
> chapter: Jim, a middle-aged slave, and Huck Finn, a boy of 14 . . .
> bosom friends, drawn together by a community of misfortune.[25]

It is doubtful whether Twain believed that the conscience could ever
be sound and the heart deformed. The terms simply justified
themselves. He brooded over them in his notebooks, just as he
brooded over his 'Ignorance, intolerance, egotism, self-assertion,
opaque perception, dense and pitiful chuckleheadedness – and an
almost pathetic unconsciousness of it all' as a Southerner of 19 or 20.[26]

Broadly speaking, conscience, then, is the 'creature' of social
indoctrination. But what of the heart? What of 'inborn nature'? That
for Twain remained a mystery, an anarchic and attractively disruptive

force, like laughter itself. It is the ultimate spiritual joke, as expressed in Pascal's great *pensée*: 'Le coeur a ses raisons que la raison ne connaît point.'[27] It is Huck's most intimate truth and secret paradox. Yet it applies equally to Twain. Though he can recognize Jim's humanity, he has no idea what to do with him. Though he is drawn to such bosom friendships as Huck's and Jim's, he has no idea how to develop them. To place an adult 'middle-aged' Black at the *centre* of his book's consciousness was simply beyond him, as it was beyond Melville to develop Queequeg as the hero of *Moby-Dick*.

For young Melville and young Clemens had much in common. Both lost their fathers while still children. Both faced adolescence in a fatherless world. Both Huck and Ishmael are outcasts, runaways, 'orphans'. Both Huck and Ishmael are trapped in cycles of death and destruction, 'involuntarily pausing' (in Ishmael's words) 'before coffin warehouses, and bringing up the rear of every funeral'.[28] Both Huck and Ishmael cross a suicidal verge in their opening chapters (or paragraphs) as if turning to ghosts who had outlived their social selves. Both opt for death by water. Both desert the shore – and the landed values of the shore – for dream-like transits by water. For both a dark-skinned companion (Polynesian or Afro-American) seems mysteriously essential. But whereas Huck is merely enrolled in the king and duke's shenanigans, Ishmael is swept off by the imperious Captain Ahab. Melville took on every conceivable intellectual challenge; Twain just one – the confrontations of the conscience and the heart.

Antigone, in this peculiar sense, in Huck's moral archetype. She, too, struggled with her conscience. She, too, had to choose between two concepts of duty: one owed to the State (in public relations); the other to an individual. The treatment by Sophocles, of course, was tragic. Twain coolly transposed the theme to a comic mode. That, in itself, was bravado. No wonder he ran into trouble. No wonder the buzz of critical debate cannot be stifled. For comedy is traditionally resolved by a recommitment to communal values, a realignment with society. But not in *Huckleberry Finn*. In the conflict between public man (as a subject of state) and private man, Twain – like Sophocles and Hegel before him – opted for the private man. He came to recognize that the highest form of freedom was not dependent on communal sanctions, but (as Antigone and Huck both demonstrate) on each man's and woman's consciousness of what is right.[29]

NOTES

1 So Huck does not 'light out for the Territory ahead of the rest' (see above, Ch. 6, n. 19). But neither is this the 'Indian Territory', meaning the future Territory of Oklahoma (1889), which Twain seems to have had in mind at the end of *Huckleberry Finn*. See Roy Harvey Pearce, '"The End. Yours Truly, Huck Finn": postscript', *Modern Language Quarterly*, vol. 24 (September 1963), pp. 253–6.

2 Her very name 'Peggy' incorporates the 'pegs' with which the Sioux prepared for a tribal gang-bang; cf. Richard Irving Dodge: 'The rule is this. When a woman is captured by a party she belongs equally to each and all . . . If she resists at all her clothing is torn off from her person, four pegs are driven into the ground, and her arms and legs, stretched to the utmost, are tied fast to them by thongs. Here, with the howling band dancing and singing around her, she is subjected to violation after violation, outrage after outrage, to every abuse and indignity, until not unfrequently death releases her from suffering' (*The Plains of the Great West and Their Inhabitants*, New York, 1877).

3 *Tom Sawyer: A Play in Four Acts* (1875/1884). Twain even considered a kind of pantomime version with an actress playing the part of Tom and/or Huck. A note among the Mark Twain Papers reads: '*Jim* can be burlesqued also – a negro boy 6 feet high.'

4 Between 1897 and 1900 Twain sketched the complex machinations of 'Tom Sawyer's Conspiracy'. From 1900 there survives the fragmentary 'Tom Sawyer's Gang plans a Naval Battle', with Tom as Lord Nelson dying on the Mississippi, murmuring 'Kiss me, Hardy'. The idea of Huck in blackface (to substitute for Jim, who is again threatened with slavery) had long haunted him. A few years before his death Twain jotted down: 'Steal skiff. Turning Huck black & sell him.' See Walter Blair (ed.), *Mark Twain's Hannibal, Huck & Tom* (Berkeley, Calif.: University of California Press, 1969), pp. 145–324.

5 Bernard DeVoto, *Mark Twain at Work* (Cambridge, Mass.: Harvard University Press, 1942), p. 92.

6 Henry Nash Smith, introduction to *Adventures of Huckleberry Finn* (Boston, Mass.: Houghton Mifflin, 1958), p. 92.

7 Walter Blair, *Mark Twain & 'Huck Finn'* (Berkeley, Calif.: University of California Press, 1960), p. 350.

8 See above, Ch. 13, n. 16.

9 Thadious M. Davis, *Mark Twain Journal*, vol. 22 (Fall 1984), p. 3.

10 Roger B. Salomon, *Twain and the Image of History* (New Haven, Conn.: Yale University Press, 1961), p. 165.

11 James M. Cox, 'Remarks on the sad initiation of Huckleberry Finn' *Sewanee Review*, vol. 62 (Summer 1954), p. 404.

12 Blair, *Mark Twain & 'Huck Finn'*, p. 123.

13 Gladys Carmen Bellamy, *Mark Twain as a Literary Artist* (Norman, Okla: University of Oklahoma Press, 1950), pp. 340 and 346.

14 *Huckleberry Finn*, ch. 18, p. 89/146.

15 Lionel Trilling, introduction to *The Adventures of Huckleberry Finn* (New York: Holt, Rinehart & Winston, 1948), p. xv.

16 T. S. Eliot, introduction to *The Adventures of Huckleberry Finn* (London: Cresset Press, 1950), pp. xv–xvi.

17 Henry Nash Smith, *Mark Twain: The Development of a Writer* (Cambridge, Mass.: Belknap Press of Harvard University Press, 1962), p. 114.

18 Leo Marx, 'Mr Eliot, Mr Trilling, and *Huckleberry Finn*', *American Scholar*, vol. 22 (Autumn 1953), p. 434.

19 Cox, 'Remarks on the sad initiation of Huckleberry Finn', p. 401.

20   Cox, *Mark Twain: The Fate of Humor* (Princeton, NJ: Princeton University Press, 1966), ch. 7, pp. 172–3, 176 and 178. See above, Ch. 8, n. 13.

21   Richard Poirier, *A World Elsewhere: The Place of Style in American Literature* (New York: Oxford University Press, 1966), pp. 193 and 199.

22   John Seelye, *The True Adventures of Huckleberry Finn* (Evanston, Ill.: Northwestern University Press, 1970), p. xii. The whole introduction is a brilliant burlesque version, in Huck's throwaway style, of the debate outlined here.

23   Thereby losing a number of subtle echoes, since Jim's paternal indignation is exercised over a case that closely resembles Huck's.

24   Seelye, *The True Adventures of Huckleberry Finn*, ch. 31, 'What happened at the saw mill', pp. 327–8 and 333; and ch. 32, 'Nothing more to write', p. 338.

25   Notebook 35, TS p. 35 (1895).

26   *Mark Twain's Letters*, ed. Albert Bigelow Paine, Vol. 1 (New York/London: Harper & Brothers, 1917), 1 November 1876, p. 289.

27   Pascal, *Pensées*, iv, 277.

28   Melville, *Moby-Dick*, ch. 1.

29   See George Steiner, *Antigones* (Oxford: Oxford University Press, 1984). It is Steiner who posits Hegel's *Phenomenology of the Spirit* (1807) as making the decisive shift in allegiance from the community, as supreme moral arbiter, to the individual. Despite his vast reach of reading, though, Steiner does not consider the case of *Huckleberry Finn*.

GLOSSARY

Henry James, in his preface to *What Maisie Knew*, wrote: 'Small children have many more perceptions than they have terms to translate them.' Huck is no longer a child, so this only partly applies to him. Some of his slang is vividly precise; but other terms scatter a kind of jovial grapeshot of imprecision. Since many of these colloquialisms are now unfamiliar, I append a short selective glossary:

Ash-hopper	Cask containing lye for making soap
'I know him by de back'	To the backbone, thoroughly
To give someone 'down the banks'	A scolding, a talking-to
Beats, or Dead-beats	Loafers, cheats
Break-down	Rapid shuffle dance (Negro style)
To have the bulge on	Have the advantage of (mining slang)
Bullyrag	Abuse, worry
Case-knives	Large kitchen-knives
Chimbly-guy	Wire to brace chimney
Corn-dodger	Hard cornmeal cake
Crawfish	Crawl backwards
Doggery	Saloon, grog-shop
Dog-leg	Cheap chewing tobacco
Fantods	Shakes, willies
Flapdoodle	Hypocrisy
Fox-fire	Phosphorescent light from decaying wood
Galluses	Braces (British); suspenders (American)
Galoot	Uncouth fellow
To give someone 'hark from the tomb'	Reprimand: cf. 'Hark! from the tombs a doleful sound, My ears attend the cry . . .' (Isaac Watts, 'A Funeral Thought')
Hive	Capture, secure
Hunch	Nudge

Pat juba	Lively tap dance, ringed by clapping and slapping hands
Knocked galley-west	Knocked sideways
Lightning-bug	Firefly
Mosey along	Move along
Mullet-headed	Trusting, stupid
'How in the nation'; 'I'm nation sorry'	Damnation
Nigger-head	Cheap black plug tobacco
Ornery	Mean
Pard	Partner
Puncheon floor	Rough log floor, chipped flat with an adze
'I'll make him pungle'	(Spanish *póngale*: 'out with it'), pay up, cough up
Round-about	Short jacket
Saddle-bags (vb)	Double round
Sand	Grit, guts
Scrouge	To crowd
'Don't amount to shucks'	Literally, the husk of an ear of corn
Smouch	Steal
Sockdolager	Knock-out blow
Spondulicks	Cash
Sqush	Collapse
Staving	Smashing
Sumpter mule	Pack-mule
To swap knives	To change tactics
Wood-rank	Pile of wood (usually half a cord)
Yallerboys	Gold coins

BIBLIOGRAPHY

The 'Definitive Edition' of *The Writings of Mark Twain* in 37 volumes (New York: Harper & Brothers, 1929) is now being overtaken by two majestic, but still uncompleted, series from the University of California Press. The first consists of scholarly editions of Mark Twain's notebooks, journals and other unpublished or abortive manuscripts deposited among the Mark Twain Papers at the Bancroft Library of the University of California, Berkeley. (The more relevant volumes are listed below.) The second consists of meticulously established texts of all previously published writings compiled by the Iowa Center for Textual Studies as *The Works of Mark Twain*. A popular standard edition of these texts has also been launched by the University of California Press under the imprint of 'The Mark Twain Library'.

EDITIONS

Adventures of Huckleberry Finn (Tom Sawyer's Comrade). By Mark Twain. A Facsimile of the Manuscript, introduced by Louis J. Budd, 2 vols (Detroit, Mich.: Gale Research, 1983).

Adventures of Huckleberry Finn, ed. Henry Nash Smith (Boston, Mass.: Houghton Mifflin, 1958).

Adventures of Huckleberry Finn, ed. Sculley Bradley, Richmond Croom Beatty, E. Hudson Long and Thomas Cooley, Norton Critical Edition, (New York: W. W. Norton, 1961; 2nd edn 1977).

Adventures of Huckleberry Finn, ed. Leo Marx (Indianapolis, Ind./New York: Bobbs-Merrill, 1967).

Adventures of Huckleberry Finn (The Mark Twain Library), eds Walter Blair and Victor Fischer (Berkeley, Calif.: University of California Press, 1985).

The Annotated Huckleberry Finn, ed. Michael Patrick Hearn (New York: Clarkson N. Potter, 1982).

The Autobiography of Mark Twain, ed. Charles Neider (New York: Harper & Row, 1959).

Mark Twain's Notebook, ed. Albert Bigelow Paine (New York/London: Harper & Brothers, 1935).

Mark Twain's Notebooks and Journals, Vol. 1 (*1855–1873*), ed. Frederick Anderson, Michael B. Frank and Kenneth M. Sanderson; Vol. 2 (*1877–1883*), ed. Frederick Anderson, Lin Salamo and Bernard L. Stein; Vol. 3 (*1883–1891*), ed. Robert Pack Browning, Michael B. Frank and Lin Salamo (Berkeley, Calif.: University of California Press, 1975–9).

Mark Twain's Letters, ed. Albert Bigelow Paine, 2 vols (New York/London: Harper & Brothers, 1917, 1935).

The Mark Twain–Howells Letters, ed. Henry Nash Smith, William M. Gibson and Frederick Anderson, 2 vols (Cambridge, Mass.: Harvard University Press, 1960).

Selected Mark Twain–Howells Letters: 1872–1910, ed. Frederick Anderson,

William M. Gibson and Henry Nash Smith (Cambridge, Mass.: Harvard University Press, 1967).

The Selected Letters of Mark Twain, ed. Charles Neider (New York: Harper & Row, 1982).

Mark Twain's Letters to His Publishers, ed. Hamlin Hill (Berkeley, Calif.: University of California Press, 1967).

Mark Twain's Letters to Will Bowen, ed. Theodore Hornberger (Austin, Tex.: University of Texas Press, 1941).

Letters of Richard Watson Gilder, ed. Rosamund Gilder (Boston, Mass.: Houghton Mifflin, 1916).

Mark Twain, Business Man, ed. Samuel Charles Webster (Boston, Mass.: Little, Brown, 1946).

COLLECTIONS

Anderson, Frederick (ed.), *Mark Twain: The Critical Heritage* (London: Routledge & Kegan Paul, 1971).

Blair, Walter (ed.), *Mark Twain's Hannibal, Huck & Tom* (Berkeley, Calif.: University of California Press, 1969).

Budd, Louis J. (ed.), *Critical Essays on Mark Twain, 1867–1910* (Boston, Mass.: G. K. Hall, 1982).

Budd, Louis J. (ed.), *Critical Essays on Mark Twain, 1910–1980* (Boston, Mass.: G. K. Hall, 1983).

Budd, Louis J. (ed.), *New Essays on Adventures of Huckleberry Finn* (Cambridge: Cambridge University Press, 1985).

Cohen, Hennig, and Dillingham, William B. (eds), *Humor of the Old Southwest* (Athens, Ga: University of Georgia Press, 1975).

Davis, Thadious M. (ed.), 'Black writers on *Adventures of Huckleberry Finn* one hundred years later', *Mark Twain Journal*, vol. 22, (Fall 1984).

Gerber, John C. (ed.), *Studies in 'Huckleberry Finn'* (Columbus, Ohio: Charles E. Merrill, 1971).

Hill, Hamlin, and Blair, Walter (eds), *The Art of 'Huckleberry Finn'* (San Francisco, Calif.: Chandler, 1962; 2nd edn 1969).

Inge, M. Thomas (ed.), *The Frontier Humorists: Critical Views* (Hamden, Conn.: Archon, 1975).

Inge, M. Thomas (ed.), *Huck Finn among the Critics: A Centennial Selection, 1884–1984* (Washington, DC: United States Information Agency, 1984).

'Mark Twain special number: a symposium on *Huckleberry Finn*', *Modern Fiction Studies*, vol. 14 (1968).

Marks, Barry A. (ed.), *Mark Twain's Huckleberry Finn* (Boston, Mass.: D. C. Heath, 1959).

Sattelmeyer, Robert, and Crowley, J. Donald (eds), *One Hundred Years of Huckleberry Finn: The Boy, His Book, and American Culture* (Columbia, Mo.: University of Missouri Press, 1985).

Schmitter, Dean Morgan (ed.), *Mark Twain: A Collection of Critical Essays* (New York: McGraw-Hill, 1974).

Simpson, Claude M. (ed.), *Twentieth Century Interpretations of Adventures of*

Huckleberry Finn (Englewood Cliffs, NJ: Prentice-Hall, 1968).

Smith, Henry Nash (ed.), *Mark Twain: A Collection of Critical Essays* (Englewood Cliffs, NJ: Prentice-Hall, 1963).

BOOKS

Bellamy, Gladys Carmen, *Mark Twain as a Literary Artist* (Norman, Okla: University of Oklahoma Press, 1950).

Blair, Walter, *Mark Twain & 'Huck Finn'* (Berkeley, Calif.: University of California Press, 1960).

Blair, Walter, *Native American Humor* (New York: American Book Co., 1937).

Bridgman, Richard, *The Colloquial Style in America* (New York: Oxford University Press, 1966).

Brooks, Van Wyck, *The Ordeal of Mark Twain* (New York: Doubleday, 1920).

Budd, Louis J., *Mark Twain: Social Philosopher* (Bloomington, Ind.: Indiana University Press, 1962).

Budd, Louis J., *Our Mark Twain: The Making of His Public Personality* (Philadelphia, Pa: University of Pennsylvania Press, 1983).

Cardwell, Guy A., *Twins of Genius* (East Lansing, Mich.: Michigan State College Press, 1953).

Carrington, George C., Jr, *The Dramatic Unity of 'Huckleberry Finn'* (Columbus, Ohio: Ohio State University Press, 1976).

Cash, W.J., *The Mind of the South* (New York: Alfred A. Knopf, 1941).

Covici, Pascal, Jr, *Mark Twain's Humor: The Image of a World* (Dallas, Tex.: Southern Methodist University Press, 1962).

Cox, James M., *Mark Twain: The Fate of Humor* (Princeton, NJ: Princeton University Press, 1966).

DeVoto, Bernard, *Mark Twain at Work* (Cambridge, Mass.: Harvard University Press, 1942).

Egan, Michael, *Mark Twain's Huckleberry Finn: Race, Class and Society* (Brighton/London: Sussex University Press/Chatto & Windus, 1977).

Ensor, Allison, *Mark Twain and the Bible* (Lexington, Ky: University Press of Kentucky, 1969).

Fiedler, Leslie, *Love and Death in the American Novel* (New York: Criterion Books, 1960; London: Paladin, 1970).

Foner, Philip S., *Mark Twain: Social Critic* (New York: International Publishers, 1958).

Gibson, William M., *The Art of Mark Twain* (New York: Oxford University Press, 1976).

Gribben, Alan, *Mark Twain's Library: A Reconstruction*, 2 vols (Boston, Mass.: G. K. Hall, 1980).

Harris, Susan K., *Mark Twain's Escape from Time: A Study of Patterns and Images* (Columbia, Mo.: University of Missouri Press, 1982).

Hill, Hamlin, *Mark Twain: God's Fool* (New York: Harper & Row, 1973).

Hoffman, Daniel G., *Form and Fable in American Fiction* (New York; Oxford University Press, 1961).

Howells, William Dean, *My Mark Twain* (New York: Harper & Brothers, 1910).

Kaplan, Justin, *Mr Clemens and Mark Twain* (New York: Simon & Schuster, 1966).

Lynn, Kenneth S., *Mark Twain and Southwestern Humor* (Boston, Mass.: Little, Brown, 1959).

McKay, Janet Holmgren, *Narration and Discourse in American Realistic Fiction* (Philadelphia, Pa: University of Pennsylvania Press, 1982).

Marx, Leo, *The Machine in the Garden: Technology and the Pastoral Ideal in America* (New York: Oxford University Press, 1964).

Pettit, Arthur G., *Mark Twain and the South* (Lexington, Ky: University Press of Kentucky, 1974).

Poirier, Richard, *A World Elsewhere: The Place of Style in American Literature* (New York: Oxford University Press, 1966).

Raban, Jonathan, *Mark Twain: Huckleberry Finn* (London: Edward Arnold, 1968).

Rogers, Franklin R., *Mark Twain's Burlesque Patterns as Seen in the Novels and Narratives 1855–1885* (Dallas, Tex.: Southern Methodist University Press, 1960).

Rowe, John Carlos, *Through the Custom-House: Nineteenth-Century American Fiction and Modern Theory* (Baltimore, Md: Johns Hopkins University Press, 1982).

Rubin, Louis D., Jr (ed.), *The Comic Imagination in America* (New Brunswick, NJ: Rutgers University Press, 1973).

Rubin, Louis D., Jr, *The Teller in the Tale* (Seattle, Wash.: University of Washington Press, 1967).

Salomon, Roger B., *Twain and the Image of History* (New Haven, Conn.: Yale University Press, 1961).

Schmitz, Neil, *Of Huck and Alice: Humorous Writing in American Literature* (Minneapolis, Minn.: University of Minnesota Press, 1983).

Seelye, John, *The True Adventures of Huckleberry Finn* (Evanston, Ill.: Northwestern University Press, 1970).

Sloane, David E. E., *Mark Twain as a Literary Comedian* (Baton Rouge, La: Louisiana State University Press, 1979).

Smith, Henry Nash, *Democracy and the Novel: Popular Resistance to Classic American Writers* (New York: Oxford University Press, 1978).

Smith, Henry Nash, *Mark Twain: The Development of a Writer* (Cambridge, Mass.: Belknap Press of Harvard University Press, 1962).

Stone, Albert E., Jr, *The Innocent Eye: Childhood in Mark Twain's Imagination* (New Haven, Conn.: Yale University Press, 1961).

Sundquist, Eric J., *Faulkner: The House Divided* (Baltimore, Md: Johns Hopkins University Press, 1983).

Tanner, Tony, *The Reign of Wonder: Naïvety and Reality in American Literature* (Cambridge: Cambridge University Press, 1965).

Wadlington, Warwick, *The Confidence Game in American Literature* (Princeton, NJ: Princeton University Press, 1975).

Wecter, Dixon, *Sam Clemens of Hannibal* (Boston, Mass.: Houghton Mifflin, 1952).

Williamson, Joel, *The Crucible of Race: Black–White Relations in the American South since Emancipation* (New York: Oxford University Press, 1984).

Woodward, C. Van, *Origins of the New South, 1877–1913* (Baton Rouge, La: Louisiana State University Press, 1951).

Woodward, C. Van, *The Strange Career of Jim Crow* (New York: Oxford University Press, 1955; 3rd edn 1974).

ARTICLES

Adams, Richard P., 'The unity and coherence of *Huckleberry Finn*', *Tulane Studies in English*, vol. 6 (1956), pp. 87–103.

Andrews, William L., 'Mark Twain and James W. C. Pennington: Huck Finn's smallpox lie', *Studies in American Fiction*, vol. 9 (Summer 1981), pp. 103–12.

Baker, Sheridan, 'Narration: the writer's essential mimesis', *Journal of Narrative Technique*, vol. 11 (Fall 1981), pp. 155–65.

Baldanza, Frank, 'The structure of *Huckleberry Finn*', *American Literature*, vol. 27 (November 1955), pp. 347–55.

Banta, Martha, 'Rebirth or revenge: the endings of *Huckleberry Finn* and *The American*', *Modern Fiction Studies*, vol. 15 (Summer 1969), pp. 191–207.

Barnes, Daniel, 'Twain's *The Adventures of Huckleberry Finn*, ch. 1', *The Explicator*, vol. 23, no. 8 (April 1965), item 62.

Barnett, Louise K., 'Huck Finn: picaro as linguistic outsider', *College Literature*, vol. 6 (Fall 1979), pp. 221–31.

Bassett, John Earl, '*Huckleberry Finn*: the end lies in the beginning', *American Literary Realism*, vol. 17 (Spring 1984), pp. 89–98.

Beaver, Harold, 'Run, nigger, run: *Adventures of Huckleberry Finn* as a fugitive slave narrative', *Journal of American Studies*, vol. 8 (December 1974), pp. 339–61.

Beaver, Harold, 'Time on the cross: white fiction and black messiahs', *Yearbook of English Studies*, vol. 8 (1978), pp. 40–53.

Beidler, Peter G. 'The raft episode in *Huckleberry Finn*', *Modern Fiction Studies*, vol. 14 (Spring 1968), pp. 11–20.

Bell, Millicent, '*Huckleberry Finn*: journey without end', *Virginia Quarterly Review*, vol. 58 (Spring 1982), pp. 253–67.

Billingsley, Dale R., '"Standard authors" in *Huckleberry Finn*', *Journal of Narrative Technique*, vol. 9 (Spring 1979), pp. 126–31.

Blair, Walter, 'The French Revolution and *Huckleberry Finn*', *Modern Philology*, vol. 55 (August 1957), pp. 21–35.

Blair, Walter, 'Was *Huckleberry Finn* written?', *Mark Twain Journal*, vol. 19 (Summer 1979), pp. 1–3.

Blair, Walter, 'When was *Huckleberry Finn* written?', *American Literature*, vol. 30 (March 1958), pp. 1–25.

Branch, Egar M., 'The two providences: thematic form in *Huckleberry Finn*', *College English*, vol. 11 (January 1950), pp. 188–95.

Branch, Watson, 'Hard-hearted Huck: "no time to be sentimentering"',

Studies in American Fiction, vol. 6 (Autumn 1978), pp. 212–18.

Brown, Spencer, '*Huckleberry Finn* for our time', *Michigan Quarterly Review*, vol. 6 (Winter 1967), pp. 41–6.

Budd, Louis J., 'Gentlemanly humorists of the old South', *Southern Folklore Quarterly*, vol. 17 (1953), pp. 232–40.

Budd, Louis J., 'Mark Twain talks mostly about humor and humorists', *Studies in American Humor*, vol. 1 (April 1974), pp. 4–19.

Burg, David F., 'Another view of *Huckleberry Finn*', *Nineteenth Century Fiction*, vol. 29 (December 1974), pp. 299–319.

Burns, Graham, 'Time and pastoral: *The Adventures of Huckleberry Finn*', *Critical Review* (Melbourne), vol. 15 (1972), pp. 52–63.

Carkeet, David, 'The dialects in *Huckleberry Finn*', *American Literature*, vol. 51 (November 1979), pp,. 315–32.

Carkeet, David, 'The source for the Arkansas gossips in *Huckleberry Finn*', *American Literary Realism*, vol. 14 (Spring 1981), pp. 90–2.

Cecil, L. Moffitt, 'The historical ending of *Adventures of Huckleberry Finn*: how Nigger Jim was set free', *American Literary Realism*, vol. 13 (Autumn 1980), pp. 280–3.

Clerk, Charles, 'Sunrise on the river: "The whole world" of *Huckleberry Finn*', *Modern Fiction Studies*, vol. 14 (1968), pp. 67–78.

Collins, Billy G., '*Huckleberry Finn*: a Mississippi Moses', *Journal of Narrative Technique*, vol. 5 (May 1975), pp. 86–104.

Colwell, James L., 'Huckleberries and humans: on the naming of *Huckleberry Finn*', *PMLA*, vol. 86 (January 1971), pp. 70–6.

Covici, Pascal, Jr, 'Mark Twain and the humor of the Old Southwest', in M. Thomas Inge (ed.), *The Frontier Humorists: Critical Views* (Hamden, Conn.: Archon, 1975), pp. 233–58.

Cox, James M., 'Humor of the old Southwest', in *The Comic Imagination in America*, ed. Louis D. Rubin, Jr (New Brunswick, NJ: Rutgers University Press, 1973), pp. 101–12.

Cox, James M., 'The muse of Samuel Clemens', *Massachusetts Review*, vol. 5 (Autumn 1963), pp. 127–41.

Cox, James M., 'Remarks on the sad initiation of Huckleberry Finn', *Sewanee Review*, vol. 62 (Summer 1954), pp. 389–405.

David, Beverly R., 'Mark Twain and the legends for *Huckleberry Finn*', *American Literary Realism*, vol. 15 (Autumn 1982), pp. 155–65.

Davis, Thadious M., foreword to *Mark Twain Journal*, vol. 22 (Fall 1984), pp. 2–3.

Doyno, Victor, 'Over Twain's shoulders: the composition and structure of *Huckleberry Finn*', *Modern Fiction Studies*, vol. 14 (1968), pp. 3–9.

Eliot, T. S., 'American literature and the American language', *Washington University Studies in Language and Literature*, new series vol. 23 (St Louis, Mo., 1953); reprinted in *Sewanee Review*, vol. 74 (January–March 1966), pp. 1–20.

Eliot, T. S., introduction to *The Adventures of Huckleberry Finn* (London: Cresset Press, 1950), pp. vii–xvi.

Ellison, Ralph, 'Change the joke and slip the yoke', *Partisan Review*, vol. 25

(Spring 1958), pp. 212–22. Reprinted in *Shadow and Act* (New York: Random House, 1964).

Ensor, Allison, 'The contributions of Charles Webster and Albert Bigelow Paine to *Huckleberry Finn*', *American Literature*, vol. 40 (May 1968), pp. 222–7.

Fatout, Paul, 'Mark Twain's nom de plume', *American Literature*, vol. 34 (March 1962), pp. 1–7.

Ferguson, DeLancey, 'Huck Finn aborning', *Colophon*, vol. 3 (Spring 1938), pp. 171–80.

Fetterley, Judith, 'Disenchantment: Tom Sawyer in *Huckleberry Finn*', *PMLA*, vol. 87 (January 1972), pp. 69–74.

Fiedler, Leslie A., 'As free as any cretur . . .', *New Republic*, vol. 133 nos. 7–8, (15 and 22 August 1955), pp. 17–18 and 16–18.

Fiedler, Leslie A., 'Come back to the raft ag'in, Huck Honey!', *Partisan Review*, vol. 15 (June 1948), pp. 664–71.

Fischer, Victor, 'Huck Finn reviewed: the reception of *Huckleberry Finn* in the United States, 1885–1897', *American Literary Realism*, vol. 16 (Spring 1983), pp. 1–57.

Galligan, Edward L., 'True comedians and false: *Don Quixote* and *Huckleberry Finn*', *Sewanee Review*, vol. 86, nos. 1–2 (Winter 1977), pp. 66–83.

Gerber, John C., 'The relation between point of view and style in the works of Mark Twain', in *Style in Prose Fiction*, English Institute Essays, 1958 (New York: Columbia University Press, 1959), pp. 142–71.

Gollin, Richard and Rita, '*Huckleberry Finn* and the time of the evasion', *Modern Language Studies*, vol. 9 (Spring 1979), pp. 5–15.

Graves, Wallace, 'Mark Twain's "Burning Shame"', *Nineteenth-Century Fiction*, vol. 23 (June 1968), pp. 93–8.

Gribben, Alan, 'Removing Mark Twain's mask: a decade of criticism and scholarship', *Emerson Society Quarterly*, vol. 26, nos. 2 and 3 (Fall 1980), pp. 100–8 and 149–71.

Gullason, Thomas A., 'The "Fatal" ending of *Huckleberry Finn*', *American Literature*, vol. 29 (March 1957), pp. 86–91.

Hansen, Chadwick, 'The character of Jim and the ending of *Huckleberry Finn*', *Massachusetts Review*, vol. 5 (Autumn 1963), pp. 45–66.

Hill, Hamlin, '*Huckleberry Finn's* humor today', in *Huck Finn among the Critics*, ed. M. Thomas Inge (Washington, DC: United States Information Agency, 1984), pp. 231–44.

Hoffman, Daniel G., 'Black magic – and white – in *Huckleberry Finn*', in his *Form and Fable in American Fiction* (New York: Oxford University Press, 1961), ch. 15.

Hoffman, Daniel G., 'Jim's magic: black or white?', *American Literature*, vol. 32 (March 1960), pp. 47–54.

Holland, Laurence B., 'A "raft of trouble": word and deed in *Huckleberry Finn*', *Glyph* (Johns Hopkins Textual Studies), vol. 5 (1979), pp. 69–87.

Hoy, James F., 'The Grangerford–Shepherdson feud in *Huckleberry Finn*', *Mark Twain Journal*, vol. 18 (Winter 1975), pp. 19–20.

Kolb, Harold H., Jr, 'Mark Twain, Huck Finn, and Jacob Blivens: gilt-edged, tree-calf morality in *The Adventures of Huckleberry Finn'*, *Virginia Quarterly Review*, vol. 55 (Autumn 1979), pp. 653–69.

Krause, Sydney J., 'Twain's method and theory of composition', *Modern Philology*, vol. 56 (February 1959), pp. 167–77.

Krauth, Leland, 'Mark Twain: the Victorian of Southwestern humor', *American Literature*, vol. 54 (October 1982), pp. 368–84.

Lamplugh, George R., 'The image of the Negro in popular magazine fiction, 1875–1900', *Journal of Negro History*, vol. 57 (April 1972), pp. 177–89.

Lane, Lauriat, Jr, 'Why *Huckleberry Finn* is a great world novel', *College English*, vol. 17 (October 1955), pp. 1–5.

Lang, Andrew, 'The art of Mark Twain', *Illustrated London News*, vol. 98 (14 February 1891), p. 222.

Lester, Julius, 'Morality and *Adventures of Huckleberry Finn'*, *Mark Twain Journal*, vol. 22 (Fall 1984), pp. 43–6.

Lorch, Fred W., 'A note on Tom Blankenship (Huckleberry Finn)', *American Literature*, vol. 12 (November 1940), pp. 351–3.

Lowenherz, Robert J., 'The beginning of "Huckleberry Finn"', *American Speech*, vol. 38 (October 1963), pp. 196–201.

Lowery, Captain Robert E., 'The Grangerford–Shepherdson episode: another of Mark Twain's indictments of the damned human race', *Mark Twain Journal*, vol. 15 (Winter 1970), pp. 19–21.

Lynn, Kenneth S., 'Huck and Jim', *Yale Review*, vol. 47 (March 1958), pp. 421–31.

Lynn, Kenneth S., 'Welcome back from the raft, Huck Honey!', *American Scholar*, vol 46 (Summer 1977), pp. 338–47.

McCullough, Joseph B., 'Uses of the Bible in *Huckleberry Finn'*, *Mark Twain Journal*, vol. 19 (Winter 1978–9), pp. 2–3.

McKay, Janet Holmgren, 'Going to Hell: style in Huck Finn's great debate', *Interpretations*, vol. 13 (1981), pp. 24–30.

McKay, Janet Holmgren, '"Tears and flapdoodle": point of view and style in *The Adventures of Huckleberry Finn'*, *Style*, vol. 10 (Winter 1976), pp. 41–50.

Marks, Barry A., 'The Huck Finn swindle', *Western American Literature*, vol. 14 (August 1979), pp. 115–32.

Marks, Barry A., 'The making of a humorist: the narrative strategy of *Huckleberry Finn'*, *Journal of Narrative Technique*, vol. 12 (Spring 1982), pp. 139–45.

Marx, Leo, 'Mr Eliot, Mr Trilling, and *Huckleberry Finn'*, *American Scholar*, vol. 22 (Autumn 1953), pp. 423–40.

Marx, Leo, 'The pilot and the passenger: landscape conventions and the style of *Huckleberry Finn'*, *American Literature*, vol. 28 (May 1956), pp. 129–45.

May, Charles E., 'Literary masters and masturbators: sexuality, fantasy, and reality in *Huckleberry Finn'*, *Literature and Psychology*, vol. 28, no. 2 (1978), pp. 85–92.

Mencken, H. L., 'The burden of humor', *The Smart Set*, vol. 38 (February 1913), pp. 151–4.

Michelson, Bruce, 'Huck and the games of the world', *American Literary*

Realism, vol. 13 (Spring 1980), pp. 108–21.

Miller, Michael G., 'Geography and structure in *Huckleberry Finn*', *Studies in the Novel*, vol. 12 (Fall 1980), pp. 192–209.

Moore, O. H., 'Mark Twain and *Don Quixote*', *PMLA*, vol. 37 (June 1922), pp. 324–46.

Moser, Kay R., 'Mark Twain – Mugwump', *Mark Twain Journal*, vol. 21 (Summer 1982), pp. 1–4.

Moyne, Ernest J., 'Mark Twain and Baroness Alexandra Gripenberg', *American Literature*, vol. 45 (November 1973), pp. 370–8.

Opdahl, Keith M., '"You'll be sorry when I'm dead": Child–adult relations in *Huckleberry Finn*', *Modern Fiction Studies*, vol. 25 (Winter 1979–80), pp. 613–24.

Parker, Hershel, 'Lost authority: non-sense, skewed meanings, and intentionless meanings', *Critical Inquiry*, vol. 9 (June 1983), pp. 767–74.

Pearce, Roy Harvey, '"The End. Yours Truly, Huck Finn": postscript', *Modern Language Quarterly*, vol. 24 (September 1963), pp. 253–6.

Pearce, Roy Harvey, 'Huck Finn in his history', *Etudes anglaises*, vol. 24 (July–September 1971), pp. 283–91.

Perry, Thomas Sergeant, review in *Century Magazine*, vol. 30 (May 1885), pp. 171–2.

Pettit, Arthur G., 'Mark Twain and the Negro, 1867–1869', *Journal of Negro History*, vol. 56 (April 1971), pp. 88–96.

Phelps, William, 'Mark Twain', *Yale Review*, vol. 25 (Winter 1936), pp. 291–310.

Piacentino, Edward J., 'The ubiquitous Tom Sawyer: another view of the conclusion of *Huckleberry Finn*', *Cimarron Review*, vol. 37 (October 1976), pp. 34–43.

Rampersad, Arnold, '*Adventures of Huckleberry Finn* and Afro-American literature', *Mark Twain Journal*, vol. 22 (Fall 1984), pp. 47–52.

Ridland, J. M., 'Huck, Pip, and plot', *Nineteenth-Century Fiction*, vol. 20 (December 1965), pp. 286–90.

Robinson, Forrest G., 'The silences in *Huckleberry Finn*', *Nineteenth-Century Fiction*, vol. 37 (June 1982), pp. 50–74.

Rubenstein, Gilbert M., 'The moral structure of *Huckleberry Finn*', *College English*, vol. 18 (November 1956), pp. 72–6.

Schacht, Paul, 'The lonesomeness of Huckleberry Finn', *American Literature*, vol. 53 (May 1981), pp. 189–201.

Schmitz, Neil, 'The paradox of liberation in *Huckleberry Finn*', *Texas Studies in Literature and Language*, vol. 13 (Spring 1971), pp. 125–36.

Schmitz, Neil, 'Twain, *Huckleberry Finn*, and the Reconstruction', *American Studies*, vol. 12 (Spring 1971), pp. 59–67.

Scott, Arthur L., '*The Century Magazine* edits *Huckleberry Finn*, 1884–1885', *American Literature*, vol. 27 (November 1955), pp. 356–62.

Seelye, John, 'The craft of laughter: abominable showmanship and *Huckleberry Finn*', *Thalia*, vol. 4, no. 1 (1981), pp. 19–25.

Smith, David L., 'Huck, Jim, and American racial discourse', *Mark Twain Journal*, vol. 22 (Fall 1984), pp. 4–12.

Solomon, Eric, 'Huckleberry Finn once more', College English, vol. 22 (December 1960), pp. 172–8.

Sommers, Jeffrey, '"I never knowed how clothes could change a body before": the dual function of clothing in Huckleberry Finn', Mark Twain Journal, vol. 20, no. 4 (1981), pp. 19–20.

Sten, Christopher, '"When the candle went out": the nighttime world of Huckleberry Finn', Studies in American Fiction, vol. 9 (Summer 1981), pp. 47–64.

Thompson, Charles Miner, 'Mark Twain as an interpreter of American character', Atlantic Monthly, vol. 79 (1897), pp. 443–50.

Towers, Tom H., '"I never thought we might want to come back": strategies of transcendence in Tom Sawyer', Modern Fiction Studies, vol. 21 (Winter 1975–6), pp. 509–20.

Towers, Tom H., 'Love and power in Huckleberry Finn', Tulane Studies in English, vol. 23 (1978), pp. 17–37.

Trachtenberg, Alan, 'The form of freedom in Adventures of Huckleberry Finn', Southern Review, new series vol. 6 (October 1970), pp. 954–71.

Tracy, Robert, 'Myth and reality in The Adventures of Tom Sawyer', Southern Review, new series vol. 4 (Spring 1968), pp. 530–41.

Trilling, Lionel, introduction to The Adventures of Huckleberry Finn (New York: Holt, Rinehart & Winston, 1948), pp. v–xiii.

Vogelback, Arthur Lawrence, 'The publication and reception of Huckleberry Finn in America', American Literature, vol. 11 (November 1939), pp. 260–72.

Wall, Carey, 'The boomerang of slavery: the child, the aristocrat, and hidden white identity in Huck Finn', Southern Studies, vol. 21 (Summer 1982), pp. 208–21.

Weaver, Thomas and Williams, Merline A., 'Mark Twain's Jim: identity as an index to cultural attitudes', American Literary Realism, vol. 13 (Spring 1980), pp. 19–30.

Wells, David M., 'More on the geography of Huckleberry Finn', South Atlantic Bulletin, vol. 38 (November 1973), pp. 82–6.

Wexman, Virginia, 'The role of structure in Tom Sawyer and Huckleberry Finn', American Literary Realism, vol. 6 (Winter 1973), pp. 1–11.

INDEX

Illustrations are referred to by figure numbers printed in *italics*

Index